WHO WOULD BE,
A MERMAID FAIR,
SINGING ALONE,
COMBING HER HAIR
UNDER THE SEA,
IN A GOLDEN CURL
WITH A COMB OF PEARL
ON A THRONE?

I WOULD BE A MERMAID FAIR;
I WOULD SING TO MYSELF THE WHOLE OF THE DAY;
WITH A COMB OF PEARL I WOULD COMB MY HAIR;
AND STILL AS I COMB'D I WOULD SING AND SAY,

"WHO IS IT LOVES ME?
WHO LOVES NOT ME?"

FROM *THE MERMAID*, BY ALFRED LORD TENNYSON, 1830

THE BALD MERMAID
A MEMOIR

SHEILA BRIDGES

POINTED LEAF PRESS, LLC.

AUTHOR'S NOTE

I realize that, like me, this memoir should have come with an instruction guide, playbook, or owner's manual. Since it doesn't, I'll quickly explain the lay of the land. It seemed absurd to change the names of my immediate family since whom else could they be? I tried to imagine Sidney as Herman and my Mom as Fran, but it just didn't seem right. I've included the real names of my extended kin—aunts, uncles, cousins, and animals, since I consider all of them members of my family. I changed the names of clients and most friends and acquaintances as well as the chronology of a couple of notable events, in order to protect the innocent—and the guilty. I have also invented addresses, switched the schools people attended, and sometimes even their workplaces, in an attempt to respect people's privacy, while still trying to maintain the veracity of my story.

I'd also like to apologize in advance in case you get bent out of shape because an event or occasion as I've described it isn't exactly the way you remember it. That's the thing about recollections: They are imperfect, just like we are. My memories are simply mine. This is not a factual autobiography but a personal memoir. It is a true account of events in my life as I remember them. Please don't feel dissed if you consider yourself a good friend but you're not mentioned in this book. I left out many significant people with no disrespect intended. Finally, I have compounded, combined, and compressed a couple of people and minor events in order to keep this book under ten thousand pages.

CONTENTS

PROLOGUE

I wasn't afraid of the water even though I should have been. It didn't matter that I wasn't a very strong swimmer. I would make up for what I lacked in skill by what filled my heart. Be it a lake, a river, or the sea, I was mesmerized. I believed the water spoke to me, that it sang a romantic siren song to me. Maybe I was fascinated by it because I was a water sign: A Cancer—the symbol for which is the crab. Maybe it was the crab in me that kept me from being afraid.

My Mother didn't like to swim. Pools were segregated when she grew up, and my grandmother told her that nice black girls didn't go to public swimming pools. My Father was a good swimmer but he was indifferent. He had worked on a Delaware River tugboat while he was in college. For him, water simply represented a means to an end—a summer job, a paycheck, a bridge to cross on his way somewhere, the earth's tidal cistern that held the bluefish he liked to catch when he went fishing.

Even though we took classes together at the Y, my brother didn't seem to care for it either. He felt the same way about those swimming lessons as he did about raking leaves in our backyard or taking out the trash. He'd rather have been dribbling a basketball. Besides, the water didn't whisper his name like it did mine.

For a little while, my family indulged my infatuation. We even established a rule that everyone adhered to when we went on road trips or vacations. Wake Sheila if you see water or horses. It didn't matter what time of the day or night it was. Neither did it matter how large or small the body of water was. It could be a big, glassy reservoir, a trickling stream, or even a muddy, stagnant puddle. Wake Sheila if you see water or horses. No matter what.

"Sheila, Sheila—wake up, look—look—there's water!" my Mother would exclaim from the front seat, as my brother nudged me with his right elbow. I would jump up in the back seat, groggy but excited, hair awry, with eyes bulging as we crossed a suspension bridge, hugged a lakeshore drive or drove past a waterfall cascading noisily over jagged rocks. I would stare out of the rear window in awe until I couldn't see it any longer, until its wetness receded into the distance and mysteriously faded, merging with the atmosphere.

In 1973, on a family vacation to Jamaica, we took an excursion in a glass-bottom boat. I was nine years old. The salt-encrusted vessel had seen better days. It was small and weather-worn, with white paint peeling away from a

OPPOSITE I was nine years old the first time my family went on vacation to Montego Bay, Jamaica. I spent most of my time at the beach.

splintery, barnacle-clad wood frame. As the old boat creaked against the ocean waves, I could see tropical fish, ribbons of wavy green seaweed and spongy, fan-shaped coral colorfully embroidering the sandy blanket below. I peered through the glass-paned hull, staring wide-eyed as schools of small, silvery fish flickered beneath the blue-green surface of the shallow water.

Where was she? She had to be down there. This was her home after all—the magical place where she spent her days cavorting with her majestic seahorse, casually luring the mariners and me. I knew what she looked like because I had seen her in picture books and on the cobalt-blue ashtray my Dad had brought back from Copenhagen. She was stunningly beautiful, with long flowing hair like Rapunzel. Even if she didn't show her face, I knew I would recognize her large, shimmering fishtail. But I never did see her.

Later that afternoon, I went back to the beach in search of seashells and coconuts. The sand was littered with them. My Mother slathered me in Coppertone, hoping I wouldn't get sunburned. I hurriedly kicked off my sandals and left them on the wood chaise under the thatched palm-leaf umbrella, right next to my inflatable pink fish that I normally wore around my waist when I went into the ocean. I dug my bare feet into the hot Jamaican sand before running away from my shadow, toward the water's foamy edge.

Suddenly I caught a glimpse of something in the water. I squinted, straining to see against the brilliant blue sky and blinding white sun. Could it be that my mysterious aquatic friend had come to visit? She was shy like me, which explained why she hadn't appeared under the glass-bottom boat earlier. I ditched my coconut and seashells before wading into the ocean. I felt that weightless sensation you get when your feet can no longer touch the bottom. I held my breath and plunged under, then opened my eyes. I could hear the hollow sound of the ocean but I couldn't see her. I spun around when I saw a flash of light and heard a loud splash. Suddenly I felt my body being dragged into deeper water. But just as I was about to start doggy paddling furiously in the opposite direction, I was gently pushed back toward the beach. Maybe it was a wave—or maybe, just maybe, something else had carried me safely ashore. I did not believe in Santa Claus anymore, but I believed in mermaids.

OPPOSITE I have always loved the art of collecting, and continue to collect antique mercury glass, clocks, and unusual seashells.

CHAPTER I

LADY SINGS THE BLUES

Like the songstress Billie Holiday, I was born in Philadelphia on the seventh day of the month. Just like her, I eventually made my way to Harlem many years later, though under very different circumstances.

My newborn skin was the shade of cauliflower, my hair the color of ginger, and I had blue eyes. I wouldn't find out until much later in life that being born black and blonde would pose its own unique set of challenges. But within my first few hours, I caused controversy as a doctor tried to pry me from my Mother's arms, insisting that a mistake had been made, that she had been given the wrong baby.

No matter how many times my Mother recounted this story over the years, her indignation never subsided. There was a new attending physician subbing for my Mother's regular obstetrician that day. He took one look at my Mother, one glance at me and was convinced I couldn't possibly be her child. My Mother had gained only 15 pounds during her entire pregnancy. Following doctor's orders, she had spent the final four months bedridden, fraught with worry she might lose the baby. When I finally did arrive healthy, there was no way she was going to let some arrogant white doctor take away her precious baby daughter.

It was the sixties, which meant that despite my pearly complexion and halo of blonde curls, since my parents and both sets of grandparents were black, I was

ABOVE My Mother saved all of my baby things, including my first pair of leather shoes.
OPPOSITE My Mom and I were photographed by my Aunt Olga's father, Mr. Leo Culmer, in 1964.

LEFT AND FAR LEFT
My paternal grandparents,
Sidney and Molly Bridges,
are posing for portraits.

BELOW This postcard picture
of my great grandfather,
James Harris, and his three
children, including Annette,
James Jr., and Azalia
(my grandmother), was
taken in 1908.

LEFT AND FAR LEFT
My maternal grandparents,
Edward and Azalia Winfrey,
were photographed in
Fairmont Park, Philadelphia.

RIGHT My Mother at age 5,
in Philadelphia.
BELOW My Father as a baby.
BELOW RIGHT My portrait
taken by a photographer
from Sears Roebuck and
Company. He was
delivering a photograph
for my grandmother, and
asked if he could photograph
me at no charge. I was ten
months old.
BOTTOM LEFT My birth
announcement, from the
Hallmark store.
BOTTOM RIGHT
My hospital ID card.

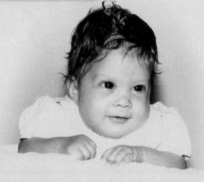

considered black. Not Negro, not Colored, and not yet Afro-American or African-American, just plain ole', straight up like the coffee-with-no-cream-or-sugar black. And while I eventually grew out of my baby blues, which turned a shade of pecan brown within my first two months, I never did outgrow my blackness. Nor do I recall ever trying. I was taught early on by my parents that the sooner I made good use of the special lenses bestowed upon the eyes of black children, the sooner I would be able to see that the true color of my own pale skin was not beige or tan or brown, but black.

My survival in blackness as a child in Philadelphia was not dissimilar to my later survival in New York—and Harlem in particular. It was predicated upon my ability to secretly hope for the best while expecting the worst, and based on maintaining my willingness to settle somewhere in between.

I was the second of two children. My brother Sidney was my Father's namesake and three years older than me. To lessen the confusion, my Father was called Sid or Big Sidney, my brother, Little Sidney. I was named after a chorus girl who danced at Club Harlem in New York City. My Uncle Jimmy, one of my Father's best friends, had introduced my parents to her while they were dating. My Mother was mesmerized by the dancer's beauty, and fascinated by her name. She had "never heard of a *Sheila* before."

My parents were introduced on a blind date by my Aunt Olga in 1958. She had known my Father since kindergarten, and my Mother since high school. It was my Father's first marriage but my Mother's second. That meant a pale-lilac silk chiffon dress instead of a full white gown, and a quick trip to the chapel instead of a long walk down the aisle of the First African Presbyterian Church.

My parents didn't serenade or shower one another with lavish gifts or public displays of affection. I never saw them gush and, in fact, I rarely saw them embrace. Their relationship seemed carefully measured, like a complicated *Joy of Cooking* recipe that needed to be precisely followed lest it explode in the oven.

My relationship with my parents was based as much on fear as it was on love; I witnessed firsthand what happened when you revolted against their regime. They had both grown up as only children and were used to doing things their own way. To my brother and me, it often seemed they spoke a different language. Things got lost in translation. As a child, I often felt frustrated by their illogical answers. Too many tears and I was being *difficult*. Too many questions and I was being *fresh*. When I asked why, their response was often "Because I said so!" When I cried my Mother would say "Stop that crying before I give you something to cry about!" or "poke that lip back in before I put it in for you."

My Mother on her wedding day, July 16th, 1960, was photographed on the front porch of her parents' house in Philadelphia. Like many brides, she had her shoes dyed to match her dress, in this case, lilac.

My Dad, on a friend's boat, loved to go out fishing.

Either behavior risked punishment, which usually meant not being allowed to play outdoors. Since nothing was more devastating than that, I tried to keep my mouth shut and my eyes dry.

Most people would describe my Mother as petite. If you asked her how tall she was, she would say, "Five-foot-one. And a half." She would always pause and add that extra half to be sure you knew she didn't want to be considered *short*. Her hair was fine but curly and naturally dark brown. She went to the hairdresser once a week and often dyed it light brown with golden highlights. I was her perfect hair alibi. So was her father, my grandfather, who was also black with blond hair and blue eyes. Thanks to us, there would never be any suspicion of her hair color coming from a bottle.

My Father was 5'11"—not tall, not short—with jet black hair, its texture thick and coarse. I never knew how it looked naturally, since most nights he slept in a black hairnet or stocking cap (the precursor to the do-rag) to ensure that his waves would lay down perfectly, like ripples on a lake, blown quietly by a slight breeze. His build was thin, and he wore glasses. Handsome but nerdish, one might say. He joked that he had married my Mother for her piano, which was a Baldwin upright, a gift from her parents.

My Mother started playing piano in the second grade, taking lessons from Mr. Hebron, who was known for having taught Marian Anderson. Every Saturday morning, my Mother walked to Mr. Hebron's home in the Fairview Apartments at 50th and Race streets, alongside her friend, Vivienne, who lived across the street. Lessons cost 50 cents. Although expensive for my grandparents, it was a price worth paying to ensure their only daughter became cultured and ladylike, something they knew little about, being country folk who had moved north from Amelia, Virginia.

My Father was also introduced to the piano as a child. His parents paid for his lessons, too, but he asked so many questions his teacher got frustrated and eventually refused to continue. My grandfather was a part-time chauffeur. He was very talented with his hands and spent much of his free time fixing things. He taught my Father carpentry, and together they enjoyed taking things apart and putting them back together. Their piano sat unused and collecting dust, so they decided to take it apart. According to family lore, my Father figured out how to put the piano back together on his own, piece by piece. Then he and my grandfather took it apart one last time, turning part of it into a headboard. So, my Father was without a piano and, even though it was my Aunt Olga who brought my parents together, it really was my Mother's piano that sealed their commitment.

My parents hoped their two children would inherit their love of piano, but it was quite simply not in the cards. I can't recall what happened with my brother's lessons but I know I dreaded mine. I'm not sure which was worse, the practicing—which I never did much of—the recitals or the actual lessons. Eventually, my parents stopped wasting their hard-earned money on my lack of talent and enthusiasm.

My piano teacher, Mrs. Goodman, was a big, fleshy woman with a heavy German accent. Each week I would sit obediently on the cushioned piano bench, squished between Mrs. Goodman and the wall, mesmerized by the ticking metronome, completely distracted by the neighborhood kids whizzing past on their bikes, or the numbers tattooed on her forearm. I desperately wanted to ask Mrs. Goodman about those numbers, but I knew that wasn't allowed. My parents explained she was Jewish and had survived a concentration camp in Germany. I couldn't stop thinking about it. I'd heard about Nazi prison camps in school, especially since most of my classmates were Jewish.

Instead of focusing on the shiny black and white keys in front of us, trying to play Debussy's *Claire de Lune*, which Mrs. Goodman never failed to remind me was in D-flat major, I kept glancing out her picture window, looking for my friends in the street. It wasn't fair. They were out there in the summer sunshine, playing, while here I was stuck indoors, being chastised about my slumping posture and long, filthy fingernails. I had spent the entire morning excavating in my backyard, digging my way to China. Having escaped Nazi Germany, Mrs. Goodman should have been more sympathetic to my dirty hands, I thought.

My childhood was largely happy and uneventful. I was no more exceptional than any other shy, awkward kid searching for a meaningful place in a world full of adult contradictions. If I were to complain all these years later, it would be hard to garner much sympathy since I had had so many privileges—from tennis camp, pony club, and swim classes at the Y, to nice family vacations in places like Nassau, Hyannis Port, and Montego Bay. There were weekends "down the shore" complete with saltwater taffy stuck in my braces, and strolls on the boardwalk in Atlantic City. And there were family dinners at Bookbinder's and Dinardo's Crab House, and lunches seated at the counter of Howard Johnson's, where I was allowed to eat as many fried clams on a toasted hot dog bun as I could stomach.

My parents made sure we got a great education, along with all the other upper middle-class privileges that a dentist and kindergarten teacher could provide. Like most black folks of their generation, they were on the conservative side of things when it came to our upbringing. There were lots of rules, particularly when my Father was around. No soda, Pop-Tarts, bubblegum or fast food. No running in the house. No bare feet. No playing dodgeball in the living room. But most of the rules flew out the window when my Dad was out of town. He was appointed by Governor Milton J. Shapp to a seat on the Pennsylvania State Board of Dentistry. He was also a member of the American Association of Dental Examiners. This meant he often traveled to Washington, D.C., as well as to our state capital, Harrisburg, for meetings and to the dental schools at places like Tufts, Harvard, the University of Chicago, the University of Michigan, Columbia, or New York University to oversee regional board exams.

My brother and I were generally very well behaved when we were young, but even the most obedient children have their limits. I'll never forget the day Sidney reached his. It was a typical Saturday, which meant my Father was seeing patients and my Mother had to shop. There was shopping and then there was *shopping*. For what, I don't know, since she had so many beautiful clothes and designer shoes that she converted two empty rooms on the third floor of our house into additional closet space, full of hanging racks and stacked cardboard shoe

My brother Sidney and I were dressed to the nines on Easter Sunday in 1967.

boxes. Her tastes ranged from Albert Nipon to Emilio Pucci, from Salvatore Ferragamo to Geoffrey Beene. Chances were, if you had seen it in a fashion magazine or catalogue, the burgundy or cerulean version of it was in my Mother's closet.

As impeccably dressed and unabashedly stylish as my Mother was, she spared no expense when it came to our clothing, either. I had my own closet full of fussy, flounced Italian linen skirts, cotton voile with eyelets, and fancy velvet dresses embellished with hand embroidery. I had patent leather shoes, purses, hats, and frilly white socks with satin ribbons to match the grosgrain ones she sometimes put in my hair.

Sidney had handsomely tailored plaid, herringbone, and Harris Tweed jackets and matching worsted wool knee pants, which to his reasonable dismay made him look like Little Lord Fauntleroy. We were two little dress-up dolls, my Mother's best fashion accessories. Everywhere we went, strangers would stop her and say, "What lovely, well-dressed children you have," or "My goodness! Your children are just so adorable and well behaved." "Thank you," she would reply, smiling demurely with maternal pride.

Typically, we started out at the Jean Madeline hair salon at 9 a.m., waiting several hours while my Mother's tresses were colored, washed, conditioned, cut, set, blow-dried, styled, and sprayed by her Italian hairdresser, Nikki. My Mother would bring a bag of art supplies to keep us occupied while she sat patiently in the stylist's adjustable chair. I would spread everything out on the tile floor and I distinctly recall the sensation of strands of hair of all different lengths, textures, and colors getting mixed in with my paper, crayons, and markers. When my Mother was finished getting coiffed, it was time to go shopping. We drove from the salon to John Wanamaker. Nothing there. So we got back in the car and drove across the parking lot to Bonwit Teller, where my Mother bought a Halston dress, then to Saks Fifth Avenue, where she saw a Bill Blass dress she liked better. So we had to drive all the way back to Bonwit Teller to return the Halston, then back to Saks to buy the Bill Blass.

Next stop was Lord & Taylor. We entered on the ground floor, through the men's department. By now it was nearly 2 o'clock Saturday afternoon, and my brother had had enough. Maybe he was hungry. Maybe his cuff links were too tight or he was frustrated carrying all those shopping bags, which bumped along the floor, pulling on his small 7-year-old frame. Maybe he was just bored and fed up after five hours of being dragged from the hairdresser to one store after another. Whatever it was, Sidney decided to take matters into his own hands, and who could blame him? He threw a tantrum like no other I have seen—before or since. It was textbook. Classic. He lay down on the carpet, face contorted, blocking the up escalator, arms and legs flailing, clenched fists banging on the floor, shrieking, determined to get the attention of every single customer in the store. My Mother and I had already stepped onto the escalator. I was clinging to her hand, staring down at my feet, well aware of how easily this metal-staired monster could eat me. (I had heard that story about the little girl who had to have her leg amputated after her shoe got caught in the treads.) My Mother shook off my hand and jumped back down several steps to grab Sidney's arm. I grasped the rubber handrail with both hands, turned and watched wide-eyed, as if I had a ringside seat at Ringling Brothers and Barnum & Bailey. *Welcome to the greatest show on earth!*

My Mother yanked my brother up off the floor and popped him multiple times on the back of his head and his backside, *POP-POP-POP-POP-POP*, in rapid-fire succession. "Don't you ever, *ever* do that again!" POP. "Did you hear me!?" POP. "Do you understand?" Then she took his hand calmly and together they stepped carefully onto the escalator, to the polite stares and mild-mannered smiles of all the white customers, who were clearly satisfied with my Mother's manner of discipline. It was the late sixties, which meant people didn't immediately get on the phone with Social Services if you slapped your kid around a little bit when he was out of line. You did what was expected, which was to handle your business, even if it was in public and even if it meant a good spanking. When my brother finally reached the second-floor landing, he was red-faced and teary-eyed, his hair and clothes completely disheveled, as if he'd been thrown by a runaway circus elephant. Sidney never did attempt a stunt like that with my Mother again—and neither did I—but from that day on he was forever my hero for trying.

When I wasn't trying to understand my parents' logic, watching the *Flintstones*, *Scooby-Doo*, and *Soul Train* on TV or following Sidney around like a golden retriever, I spent much of my after-school time on the private golf course behind our house, catching salamanders and frogs from the muddy stream near the third hole. The knees of my high-water bell-bottoms were always grass-stained, and my hands and elbows dirty. I spent countless hours riding my white Free Spirit bike alongside Cynthia and Jade, my two friends who lived around the corner. Even though we traveled the same route every Saturday afternoon, the journey was always exhilarating. A quick right turn out of my driveway then a right at the stop sign onto Wynnefield Avenue, pedaling at meteoric speeds, navigating the cracked, uneven sidewalk to get to Leoff's (our neighborhood drugstore) in time to buy a pack of Watermelon-flavored Now-and-Laters, Sugar Babies, and a large Charleston Chew before they closed.

During those wonder years, the only real responsibility I remember having—aside from clearing the table, packing and unpacking the dishwasher, sweeping the breakfast-room floor and keeping my room clean—was to be home by dark. We didn't have bike helmets or cell phones, but our parents never seemed to worry about our photographs ending up on the back of milk cartons. Or if they did, they were wise enough to keep it to themselves.

My Mother hated to cook. With the exception of Thanksgiving and Christmas, almost everything she prepared for our family was zapped in the microwave. Baked potatoes, bacon (lined up perfectly between two Bounty paper towels, to soak up the grease), and Uncle Ben's Minute Rice were her specialties. It wasn't until after college that I learned you could actually make corn on the cob in a pot of boiling water. Occasionally, my Mother made dishes like spaghetti with Ragú sauce or baked pork chops but more often than not everything came from the microwave. She dropped a frozen brick of Acme-brand vegetables into a Pyrex dish, covered it with Saran Wrap, and after a mere five minutes of steady spinning and humming—*poof*—it would be magically transformed from a solid green mass into something edible, albeit with the consistency of baby food. Now at least it could be identified as broccoli, spinach, or string beans.

"Stand back!" she would warn if I approached the kitchen while she was cooking. Everyone knew that microwaves gave off radiation and caused cancer if you stood too close. She reliably put those nutritious dinners on the table every night by 6 o'clock, but when my Dad went out of town on business, she decided she deserved a break. My Father's car would have barely backed out of the driveway before my Mother would pile us into the back seat of her grey 1970 Chevy Camaro, driving six blocks at breakneck speed to the local Roy Rogers.

Sidney was obsessed with hamburgers, tennis, and basketball while I was totally preoccupied with cowboys, Indians, and horses. He would focus on his bacon cheeseburger smothered in ketchup or his roast beef sandwich, while all I wanted to do was sit quietly at the wagon wheel table, eating French fries and sipping my large birch beer through a bent plastic straw. My Mother was simply relieved we supported her non-violent protest against Shake 'n Bake.

The restaurant was filled with Western paraphernalia and autographed movie memorabilia. I would stare at the posters of Roy Rogers on horseback. Who cared about Dale Evans when you got to wear a fringed shirt and rode a beautiful palomino horse named Trigger who could do tricks? Roy was one lucky son of a gun. I fantasized about what it might be like to own a horse and wear dungarees every day.

"Don't tell your Father!" my Mother would say as we jumped back in the car and drove away. She insisted on taking a circuitous route home in case we were being followed. Sidney and I used the longer journey as an opportunity to shoot spitballs at each other through the striped plastic straws we collected at the restaurant. He would pin me under him on the hump in the middle of the back seat and fire at me from point-blank range. I would end up with wet wads of straw wrappers stuck in my two thick plaits.

"Stop it. Stop it, right now, you two!" my Mother would fuss, nervously checking her rearview mirror. "If you say anything, I mean *anything* at all, no more trips to Roy Rogers. And take that stuff out of your hair and throw it in the trash as soon as we get in the house!" I'm not sure exactly what my Father would have done if he had found out about our illicit fast-food outings but my Mother made it very clear they had to be kept a secret. Given my quiet nature, that part was always easy.

ABOVE Sidney, my Mom, and I were photographed in front of the red azaleas in our yard in 1966.
I was two, and Sidney was five years old.
OVERLEAF LEFT My grandmother Azalia, Sidney, and I were photographed near our sun porch
in Philadelphia. OVERLEAF RIGHT My Mom thought I was pretty in pink—with my matching hat,
patent leather purse, and shoes—in front of our pink azalea bushes.

CHAPTER 2

BEARDED UNICORN

Looking back, I realize many of my fondest childhood memories revolve around holidays and weekends, although they have little to do with presents from Santa Claus or Fourth of July fireworks. Instead, they have everything to do with what happened when my parents had company. Whether it was because they lost their parents young or because they lacked siblings, they had a need to surround themselves with good friends. And they developed a knack for entertaining. I grew up calling all of their close friends "Aunt" and "Uncle" and believing we were related, although I didn't fully understand how. Instead of the traditional family gatherings most of my friends had with their parents, grandparents, cousins, in-laws, nieces and nephews, the Bridges family gatherings were bound less by blood and more by George Benson and Dave Brubeck.

Both of my parents loved music, and our house was always filled with it. Jazz from the likes of Miles Davis, Stan Getz, Bobbi Humphrey, Lionel Hampton, Shirley Horne, Ella Fitzgerald, and Modern Jazz Quartet played loudly in the best stereophonic sound the seventies had to offer. My Father's expensive stereo equipment was housed in two custom wood cabinets he had built. One looked like the cockpit of an airplane. Its doors opened to reveal shiny metal boxes with glass gauges, their needles flicking back and forth, and a series of illuminated knobs, some pushed in, others out. The other had shelves packed so tightly with albums that my Father built wood reinforcements underneath to help ease the sag. Although his leanings were toward classical piano, he was equally passionate about jazz. They were the only types of music he played at home or in his office, with the exception of a few soulful singers like Marvin Gaye, Roberta Flack, Donny Hathaway, and Minnie Riperton.

My parents and their friends often had jam sessions, with my Father seated at his baby grand piano in our living room, Aunt Dodie playing her flute, Uncle Bill playing his violin, and Uncle Victor strumming his guitar, always lagging behind. Everybody joked that the only song Uncle Vic could really play was Duke Ellington's "Satin Doll." My Mother played the piano proficiently and would sometimes try to sing, but she was definitely no Billie Holiday. No Lady Day. She was too busy running back and forth to the kitchen, in search of toothpicks for the

OPPOSITE I couldn't resist purchasing this white unicorn-head costume for Halloween, but I nearly suffocated in the hot, unventilated rubber mask.

Marvin Gaye and Dave Brubeck were two musicians whose music my parents played constantly. They stored hundreds of their favorite albums in cabinets my Father designed and built in the living room of our house in Philadelphia.

new batch of pigs in a blanket that had just come out of the oven on a cookie sheet.

Sometimes I played games with the children of my parents' friends, but more often I lay in the middle of the living room floor, surrounded by music, conversation and commotion, with a stack of white paper and colored pencils, drawing album covers. My parents were of the generation that firmly believed children should be seen and not heard. As long as I wasn't disruptive, I could stay in the room. All the adults just stepped over or around me. I was content not to be the center of attention. My brother, on the other hand, was usually in the basement with a bunch of his friends, watching the game, arm wrestling, or giggling about the usual boy stuff, such as who cut the loudest or smelliest fart.

My parents had an eclectic collection of friends, some married couples with children, some divorced, some single. The only time-honored family tradition we kept was to spend every Thanksgiving with my Aunt Olga, my Uncle Ben, and their son Alan, who lived in New York. We alternated years between their house and ours. Aunt Olga wasn't related to my parents, but she might as well have been. She grew up in North Philly with my Father, went to The Philadelphia High School for Girls with my Mother, and introduced them much later.

My Father and Aunt Olga argued about everything from who was smarter— they had both skipped one grade in elementary school, but my Dad had completed college in two years after receiving the Philadelphia Mayor's Scholarship, then went directly on to dental school; she held a doctorate from Columbia University in education, so it was debatable—to sports, race and politics. My Father drank Myers's Dark Rum and Coke with a twist of lime. My Aunt Olga,

My parents loved to entertain, and often invited friends over for cocktail parties and makeshift jam sessions. These photographs were taken around 1966.

Tanqueray and tonic. Both smoked packs and packs of cigarettes (Lark for him, and Pall Mall for her), a habit they had both picked up as teenagers. By the end of the night they had been either too tired or inebriated to remember whatever it was they were debating so they would call a truce. The rest of us would have long since gone to bed, driven upstairs by their thick clouds of toxic smoke.

Whether it was Thanksgiving or a cocktail party, our house transformed from a place that often felt stiff and formal to one that felt completely unbuttoned and relaxed. Maybe it had something to do with the music and the drinks. The fact is, when my parents had company they both seemed to exhale deeply. With that one intentional, shared breath, their demeanor softened and their rules slackened. Ordinarily, my Father was strict about not allowing my brother and me to drink soda. After all, he was a dentist and knew it would rot our teeth— not to mention make us fat. Bottles of America's favorite brown carbonated beverage with the red label were stored like Kryptonite in the basement and in the cabinet below the sink of the first-floor powder room. When company arrived, suddenly Coca-Cola flowed from those bottles like tap water from the kitchen faucet, not just for our parents' cocktails, but for all us kids.

My Mom's favorite cocktail was a Whiskey Sour, which she made in the blender, using packets of mix. (But for the ice, she probably would have made it in the microwave.) The first time I tried alcohol was when she gave me a sip. I didn't like the taste but I was excited to have the maraschino cherry, which was sweet and cool, having been stored in a jar in the door of our fridge since the last cocktail party.

Our home was filled with so much life and laughter and music during those "holiday evenings." My parents seemed truly happy, and it was at those times I could see the glue that bound them together. There was something intangible in their connection. I couldn't quite put my finger on it, but I could sense it. It was never evident on Tuesday evenings or Thursdays after school, after my Father came home late from his office. Her warmth to his cool distance; his intellect to her common sense. Her outgoing nature bringing his introverted personality out to play. Like a short jazz riff on piano, changing chords quickly and unpredictably, somehow surprisingly finding balance and harmony. Love was hidden deeply in the melody if you listened closely.

By the time the last cocktail glass was loaded into the dishwasher, everything reverted to "normal." Opened bottles of Coke were sealed tightly and put away, the empty ones tossed into the garbage bin. The stereo was turned off, all the records slid back into their colorful cardboard sleeves, the cabinet shut tight. All the rules, formality, and expectations fell back into place. Order was restored.

I first became fully aware of my blackness in the second grade. It started near the seesaw during recess, when Keith Saltzman called me the N-word. Even though both of us were too young to understand what it really meant, I was smart enough to know it was no compliment. So I did what any self-respecting second grader would do under the same circumstance: I beat him up. In fact, I beat him up so badly he cried, which was a shock because he was one of the cutest and most popular boys in our class. I remember being even more shocked at how easily those punches came from my body, as easily as the word *Nigger* had spilled from his lips. It was the only time I ever sat on that infamous blue bench outside our principal's office. I never told my parents, and Mrs. Horowitz never called home to tell them, either. And I always thought Keith Saltzman should have had to sit on the blue bench with me that day.

Things became a bit more complicated during my adolescence. Like most children who grow up clamoring for attention and recognition from their parents, by the time I became a teenager I felt slightly invisible and grossly misunderstood. Those feelings were probably further exacerbated by me attending a small, private Quaker school, where most years, I was referred to either as "Sidney's little sister" or simply as "the black girl" in my class. As benignly true as those distinctions were, I cringed when I heard them, and I recognized their subtle contributions to my feelings of invisibility.

On top of the usual teen angst, I felt as though I constantly straddled two opposing hemispheres—the white one at school and the black one in my neighborhood—eventually becoming wedged in between. It was a tricky existence, but I managed it deftly—on the surface. I certainly wasn't the first black child to delicately balance what scholar W.E.B. Du Bois referred to as "double consciousness," in his book *The Souls of Black Folk,* nor would I be the last. At school I was surrounded mostly by *uber*-smart, privileged Jewish kids (with a few WASPs thrown in for diversity) who loved to touch my Angela Davis-inspired Afro and make jokes about my round "basketball booty." It also brought them great pleasure to compare our skin tones whenever they returned from vacation at their grandparents' in Boca Raton. "Look, Sheila! Oh my God, look. I'm darker than you are!" they would say, grabbing my arm and pulling it next to theirs. It didn't take much, since my skin tone, particularly in the winter, was barely the color of sandpaper.

"You're different than other black people," they would often say, as if I needed reassurance that my blackness would eventually fade like their Florida tans. "I mean...you aren't *really* black." I wasn't exactly sure what they meant by those

TOP I am horse-show ready with a dapple-grey horse named Bonne Belle.
I was outfitted in proper jodhpurs, leather boots, a white dress shirt, and a riding helmet.
ABOVE In 1974, I sat atop Copper Penny for my weekly Saturday morning
English riding lesson with Lorna Hoopes, my instructor.

comments, but I do know I felt as though instead of seeing me, many of my classmates looked right through me. Both my parents reminded me from time to time why this was. My Mother in particular wanted to be sure I fully understood: "You do realize that other than their maid or the man who paved their driveway, you are probably one of the few black people they know."

While I think my Mother's motivation was to protect me from getting hurt, ultimately her assertions only helped create a foundation of mistrust. I took her words to heart, which meant I could never really confide in my white schoolmates or develop the type of friendships that should have lasted a lifetime. It worked both ways. While I was invited to their homes and to various functions, their parents usually maintained a polite distance, often referring to me in the third person as if I weren't in the room. "Sheila wears such nice clothes. Look at her pretty blue espadrilles! She comes from a nice black family."

I felt a bit like a Shetland pony in a petting zoo. A cute, immaculately groomed and well-behaved animal that was best kept behind a fence, tame enough to invite to birthday parties, bar mitzvahs and "Sweet Sixteens" as long as she wore a proper halter and was held on a strong lead rope, just in case she might bite.

I would go back to school on Mondays, and if my white classmates or teachers asked how I spent the holiday or the weekend, I might tell them about my parents' parties and dinners with all my uncles and aunts. "How can you have aunts and uncles if your parents don't have any brothers or sisters?" they would ask. I tried to explain that even though my parents' friends weren't technically related we were still family. This was generally met by puzzlement or incomprehension. It didn't help that I pronounced the word "aunt" to rhyme with "font" rather than "ant," as they did. I would tell them my godmother, Aunt Jackie, had stopped by, that Sidney's godbrother, David, had joined the festivities or that I had gone with my Mother to pick up shortbread cookies my Aunt Baby had baked for me. I remember the funny looks when I brought up her name: "Aunt *Baby*! What kind of name is that?" or "Huh? Why would someone who is 80 years old be called *baby*?"

It was just one more reason on my growing list of differences that convinced me why it was better—easier—not to share anything about what happened at home with my classmates. From what I said to the way I said it, I always seemed to stand out, like a white-bearded unicorn amongst a herd of black horses.

The other world I straddled was that of my neighborhood, which was racially mixed but predominantly black. Once blacks moved to the Wynnefield section of Philadelphia in the mid-sixties, many of the Jewish residents escaped to nearby suburbs, following Har Zion Temple (our neighborhood synagogue), which had moved to expand. They didn't go far, just beyond City Line Avenue to Bala Cynwyd, Wynnewood, and Lower Merion. Our tree-lined street of stone houses bordered The Bala Golf Club, which was founded in 1897 and had a private 18-hole course. The club was famous for having hosted the 1952 U.S. Women's Open, but none of that mattered to me. I cared only that it was an extension of my own backyard. The perfectly groomed slopes made for great sledding in the winter, and an outdoor science lab in the summer, where I spent hours on the pristine greens, narrow fairways, and in the sand traps and streams. When the white golf carts zoomed around the bend on pebbled paths, I would run and hide with my containers full of crayfish, newts, and the occasional turtle.

Balls frequently ended up in our yard, and even occasionally broke a window. My Father kept a large container on the floor of our breakfast room, where we dumped all the strays we found. The club's policy barring Jews and blacks bothered me. If golfers ever saw me on the course, they would wave their clubs shouting "Get outta here!" which I promptly did, running back up the embankment to the safety of my backyard. At some point, when I was around nine years old, I was tired of being complicit and decided to take my anger about their membership policies out on the golfers themselves.

I would hide behind a large oak tree, waiting for the men to tee off. As soon as a ball landed on the flat behind my house, I took off running as fast as I could across the perfectly manicured rye grass, and stole the ball. Sometimes I could grab two. I would watch as the men, in their colored pants and white-collared shirts, got out of their carts, took their visors off, scratched their heads and searched for the balls. They sometimes cursed loudly or even threw down their clubs, frustrated they had messed up this short, strategic par 4. Every once in a while, a golfer would spot me crouching behind mature plantings or in high grass near the pot bunker, and a chase would ensue. But by the time they got back into their carts and sped after me, I could always outrun them. I knew the entire course like the back of my hand, including all the holes in the chain-link fence that separated it from our neighborhood. I felt a sense of power and victory, of righting a wrong, as I ran away fast, tightly squeezing that white, dimpled Titleist ball in the palm of my little black hand.

Because I went to private school just beyond the city limits, I was told by some of the black kids in the neighborhood that I sounded and acted "like a

The Bala Golf Course was situated directly behind our backyard in Philadelphia. I spent a lot of my free time there as a child, looking for insects, salamanders, and other critters to bring home. My Father took this photograph in 1979.

white girl." Again, I didn't understand exactly what that meant, but I was quick to notice that cute black boys wearing suede Puma sneakers riding banana seat bikes showed absolutely no interest in the finer points of field hockey or the rules of lacrosse. None of the kids on my block understood why I was so insistent on going to my English riding lessons on Saturdays instead of hanging out with them at the mall. While I never remember being called an "Oreo" directly (a name usually reserved for my darker friends suggesting they were black on the outside but white on the inside, just like the cookie), it did mean that the more I said, the greater the likelihood that I would be mimicked for it.

If I talked about horseback riding with my friends from the neighborhood, I was too white. If I told my high school classmates about the latest dance moves I had learned on Saturday night at The Cornucopia (our neighborhood banquet hall), I was too black.

DJ Lady B would be spinning records like Grandmaster Flash and the Furious Five's "Super Rappin'" or Kurtis Blow's "The Breaks." When my neighborhood girlfriends and I hit the worn wooden dance floor, I would sometimes slow down, whispering in my friend Jade's ear that I "couldn't find the beat." She would just laugh and say, "You'll get it back." I remember one time it was easy to figure out where I'd lost it—at a white classmate's birthday party the night before. After watching Lisa Rosenthal tear up the dance floor all night like a Fair Isle Sweater caught in the "permanent press" cycle of the washing machine, I lost my own rhythm. I never understood all that herky-jerky dancing to the words. Those girls flung their bodies and Laura Ashley prairie skirts back and forth to Lynyrd Skynyrd's "Free Bird" like they were being hit from all sides by bumper cars at Great Adventure. As soon as I could relocate the drumbeat, I'd be fine.

It dawned on me early that it was far less complicated to keep my endeavors and inclinations to myself rather than offer inadequate explanations—to either side. That way, there would be no expectations of how I should behave and consequently less of a risk of anyone questioning my racial authenticity. I was far more concerned about disappointing everyone in both worlds than fitting in completely in either. There was safety in not sharing. And whenever I was offered one of Nabisco's famously distinctive Oreo sandwich cookies by either white or black friends, the answer was always the same. "No, thank you."

I often spent my time with Sidney and his friends, playing touch football in the street or games of P-I-G or H-O-R-S-E on the makeshift basketball court in our driveway. I made a great wide receiver but was a terrible basketball player. My shots would fly all over the place, hitting the glossy, dark leaves of the copper beech tree and the window of our carriage house, often missing the backboard completely. While short for his age, time after time, my brother managed to get nothing but net. *Swoosh!* Since I always lost, I would quickly grow bored and make my way up the three flights of carpeted blue stairs to my bedroom, where I would happily entertain myself, alone, creating kaleidoscopes of make-believe.

I designed and built elaborate worlds from facial tissue, fishhooks, dry elbow macaroni, and anything else I could get my hands on. All I needed was a little Elmer's Glue to shore it all up. My parents and their friends gave me knitting needles and crochet hooks, balls of yarn, complicated rug patterns, paint-by-numbers canvasses, and needlepoint kits. My Father set up a card table in my bedroom so I could work on the series of 6,000-piece jigsaw puzzles of cats and dogs I was given for my birthday. I would listen to Earth, Wind & Fire or Stevie Wonder's "Innervisions," rushing to get the puzzle done before my Father's Friday night Pinochle game, when he needed his table back in the basement so he and his friends could drink, play cards, and pass girlie magazines around.

I also learned from the books my Father gave me on string figures, macramé, and origami. I would spend much of the day weaving cotton twine into Jacob's Ladders, tying double half-hitch knots to make geometric patterns or neatly folding poppy-red paper into blossoming lotus flowers and flapping birds. I also learned subconsciously how to apply those same techniques to my own emotions—whenever I felt crippled by my shyness or had my sensitive feelings hurt by the words of my schoolmates or my parents and brother.

The landscape of my fantasy world was vast, always brimming with infinite possibility. It was an amalgam of all the things that made me comfortable in my own skin: I loved books, drawing, puzzles, nature, animals, and sports. In high school my two favorite subjects were biology and art. I wanted to be either a veterinarian or a marine biologist when I grew up. But once I found out how much math and chemistry were involved, my plans to work aboard the *Calypso* alongside Jacques Cousteau were squashed.

It was around the same time that I began to set my sights beyond Philadelphia. Ever since I started staying up late Saturday nights to watch *Saturday Night Live* with Sidney, fantasizing about hosting the show and doing a skit with Dan Aykroyd and John Belushi, I quietly decided I wanted to live in New York City. And while the likelihood of my becoming a *Not Ready for Prime Time Player* was in itself comedic, I secretly clung to my adolescent dream by keeping a postcard of Manhattan tucked into the upper right corner of my bedroom mirror, sandwiched between the shiny brass frame and my autographed fan photo of Michael Jackson. Every day, when I looked in the mirror to get ready for school, I saw that five-cent souvenir I had bought on a family trip to New York City. My parents and brother walked in and out of my room several times a day, completely unaware that by the age of 13, Michael and I were steadily scheming how to make a clean getaway from my tiny third-floor bedroom with its purple cut pile, wall-to-wall carpet.

When I was in high school, I spent many hours washing, blow drying, and curling my hair, hoping it would resemble movie star Farrah Fawcett's. Unfortunately, it never did.

CHAPTER 3

TRAGIC MULATTO

It was just the two of us, speeding north on I-95 in my Father's white Oldsmobile Toronado. He drove and I was the copilot. Dad smoked his Lark cigarettes and fumbled with the car radio to find the classical music stations while I pored over the AAA road maps that filled his glove compartment. I had narrowed it down to Mt. Holyoke, Dartmouth, University of Virginia, and Brown. Except for the visible absence of testosterone at Mt. Holyoke, all of the campuses had begun to look the same. Stately old brick edifices surrounded by manicured grass lawns peppered with students circling up casually to play Hacky Sack or lounging next to their knapsacks. There was plenty of variety in hairstyles and fashion statements—from hippie to preppy to jock—but I rarely spied a black person. I quickly came to realize the sight of a black Labrador Retriever chasing a Frisbee seemed to be far more common.

As we drove up the steep hill toward Brown's campus and first caught a glimpse of the Van Wickle Gates, I experienced that inexplicable feeling you get when you know something is right. At 17, I'm not sure I fully understood the concept of a hunch or intuition, but I certainly felt its power. It grabbed hold of me and wouldn't let go. And so, when things worked out after the ensuing months, I trusted it and went to Brown. It was my first choice.

Karen and I became fast friends after meeting during "Third World Transition Period." As Brown University "students of color," we were required to arrive on campus a week before the other freshman for a special orientation. Apparently, the assumption was that many of us would need extra time to adjust to life around white people, in case we hadn't had that experience before. Karen and I bonded over the irony. I was from a place called Philadelphia, far from the Sudan, and she hailed from the distant land of Montclair, N.J.—not Papua New Guinea. I was the daughter of a prominent dentist and she of an orthopedic surgeon with a lucrative private practice in Manhattan. We hardly qualified as Third World.

No doubt there were students from other countries who benefited tremendously from this well-intentioned program. But most of us simply appreciated the chance to snag the better beds before our roommates arrived. In my first 17 years, I couldn't recall a specific instance when it had actually been a plus to be black, so I took full advantage and occupied the bigger closet, all the better to hang my Masai headdress and lion's tooth necklace right next to my colorful collection of Ralph Lauren polo shirts from Saks.

After our Third World Transition Period was over, everybody else arrived on campus. During my first week, I was chased down by a petite, curly-haired young woman as I hurried across the green. I had overslept and was late for my psychology class in Sayles Hall.

"Excuse me, um, excuse me," she said, catching her breath. "Sorry to bother you but I was wondering if you'd like to join the Interracial Support Group."

"The *what?*"

"The Interracial Support Group."

"What's that?"

"It's a group of biracial students who support one another through the challenges we face having parents of different races. I'm sure you've felt sometimes how hard it is to fit in, the extra pressures. We get together and talk about how we have different experiences from other Brown students. My Mother's white and my Father's black. How about you?"

I didn't get it. I had never seen this girl before and she was already making assumptions about my family. She was right: Sometimes it felt hard to fit in, but that had nothing to do with one of my parents being white.

"Me? No. Sorry, but both my parents are black."

I had ditched my nappy, unkempt 'fro a couple years back and opted for straightening my hair with a chemical relaxer, proudly paying homage to Farrah Fawcett, wearing my hair in a modified version of her famous long shag look, complete with "wings." Early eighties fashion demanded I trade in my double-fisted plastic pick for a blow dryer and curling iron. Maybe that's where the misunderstanding lay.

"Really? Wow. Then I'm the one who should be sorry. You really look biracial. Your skin coloring, your hair…"

"True, but where I come from we just called it light-skinned. Hey, I'm late for class—gotta go."

I walked away from my support-group recruiter, perplexed. *Biracial?* I had never even heard the word before. Good thing it hadn't shown up on the SATs. I'd been called "light-skinned," "high yella," "light-bright," "beige," "light-complected," and "redbone," but never "biracial." When it came to matters of race, my small Philadelphia world was easy to navigate: You were either black or white, simple as that. I knew people with red hair and freckles, others with green eyes and skin the color of pumpernickel, and they were all black. Around

The Octoroon Girl was painted in 1925 by New Orleans-born artist Archibald John Motley, Jr.

Philly, we adhered to the One Drop Rule when it came to determining race. Or as my Mother used to say jokingly, "It doesn't matter how much milk you put in your coffee. Coffee with milk is still coffee."

I knew the difference between Jewish and WASP, but not much beyond that. With the exception of Mrs. Horikawa, our Japanese high school librarian, I didn't know any Asians. It wasn't until my freshman year of college that I learned from a Chinese woman on my hallway that the word "Oriental" should be used to refer to carpets, not people.

Almost all of my parents' friends were black. My godparents and their spouses were black. All our extended family, including my "aunts" and "uncles," were black. I wasn't sure if I actually knew any "biracial" people. I had read about fictional quadroons and antebellum octoroons in poems and novels by Langston Hughes, Faulkner, Harriet Beecher Stowe, and James Weldon Johnson. I had seen their faces poised in portraits, prints and drawings, romanticized by African American artists like Dox Thrash and Archibald Motley. I had even watched that film *Imitation of Life*, with the Sarah Jane character, smart and

This photographic still is from the 1959 version of *Imitation of Life*, one of my favorite films, which starred Sandra Dee, *left*, and Susan Kohner.

stunningly beautiful on the outside but denying her blackness, trying to pass for white, and ultimately sending her poor, heartbroken black housekeeper-mother to the grave. What a sad, melodramatic story that was. I sure as hell didn't want to end up like her, or worse—a tragic mulatto. I wondered if that's what the students in the interracial support group did: sat around feeling sorry for themselves because, ultimately, they couldn't pass.

I was having a hard time focusing on the lecture—"Carl Jung's Theories of Analytical Psychology"—as I stared at the gilt-framed oil portraits of wrinkled, old white men lining the walls above the mahogany wainscoting. *Did I really look as if one of my parents was white? And if I did, what was the big deal? Why did it bother me so much that that girl thought I was biracial? I mean, it wasn't like I didn't have any white blood. We all did. For all I knew, I could be related to one of these crusty old men on the wall. And why did mixed-race students need a special support group? I could see how having one white parent and the other black could be a bit tricky, but come on. Were their problems really so much worse than anyone else's?*

I'm not sure I ever figured out the answers to all those questions. I do know they began to open my parochial mind to the notion that the question of racial identity was far more complex than I could ever have imagined. Maybe I wasn't learning everything my parents expected me to when they wrote that big, fat tuition check each semester, but I was definitely getting an education.

While my first semester was an adjustment, overall my college experience was all I had hoped for. I flourished under Brown's unique pass/fail grading system and relished my independence from my parents and brother. Like most girls, I gained the requisite "freshman fifteen," downing slices of pepperoni pizza and hot pastrami sandwiches at 1 a.m. shortly before hitting the light switch and diving under my floral Marimekko comforter. I went home for Christmas looking positively aglow and also confidently elephantine.

In my second semester I was "swooped on" and started dating a corny but handsome upperclassman named Kevin, who lived down the hall in my dorm. He told Knock Knock jokes with confidence and wore painter's pants with Argyle socks and suede bucks. He was a 6'4" pre-med who happened to be the captain of the track team—my first *real* boyfriend. It was perfect: I was a virgin and he was a closeted Christian, so there was never any pressure to have sex. There was a lot of kissing and dry-humping to Maxell mix tapes of David Sanborn, Steely Dan, and Spyro Gyra on his loft-style twin bed above stacks of orange plastic milk crates stuffed with biology and organic chemistry textbooks. The first time I went to visit Kevin at home in Baltimore, we decided to go to Harborplace Mall. It was one of those touristy shopping malls on the water's edge with a big food court on one level and stores on the other. When we paused in front of the Bagel Express, contemplating what to eat for lunch, a woman started yelling at us.

"Hey you, you! You! I'm talking to you, Blondie!" Kevin and I turned to see what was going on. Sure enough, the brown-skinned, roly-poly girl in the red-and-black striped apron and matching baseball cap behind the Bagel Express counter was pointing at us. We both froze.

"That's right. I'm talking to you, bitch! Who the hell do you think you are, huh? Messin' with my man!" She was waving a big, shiny knife in her right hand. A crowd started to gather. I glanced nervously at Kevin. This was his home turf, not mine. A brawny, buff, All-American hammer thrower, Kevin weighed 225 pounds. I expected him to do something or at least *say* something. He just stood there, looking like the Jolly Green Giant on a box of frozen peas.

Kevin finally bent down and whispered toward my ear: "Dag...I think you'd better get out of here." I started slowly backing away, as if I'd encountered a grizzly bear. Maybe if I let her know I wasn't a threat, got really small and didn't make eye contact, she would leave me alone. She noticed my retreat and started screaming again, pointing her knife at me.

"Don't you try to run away, skank bitch! I see you! I'm talking to you! That's right—*you!* I should come around this counter and cut you!"

All eyes were on me. There was no place to run, no trees to climb, no place to hide. By the way people were rubbernecking, they obviously thought I had a pretty good chance of getting stabbed. When Kevin finally stepped forward to defend me, I turned and made a run for it. He eventually found me cowering by the entrance of the Phillips Seafood restaurant at the other end of the food court.

"Where *were* you?" he asked.

"What do you mean *'Where was I?'* Hiding out here, trying to not get killed by that crazy bagel lady. Oh my God! Why didn't you do something or say something! I have no idea what she was talking about. Holy shit!"

"I *did* say something. I told her you were my girlfriend and this was the first time you had ever been to Baltimore."

"What did she say?"

"She didn't believe me. She said you were the one sleeping with her boyfriend. She said she knew that look anywhere. I told her you were with me, you're my girlfriend, you are from Philadelphia and we go to college together in Providence. You didn't know any guys from Baltimore and even if you did you weren't sleeping with them."

"So then what did she say?"

"She asked me if your name was Valerie and I told her no. Anyway, I finally got her calmed down. She wants you to come back and meet her."

"You've got to be joking. Why would she want to meet me? Oh my fucking God! I am not going back there."

"Sheila, I wish you would stop using the Lord's name in vain."

Great, I had almost been stabbed, and now I was being scolded by my boyfriend. "OK, oh my *gosh*, then. Sorry, but I'm a little upset. I really thought she was going to attack me with that knife."

"All right, I know, but come on. We're going back there. She wants to apologize. I think you'll both feel better once she does." Apparently, it was the Christian thing to do. Kevin took my hand and started to walk me back to Bagel Express. I had to admit I was a little curious as to why she was so sure I was having an affair with her man.

"So this is my girlfriend, Sheila," he said, putting both hands on my shoulders and gently but firmly shoving me toward the counter. Crackpot Bagel Girl was using her big knife to spread cream cheese on an onion bagel. She put it down and offered her hand.

"Hi, I'm Sheri. Nice to meet you. Do you know you have a twin sister living here in Baltimore? I'm totally serious! There is a girl who looks just like you named Valerie. She has that sandy brown hair exactly like yours. Same style and everything. I'm sorry about cussing you out, but I know Valerie has been fooling around with my man and I could've sworn you were her."

I smiled nervously and shook her hand. She looked like a much nicer, friendlier bear now that she wasn't screaming and threatening me with her knife.

"No, I definitely don't have a twin and this is my first time in Baltimore." I couldn't think of what else to say.

"Well, welcome to Charm City, honey. But you should be really careful while you're in town because you look just like Valerie and she's a big ho who sleeps around. I can't get over how much you look like her. Anyway, I'm real sorry and I want to make it up to you guys. So you can both have any bagel sandwich you want for free. On the house. My treat."

I had lost my appetite. The idea of having a bagel sandwich prepared by Sheri-Bear with that knife of hers held no interest for me. I just wanted to go back to the safety of Kevin's parents' house, but Kevin was hungry. Besides, the sandwiches were free and Kevin was squirreling his money away for med school. I soon learned that pinching pennies was his favorite hobby, second only to clipping coupons from the Sunday *Baltimore Sun*.

"Sure, we'd love a couple of sandwiches," he said.

We scanned the menu board above Sheri's head and a few minutes later walked away with a final apology, one tuna melt and one sliced turkey on a plain, white bagel. I picked at the Muenster cheese on my tuna melt while Kevin wolfed down his sandwich as if he hadn't eaten a real meal in days.

When he was done, all he could say, looking at my lunch, was, "Are you going to finish that?" I was silent during the car ride back. I stared out the passenger window and thought about what had just happened. What was it about my appearance that was suddenly attracting so much attention, and not in a good way? No one had ever said anything out of the ordinary about the way I looked when I lived in Philly. *"Blondie" for God's sake? Was she for real?* While I didn't always feel like I completely fit in, I had never thought I stood out all *that* much. It wasn't like my hair was the color of Marilyn Monroe's or anything.

I hated it when people made assumptions about me based on how I looked. I wanted to believe that what made me stand out was my personality and my interests, not my complexion or hair color. I wondered if my slutty Baltimore twin, Valerie, ran into the same problem. It was 1983, and Vanessa Williams had just been crowned Miss America. She was black but had big blue eyes and sandy brown hair that was blown dry and curled with a curling iron, just like mine.

CHAPTER 4

"LIKE NO OTHER STORE IN THE WORLD"

I considered myself lucky. Unlike so many young people who move to New York City in their early twenties with pockets full of dreams, I was armed with an expensive Ivy League degree. I majored in sociology and had the distinction of having studied abroad in Rome during my junior year without becoming fluent in Italian. My youthful enthusiasm coupled with my impractical academic skill-set meant I wasn't qualified for much of anything, including kneading the dough or taking out the garbage at Ray's Original Pizza.

The only practical work experience I did have was in retail. So the first "real job" I landed was in the Executive Training Program at Bloomingdale's. I had worked as a salesperson at The Narragansett Clothing Store in Baltimore after my sophomore year. I spent the summer selling preppy sportswear so I could live with Kevin, who was in med school by then.

My initial days at Bloomingdale's were spent shlepping boxes of cotton mock turtlenecks out of the stockroom and onto the selling floor, and marking down furry pale pink Liz Claiborne angora knit dresses from $79.99 to $59.99. Thanks to an additional 20 percent employee discount, I was able to buy one and wear it home that first Easter, leaving a trail of pink fuzz all over my parents' house. They were proud to see their hard-earned tuition money finally paying off. Their only daughter was well on her way to becoming a top New York Fashion Buyer. Or so they thought.

Looking back, I could never be sure whether it was a serious career misstep or just a bad joke. Either way, I sucked it up and paid my dues, living in an over-priced Brooklyn shoebox with water bugs that were fatter than my paycheck. I celebrated my newfound independence by ordering Chinese take-out through a small hole in a smudged, bulletproof glass window at Wing Wah Restaurant at least three nights a week. I would wash it all down with a carton of Tropicana Fruit Punch that my roommate, Pat, or my new boyfriend, Eric, had bought from the tiny bodega across the street. Several years (and thousands of milli-grams of MSG) later, I learned from an article in the *New York Times* that my "healthy choice" of chicken with broccoli had more fat calories than two Big Macs, a large order of fries, and a vanilla shake.

This is the entrance to the Bloomingdale's department store in Manhattan, at Lexington Avenue and 59th Street. I worked at Bloomie's after I graduated from Brown University in 1986.

Every night I arrived home from work exhausted and raggedy. Bloomingdale's was open until 8:30, which meant I often didn't make it back to the apartment until after 10. My pantyhose would look as if my legs had been used as a scratching post for a kitten trying out its new claws. My headband was always crooked and my head throbbed. I would march straight to the medicine cabinet for the bottle of Extra Strength Tylenol. (I hadn't discovered vodka yet.) Then I would collapse onto my roommate's overstuffed beige Jennifer Convertibles sleeper sofa.

"Why don't you just quit the fucking job?" Eric would say as he took turns stroking my hair and rubbing my aching feet. I was only 23, but already had a standing monthly appointment with a podiatrist to treat the painful corns I was developing from spending 10 hours a day on my feet in mandatory stockings and heels.

"I can't. How the heck am I going to pay my bills? And what else am I supposed to do?"

I was unclear about my career path. Meanwhile, every one of my friends seemed to be right on track; they had all started medical school or law school or scored fancy jobs on Wall Street. Eric was in the Sales & Trading Program at Goldman Sachs. He made three times as much as I did, but when we moved in together we split our thousand-dollar rent: his six hundred to my four hundred.

One night after getting home from work and plopping down on the couch I had an exciting new development to share with Eric: I could finally change my tune from "I can't quit" to "I don't need to quit."

"It's all gonna change *very* soon," I told Eric. "I saw my written review in Sandy's office today and I'm about to get promoted. Do you know what that means?"

"Do I know what it means to get promoted? Yeah—new title, more money, less shitwork."

"I'll be off the selling floor and in the Buyer's Office by Christmas! No more crazy hours, no more dealing with those stupid salespeople."

Those stupid salespeople I referred to was actually only one in particular. He was from Staten Island, his name was Kimon, and he was the first openly gay person I had ever met. When my boss, Sandy, introduced us, he offered a limp handshake then, with a squint, stared me directly in the eyes and asked, "What *are* you?" As if my spaceship had just touched down in the Men's Designers department from another planet.

"Excuse me?" I replied. *One Mississippi. Two Mississippi. Three Mississippi.*

I always liked to give people a moment to reconsider. Usually, they would rephrase the question.

"What *are* you?" he asked again. My three-count hadn't worked. I answered anyway, knowing exactly where he was headed.

"I'm black."

"Black? Really? You're *black?* You don't *look* black. What—did your father fuck a *Swede* or something?" he added, with a snide chuckle.

Wow. I hadn't expected him to take it *that* far.

Sandy jumped in before I could even think what to say: "Kimon, you can't say things like that. It's just too rude!"

"Rude? What's so *rude* about it? I mean, c'mon, look at her. She practically has blond hair. She's no darker than me. She's not really *black* black."

Was that how white people thought of me and my blackness? Was being black sort of like a Clinique free-gift-with-purchase that didn't really count because melanin didn't cost anything? Since my complexion was lighter than a lot of other black folks', did it somehow mean that I should feel *less* denigrated whenever someone bluntly said something offensive, callously disregarding my ethnicity? What exactly does it mean to be "...not really *black* black?" Why were we often made to feel invisible, deferred to the third person or consigned to insignificance? There were days at Bloomingdale's that the thinly disguised racism made me feel is if I were reduced to a mere pose, frozen still and translucent like those mannequins in our storefront windows along Lexington Avenue.

I desperately wanted a witty comeback, harsh and cutting enough to put Kimon in his place. But the right words never came. Part of it had to do with being caught so off-guard, but mostly it was not wanting to show "negritude" at work. It was my first day as Assistant Manager in Men's Designers, and I needed to make a good impression. Be professional. Throwing shade on my first day in the new division would amount to self-sabotage. From that moment forward, I made a conscious effort to steer clear of Kimon. Whenever I saw him on the floor, though, I felt my anger percolating like the pot of boiling coffee I wanted to throw in his face. See if he recognized *black* black, then.

Even with somebody like Kimon in its midst, Men's Designers was a step up from my previous outpost in Better Dresses, where I had to work weekends, evenings, and holidays, plus deal with rude customers returning rank merchandise. Bloomingdale's' policy was to take back any garment, even if it was stained or smelled like dirty sweat socks. As long as the tags were still on, my job was to smile while I rang up your return.

E ric was about to run out the door to pick up Chinese. We took turns, depending on whose day was worse, which meant it was always his turn. "So how did you manage to see your review?"

"I went upstairs to Sandy's office to check on an Armani shirt a customer wanted. She was out to lunch. I was looking through a bunch of papers on her desk trying to find a stock report, and there it was." After nearly a year of constant retail drama and crisis management, I had finally been labeled "promotable." Soon I would be out of the store and down the street in the Buying Office, which was a big step up. Eric and I celebrated prematurely that night with an order of shrimp fried rice and pork dumplings. We toasted my new promotion with a couple of Bartles & Jaymes wine coolers.

The following week I was summoned to Sandy's office for my official review. She was there, along with the division head, Saul Epstein. The same piece of paper I had seen was on her desk. Reading upside down, though, I immediately noticed all the check marks down the "Excellent" column had been whited out like typos and switched over to "Satisfactory." "Promotable," which was origi-nally hand-written above her signature, was gone. *How could this have happened?* Obviously, there was nothing I could say: I wasn't even supposed to have been in Sandy's office, let alone rifling through confidential papers on her desk.

Sandy and our division head took me through my review step by step. It had very little relation to the glowing endorsement I had scanned the week before. I sat there, biting my tongue, trying to hold back my emotions. When they were done, I couldn't help but challenge them. I had busted my ass for months, working virtually nonstop, carrying out every little task I was asked to com-plete no matter how tedious or onerous. I told them I didn't agree with the review, that I felt I had earned this promotion and deserved it now. Sandy sat there in silence; for all I knew, she agreed with me. The division head shot back, "Well I don't know exactly who you think you are or what makes you think you're so special, but nothing is going to happen regarding your promotion now, and at least through the holidays."

I could feel the tears welling up. I dropped my head and nodded as they chimed on in tandem, explaining how they needed every able-bodied person on that selling floor right through the Christmas season—no exceptions, not even Little Miss Executive-in-Training. But their explanation fell on deaf ears. I had already tuned them out.

After the ordeal was over, I retreated from Sandy's office stunned. Skipping my normal 20-minute lunch outing, I grabbed my purse, then snuck into the stockroom and hunkered down on the edge of a splintered wooden pallet, comforted by boxes of brown Calvin Klein cable-knit sweaters waiting to be shelved. Maybelline tears flooded downstream from my eyes, smearing my face and chin, splattering my nude pantyhose and starting a miniature Jackson Pollack in my lap. Once I had composed myself enough to reemerge onto the selling floor, of course, I immediately ran into Kimon.

"Oh, *ahem*," he enunciated with an eye roll, ostentatiously avoiding the apparently distasteful act of actually pronouncing my name. "I should *remind* you, Goldilocks, we just took delivery of three full skids and a rolling rack that need to be signed for and unpacked." I ignored him and walked out of the department—past the black Jean Paul Gaultier leather pants, past the Valentino sweaters, beyond the bank of elevators, and out the 60th Street Employee Exit. Picking up speed, I turned onto Lexington, headed downtown and just kept walking. It was over.

I did not set foot in Bloomingdale's until almost a year later, when my friend Janet dragged me back to return a DKNY dress. She had worn it twice, then changed her mind because it made her look too "hippy." "I have to return this but I can't find the receipt," she said. "Will they take it back?" I assured her they would and reluctantly agreed to show her exactly where and how to do it.

Despite a few more professional hiccups—including stints at Giorgio Armani and BASCO (Barney's All-American Sportswear Company), I found New York to be strangely comforting during those novice years. The city allowed me to define and redefine myself enough times to the point where I eventually felt like I fit in. Just as I was getting comfortable, though, my core circle of friends started trading New York for destinations like Boston and Washington, the Peace Corps and B-School. A few were already making the swap for husbands, babies, and minivans in places like Atlanta and the New Jersey suburbs. Neither choice particularly appealed to me. I was no longer in a serious relationship and I certainly wasn't ready to settle down.

I kept telling my friends the bigger picture was "I loved Eric but wasn't *in love* with him." I felt the distinction was important. I could live with someone I wasn't in love with for a couple of years, but settling down and getting married was probably out of the question. Eric wanted to marry me, but I was newly infatuated with Greg. Eric and I broke up after I cheated on him, a sordid saga I'd rather not belabor in the current telling. Suffice it to say he was suspicious enough that he ended up following me from Brooklyn to Greg's apartment above Café Un Deux Trois on West 44th Street in Manhattan. When the doorman let him up and he knocked at the door, I hid in the guest-bedroom closet like he was a Jehovah's Witness instead, convinced that he wanted only to have a heart-to-heart with Greg. Eric and I had both met Greg, together, a few months before at a party, and they seemed to hit it off. Greg even knew Eric's older brother from law school.

Needless to say, I was wrong; Eric was looking for me. And sure enough he found me, right behind those white bifold doors, crouched below Greg's winter coats and down jackets. Our argument was epic, moving from the guest room to the kitchen, then escalating out to the hallway by the elevators. Eric moved out of our Brooklyn apartment and eventually relocated to Cambridge, Massachusetts, for Harvard Business School. We were growing up and life had suddenly become more serious, more *adult*.

As I helped some of my closest friends pack up their apartments and leave the city, I felt a sense of abandonment. They were my extended kin, my makeshift New York family. We would reminisce about all the fun we had had, hanging out at The Tunnel and Paradise Garage, dancing all night, coming home with clothes reeking of cigarette smoke, eyes red and burning, showering and changing into work clothes without ever going to bed. Someone needed to stay in the trenches, to soldier on, to keep those memories intact. I figured it might as well be me. I wrote letters, keeping everyone who had moved out of New York apprised of what was happening in The Big Apple. I made a career switch, taking a job listed in the Sunday *New York Times* classifieds: "Small, prestigious architectural firm seeks administrative assistant." I applied to Parsons School of Design, attending classes nights and weekends. With the exception of my futon mattress, I put most of my belongings in storage and moved into a tiny studio apartment. To pay my tuition, I took out my first student loans and sold the designer clothes off my back to friends, and friends of friends.

My Mother and Father no longer supported the direction my career was taking. The only thing my parents did appear to be happy about was that I was no longer shacking up with my boyfriend. Another benign, handsome, athletic, All-American–looking, 6'1" Ivy-educated black man (like all my boyfriends), Eric was respectable enough. But they had a problem with us living together. My Father refused to visit me in New York, and in fact he never actually acknowledged the relationship existed. When we visited Philadelphia, I slept in my twin bed on the third floor and Eric slept in the guest bedroom on the second—directly across from my parents' room, where the door would remain strategically ajar, just in case we were tempted to break their house rules.

My parents could not fathom why I had walked out of a perfectly respectable job with health benefits. I was told I was being "silly" and "impetuous." I remember my Father shaking his head in disapproval: "For goodness sakes, Sheila. Bloomingdale's is a huge conglomerate with all kinds of career opportunities and you were in their *executive training program*. You can't just quit a job when things don't go your way. Exactly how do you plan on supporting yourself?" my Father asked, making it crystal clear he would not help out in any way.

"I don't know exactly how I'll make it work, but I will," I said. "Trust me."

I felt things were starting to click and I was on the cusp of something good. For the first time in my life, I was standing upright on my own two feet and making my own decisions. It was scary and exhilarating at the same time. I was ebullient, my happiness indulgent, my giddiness palpable. Even though the pay was abysmal and one of the partners was a schmuck, I loved my new job at the architectural firm. While one partner would stiff me for cab fare and petty cash, the other was kind and generous to a fault, the Yin to his Yang. He was brilliantly creative, slightly misanthropic, and wore a "uniform" of khaki pants, a tattered tweed jacket, and white Jack Purcell sneakers. I gave him haircuts with blunt office scissors purchased from Charrette and he gave me my very first Macintosh computer. I became a sponge, soaking up every drop of knowledge and bit of information about design and architecture that I could. My classes at Parsons were fascinating and absorbing; I was learning color theory and how to hand-draft elevations, sections, and door swings, which I initially found difficult but soon got the hang of.

Most importantly I was in love with Greg—a smart, athletic, funny black attorney who wore a flat-top fade and was a graduate of Dartmouth College and Stanford Law School. I had a wildly positive outlook about my new career path and the new man in my life. Despite teasing me that I "couldn't do doors," referring to the confusion I initially had determining whether a door should swing inward or outward, he gave me a dozen long-stemmed red roses for my birthday and, with the card, enclosed a round-trip airline ticket to the South of France. He had rented a tiny villa with a rooftop garden for ten days in Seillans, a medieval village not far from Nice. It would be the first time I had flown first class or visited the French Riviera. He told me that "we were made for each other" and said he believed he was a better person with me than without me. I felt as though the Universe had sprinkled me and everything in my path with a combination of confectioner's sugar and magical gold dust. If this was what being a grownup was like, I wanted more of it.

NICE

On my first trip to the South of France, my boyfriend and I spent a lot of time in Cannes, Nice, and Monaco, going to the beach and museums, eating French food, and drinking lots of rosé.

that lawyer chris ▓▓▓▓ or chris ▓▓▓▓ i can't even remember his last name- which is ok because he definitely is not my husband or even teh kind of guy that would know my husband if you know what I mean. we had brunch at *good enough to eat* on amsterdam. i had an omelet and he had pancakes and bacon (love their strwaberry butter!0. the conversation was so boring i swore i heard crickets in the restaurant. i tried to be polite and act interested in what he was talking about (himself mostly) but if he calls me im not going out with him again. no sense wasting his time or mine.

but even the snorefest with chris ▓▓▓▓ was better than the date i had last thursday at a restaurant on 22nd street called Alva with a guy named ▓▓ ▓▓▓▓▓ who my friend ▓▓▓ set me up with. anyway he was a 55 year investment banker with a big bald spot, 2 afro puffs and thick mutton chop style side burns. totally old school-looking like he was one of the isley brothers. ronald's older brother but in the navy pinstripe instead of the skin tightt polyester bell bottoms and a suede fringed vest. so when he was dropping me off after teh date ▓▓▓▓ (my ex) was in front of our apartment building. i panicked because i didn't want him to see me with some old man with afro puffs so I tried to stall getting out of ▓▓'s car. the only thing i coudl think to do was to duck and pretend to lose my contact lens on the floor so i bent down and felt around on the dirty car mat even though i don't even wear glasses or contact lenses. luckily by the time i finished, ▓▓▓▓ had already gone into the building. talk about a close call!

meanwhile...why did i find out after the date that grandpa was married!!! i called ▓▓▓ and read him the riot act. why in god's name would you set me up on a blind date with an old married man? because you are a knucklehead. because you are an asshole.

hey- just read my horoscope in elle magazine and harper's bazaar!

"If you're bold enough to demand it, the coming year offers a turning in your intimate life. A pattern of nebulous instability has reigned there for many years. it may be a relationship with someone who's been emotionally evasive, or simply manifested in a long line of scoundrels cleverly disguised as sensitive, romantic, self-help graduates. Whatever the storyline, you're ready to change it. You're feeling pluckier, more direct. Trust those feelings! You've been settling for too little for too long."

harper bazaar says: *Jupiter and uranus will occupy your house of marriage from the 3rd to the 11th giving you a brief chance to improve every important partnership. Your stars will send you into an emotional fever around the 5th and 6th, but by the 15th you'll feel calmer, cooler and willing to appreciate a fabulous new relationship. Driven by financial*

CHAPTER 5

DEGREES OF ASSHOLE

I spent most of my late twenties and early thirties kissing frogs. Where did all the love go? Where did all the starry-eyed romanticism and pixie gold dust suddenly disappear to? Part of the answer is that my focus had shifted: I started my own design business and my on-again off-again, revolving-door relationship with Greg had run its course. We had some amazing times together, and it was the closest I came to settling down with someone. But when it was finally over, I felt as though he had wiped his feet with my heart; he left all of his good intentions and sincere promises unfulfilled, and I walked away feeling gypped.

After Greg, I dated a series of guys who, instead of turning into princes and whisking me away atop strong stallions, merely remained the handsome, well-educated, self-involved narcissists they already were at the core. What did I expect? Most could shoot hoops, they all had swagger, their Buppie credentials were unassailable, but let's face it, none of them really knew how to ride a horse—let alone play Prince Charming to my Cinderella.

I met them in a variety of ways, but mostly at parties. In fact, there were so many parties and so many men I decided to keep a detailed journal, chronicling everything for several years. The pickup lines were so ripe and the break-up talks so clichéd that I needed to scribble them all down. You never know, I thought: One day I might want to remember all this stuff.

My single girlfriends and I went to at least two parties every weekend, many times without knowing the host(s). When we arrived, we would immediately scan the room, assessing the cuteness of the men, the danceability of the music, and the quality of the snacks. If we agreed that all three were up to par, we stayed. If not, we bounced—in search of a better scene.

In my twenties, I was typically the one who could be located hovering by the snack table, spearing neon-yellow cheese cubes with toothpicks, or dunking Ruffles potato chips into homemade sour cream onion dip. Perhaps the fact that I wasn't embarrassed to eat in public made me seem like easy prey. Maybe, but I had to hand it to them: They looked good, and talked an even better game. So I put on my floppy pink hat and Wayfarer sunglasses, ready for the boat ride. Predictably, like the innumerable prospects before me, I often ended up thrown

OPPOSITE This entry in my personal journal is dated January 18th, 1996.

overboard like chum, attracting the next round of unsuspecting victims. Sometimes, I jumped from the slippery deck on my own, even with no land in sight. Either way, I ended up in the chop, treading water in the wake of their shiny cigarette boat as it roared off into the distance. Fortunately I was buoyant and in no danger of drowning. But I was almost always left wondering what exactly had gone so terribly wrong with the ride.

I attracted so many men, I had to swat them off like flies. Which enabled me to move from one impressive résumé to the next even more impressive one. Ivy educated BAs, MAs, MBAs, MDs, and JDs. There was a managing director, an attorney, a surgeon, an architect, several investment bankers, and one Indian chief. Most were far more interesting on paper than in real life. Like varying degrees of lactose intolerance, I figured out there were varying Degrees of Asshole. A little crumbled feta on your side salad might make your stomach grumble, but a pint of vanilla Häagen-Dazs would send you sprinting to the nearest john.

It worked the same way with the assholes. On a 10-point scale, most guys started at a 1 or 2 simply because they were men. They couldn't help but piss on the toilet seat. If they bothered to lift it up at all, it stayed there. On the highway, they hogged the left lane, chronically refusing to move over. Whenever they got lost, they would *never* ask for directions, especially from another man.

Most men moved quickly up my Asshole Scale, usually in direct proportion to their level of narcissism. Often their rating depended on more essential matters such as cheating on your pregnant wife, not paying child support, or giving your girlfriend a black eye.

Imagine how boring the world would be without assholes. Many favorites come to mind. Public servant assholes include former congressman Anthony Weiner, former governors Arnold Schwarzenegger and Elliott Spitzer, and former Senator John Edwards. Bernie Madoff, Rush Limbaugh, and Supreme Court Justice Clarence Thomas. *Assholes.* O.J. Simpson and Tiger Woods. *Big assholes.*

Assholes come in all colors, shapes, and sizes, but mine were always black and most were six foot-something. I preferred mine tall and preferably buff enough to bounce a quarter off. I should have prefaced all this by saying that just because *I* think you are an asshole doesn't mean you are one. One woman's asshole is another's Prince Charming. I'm betting Melania Trump would agree. And since I know I trampled quite a few hearts back in the day, there are a few men who might even call *me* an asshole. My personal list of assholes was longer than my hair. Close friends usually knew their real names but not always. That's because

• Twenty-five years of cover art
• Solving a lead-poisoning mystery
• A literary pioneer retires

May/June 1999

BROWN

ALUMNI MAGAZINE

Designing Woman

Sheila Bridges '86 is one of New York's top interior designers. Now if only people would stop calling her the black Martha Stewart.

I landed on the cover of the Brown Alumni Magazine in the May/June 1999 issue. The spooky, unflattering photograph could have been used by Stephen King for one of his scary novels.

I almost exclusively referred to them by the nicknames I gave each of them.

In no particular order, there was The Pathological Liar, a trader who had a Biedermeier furniture fetish, lived in TriBeCa and used to leave the trading floor in the middle of the day to have phone sex with me. There was Mr. Coffee, a bond salesman I met at a house party in Brooklyn, who, after seeing me in a Millstone Coffee advertisement in a national magazine, kept inviting me over for a cup of joe. He neglected to tell me—before or after I slept with him—that he

My first interior design book, *Furnishing Forward: A Practical Guide to Furnishing for a Lifetime*, was published by Little, Brown and Company, in 2002.

had herpes. Thankfully, I had enough good sense to practice safe sex. There was the Army Ranger-turned-internet entrepreneur, whom I met snowboarding in Vail. He was so seductive and charismatic that wherever we went, people stared. I couldn't keep my eyes off him, either. The first time we had sex he pounded me so hard I swore I could feel his dick hitting the inside of my face. I was worried my left eyeball might spring from its socket, but when I found out he had a fiancée who lived in Knoxville I quickly became much more concerned about what *I* might do to *him*.

Then there was The Actor. He had the most impressive educational credentials of all: An undergraduate degree from Brown, an MFA from Yale School of Drama, and a PhD in economics from MIT. Both of his parents were doctors. He sent me a note after my photo appeared on the cover of the Brown Alumni Magazine with the caption *Sheila Bridges, Designing Woman. Now if only people would stop calling her the black Martha Stewart.* I saw him a year or two later at a magazine party and introduced myself. Although shortish—Lilliputian almost—he was handsome and the color of caramel. Being the sugar addict I am, it's no surprise I fell hard.

The Actor turned out to be super-smart, funny, athletic, and a good dancer.

He lived in Los Angeles but eventually wanted to move to the Washington, D.C., area. He had political aspirations—or at least that's what he told me on our first date. There were a few red flags, but that should have been the biggest of them all. That and the fact he was estranged from his only brother, wore sunglasses at night, *and* lied about his age; as I got older by the year, he continued to get younger by dog years.

"You are one incredibly lucky lady!" an acquaintance told me after she'd seen us together. The Actor was still struggling, doing theater, and landing a few roles in some unmemorable films and television shows. He was waiting for his "big break." The first time he spent the night at my apartment, we stayed up late. He read me poetry and passages from my favorite book, *Letters to a Young Poet* by Rainer Maria Rilke, which sat on my bedside table. He seemed different from most of the other assholes I had dated. He had this spiritual side, and he wanted to take it slow. He was very open and had nothing to hide. He would even play his voicemail messages on speakerphone with me in the room. There would be no secrets. He wanted me to trust him. And I did.

A couple of months after he dumped me, he reappeared, sending me a beautiful silver ring by Robert Lee Morris, via FedEx, for my birthday. My friends ooh'ed and aah'ed. He claimed that he was "tortured" and "carrying pails of sadness" without me. We decided to give it another try. But something was still off.

"I love you, but I don't know what to do with my love," he said dramatically. I thought, *Maybe you should put it in the laundry room, right next to the washing machine, below the box of Tide.*

The Actor moved right up my Asshole Scale because everything always had to be about him. "When are we going to meet him or when can you guys come over for dinner?" my friends would ask. They never did meet him. We never could go out with them. They might be able to catch him on *Jeopardy* or *Real Time with Bill Maher* if they wanted to, but we could only have dinner when and where he decided, and do things with people he wanted to do them with. His parents were divorced. I met his mother, who was soft-spoken and lovely. I drove with him from L.A. to Vegas in his new Mercedes sedan. We got massages, went to see Cirque Du Soleil and crashed a bachelor party. His father had lived in Vegas and recently passed away, so I went with him to the house and spent an afternoon helping him get the place organized.

When I published my first design book, I felt proud, but I couldn't ever get The Actor to buy it or, for that matter, *any* of the magazines or newspapers featuring my work. He invited me to be his date at a wedding in New Orleans.

The bride was a well-known actress who was marrying a high-profile professional athlete. At the reception, if he bothered to introduce me at all, it became obvious that none of his L.A. friends had heard about me, even though we had been dating for several months. *Big Red Flag.* "Now how do you know X, again?" they would ask. Wedding guests who were in his fan club handed me their digital cameras and asked if I wouldn't mind "taking a shot or two" of them together with him.

I smiled and obliged. *Click-click.*

"I don't think the flash went off. Would you mind doing it again, just to be sure?" a few of them asked.

Mostly I just stood around by myself at the buffet table, piling more steamed shrimp seasoned with Old Bay and mini crab cakes onto my plate. The Actor seemed ashamed of me. Behind closed doors he was all over me, but in public he treated me like an acquaintance. I wondered why he had invited me to the wedding in the first place. What was I doing here? By the end of the weekend, I decided all he really needed was a valet.

Our relationship ended and we eventually lost touch, which wasn't really a bad thing since the loneliest I have ever felt was when I was with him. The next and last time I saw The Actor I was on an airplane. I was headed on a ten-day cycling trip to Vietnam. My carry-on was stuffed with my iPod, *Lonely Planet* guidebooks, trashy magazines, and too many boxes of Good & Plenty in anticipation of the twenty-hour flight to Hanoi. After dinner, I pulled out my *People* magazine and a box of candy. Jude Law was on the cover. According to them, he was the "Sexiest Man Alive," but there were plenty of others. I flipped page after page under the pin-sized overhead reading light. Everyone else was finishing their ramen noodles or nodding off to sleep. My Ambien hadn't kicked in yet. There he was, The Actor, all of a sudden staring up at me from the glossy page with those big brown eyes. Yes, he was sexy, but boy was he an asshole.

Then there was The Celebrity Chef, who wasn't really much of a celebrity himself but did have a penchant for sleeping with them. He was 6'4" and handsome, maybe even considered "fine" by Old School standards, which meant light-skinned with wavy hair. Oprah's Stedman was the prototype. I met him at a party and he asked me to play tennis with him. He told me his mother had cut an article about me out of *House Beautiful* magazine. She approved of how I looked and remarked, "Why don't you date her?" Maybe I had passed the paper bag test—meaning that my skin tone was lighter than a paper bag, which made me acceptable dating material. We never did play tennis, since his favorite

This photograph of Dolby, my Jack Russell Terrier and me is from an article in *House Beautiful*, April 1999. We are sitting on the front porch of my house in upstate New York.

sport turned out to be name-dropping. He beat me badly at that, forty-love. While I never actually saw any evidence of a book around him, he was proud to remind me that his name was mentioned in one sentence of Anthony Bourdain's *Kitchen Confidential*.

"I have a huge problem with you making more money than I do," he once told me. Well, at least he was honest; I automatically subtracted two on The Asshole Scale for that. This statement seemed odd coming from him, however, since the woman he dated before me was a bona fide celebrity, far more successful than me, co-hosting a network, morning TV talk show and no doubt making a lot more money than the both of us. What was I supposed to do—quit my job?

The first time The Celebrity Chef cooked for me, he burned the filet mignon

CLINTON FALLS FOR 'DESIGNING WOMAN'

Successful Harlem-based interior designer Sheila Bridges has caught Bill Clinton's roving eye

BILL CLINTON has his sights set on a beautiful designing woman!

The former president is lusting after Sheila Bridges, the sexy interior designer he personally tapped to decorate his new New York office, pals say.

"He's taken by her – no doubt," says one insider.

"He can't stop talking about her. She's beautiful and he's Bill Clinton. Need I say more?

"Sheila's an incredibly successful designer. But when Bill talks about her, he doesn't exactly discuss her resume.

"He just can't get past her looks. It's really amazing – he's like some high school kid.

"Bill's vowing to win Sheila

over w
unlike
fast-lar
to, she
sional
out to de
And
"Whoe
would g
redoing
course,
the des
beautifu
Bridge
describe
answer t
reported
track o
all alor
The Ph
is a
54-year-
ton's go
Vernon J
"Once
eyes on
a done
insider sa
"Believ
that's all
Bridge
clients
spy-thril
Tom Cla
Sean "P.
She re
with Con
his tastes
mogul's
initials "F
everythir
little too
source.
Her su
firm has
fame amo
entreprene
Bridges'
such proje
an apar
ultra-luxe
building
City.
Now, the
is trying
hand at Cl

I was in the checkout line at my local grocery store when I first saw this tabloid feature. I had gone into the store to buy ice cream but came out with a stack of trashy magazines instead. Obviously, the story was completely fabricated and untrue.

'a smart,
iful, young
r decorator
e's like a
CHOOL KID'

the best advice I could."
Bauer, 44, who was
Melanie's second hus
has remained
with

HOLLYWOOD MURDER

Robert Blake
on night of
shooting

BARETTA WIFE'S CHILLING LAST WORDS

GLOBE

$1.89 / $2.29 Canada

May 22, 2001

COP'S SHOCKING FILE

CRIME SCENE

NEW JONBEN CRIME SCENE PHOTOS

CLINTON CHASING SEX
NEW 'DESIGNING WO

's
ving to
Sheila
r with
charm'

But   office. T
her   f

woman he fin
tive to work
another source
the former presid
GLOBE.

"It's his preferre
when he's in a positi
have anything to
about it.

"And with his v
Hillary fading from
life, his eye is alread
wandering – and he likes
when it doesn't have to
wander far.

"Hillary's not surprised
Bill is smitten with
Bridges, but she believes
anyone who gets involved
romantically with him at
this point would have to
be insane."

— STEVE HERZ

and put too much salt in the vinaigrette, but made the best flourless chocolate cake I'd ever tasted. He told me he loved me and asked if I wanted to have his baby. I told him I didn't. He was plagued by insecurities about me getting back together with The Actor. Therefore, I was required to talk dirty every time we had sex. Bottom line, I had to worship The Johnson: "Oh, X, you have the biggest cock! Oh baby, I love it inside me, it feels so good, please don't stop, don't stop." And so on and so forth, with each stroke pretending that his penis was as big and as hard as a Duraflame log: You know the routine. I moaned and writhed, pretending to be turned on, meanwhile rolling my eyes under closed lids. I crept out of his arms and his life as soon as his snoring shook the sconces off my bedroom wall.

Please don't get me wrong. It's not like I didn't ever meet nice guys or date them in between The Assholes. The problem was that most assholes, with their big egos, were much more confident, more willing to ask me out, and more capable of showing me a good time. And let's face it: They usually *were* more interesting. Back then I didn't ask men out. While I was definitely particular about whom I dated, there was a strong chance that if you liked me, I would probably like you back. I liked nice guys, too. It's just that most of them were already taken. There was even a category of nice guys who wanted to be assholes but didn't know how. I briefly dated an asshole wannabe. My friends only knew him as The Horse Whisperer. He was a surgeon-turned-horse breeder, the only black man I ever met who was a serious rider and loved horses like I did. Right up my alley. It didn't matter that I had my period. He was a doctor and therefore accustomed to blood. He wanted to go down on me so badly that he pulled the tampon out of me by the string with his teeth, which meant he could never, ever be an asshole. But I ran roughshod over him like I did most of the nice guys who wanted to get with me.

Here, I've saved the biggest asshole for last—although I dated him first. He was my first asshole and set the bar so high it was tough for the others to measure up. My close friends knew him simply as The Original Asshole. They still do. He was bald like Michael Jordan and worked at Salomon Brothers. We didn't meet at a party. I was still in design school at Parsons but had picked up my first and only freelance clients, a couple. We met through them.

The Original Asshole lived in Brooklyn. So did I. He had a beautiful duplex in a brownstone and I lived in a roach-infested studio a few blocks away. Since I was still a student, I was always broke. He had money and shopped at Charivari.

We became friends first, getting together every few nights for a beer, talking about how we were "losers" because we were both still single. He started leaving messages on my answering machine every day so I wouldn't come home to a "goose egg" as he called it. He was funny, caring, very attentive but a little intense. I was accused of being the same. We started spending all our free time together. One night he admitted he was falling for me. "Don't worry, it happens all the time," I joked. Our friendship suddenly turned into a relationship. I had keys to his apartment. We got HIV tests. Mine was an ordeal because the nurse had to poke half a dozen holes in my arm before she could find the right vein.

The Original Asshole took me to ABC Carpet and Home, where he plunked down 1,000 bucks for plush pillows and fancy new bed linens since (he made a point of informing me) he didn't want me sleeping on the same sheets his ex, Ann, had. He even let me pick them out. "I want you to feel like it's our bed," he said, "Like it's your home." As an aspiring interior designer, he had me right there.

My single girlfriends were jealous. "Wow. He seems really into you," they said. It was autumn. We wanted to get out of the city so we went apple picking at Greig Farm, an orchard in upstate New York. We picked so many apples we couldn't figure out what to do with them all. Since The Original Asshole always paid for everything, I felt I needed to compensate by showing my domestic side. So I frantically baked. And baked. And baked. Apple Betty, apple crisp, apple pie, and apple crumble. I told my Mother on the phone. She said, "If you don't stop, Sheila, you're going to turn *into* an apple." The only thing I didn't make was candied apples. They didn't need much baking but the recipe was complicated. It called for sticks and wax paper. I loved artistic craft projects but this one required eight drops of red food coloring, which everybody knew gave you cancer.

"We are clearly in the presence of love," The Original Asshole liked to say whenever he pulled me close, usually in front of the downstairs hallway mirror, hugging me from behind. "We make a perfect couple and we will have beautiful babies with sandy-brown hair." I told him we wouldn't because my hair color wasn't a dominant family trait.

"How do you feel about living in a brownstone in Brooklyn and having a house in Martha's Vineyard?" he frequently asked. He told me he wanted to "give me the best of everything" and "take our children all over the world and teach them things." What those things were, I'll never know.

It was all happening so fast, I was a little apprehensive. I had been heartbroken by Greg the previous year. I still had feelings for him but he had been wishy-washy, noncommittal, always needing time to "get things in order." Suddenly, a few months into my new relationship with The Original Asshole, Greg reappeared, leaving five urgent messages on my answering machine, which I picked up remotely, calling in from The Original Asshole's house. "Call me as soon as you get this message. I have to speak to you!" It was a Thursday and he was headed down to Washington, D.C., for the weekend. He needed to give me something before he left. I ran home early Friday morning from The Original Asshole's so my ex could drop off whatever it was that was so urgent on his way to work. It turned out to be a handwritten letter.

> *Dear Sheila,*
>
> *Hello. I'm sure you are surprised to get a letter from me. Well, I am writing because the things I wanted to talk about today are too important to wait until tomorrow or whenever.*
>
> *Basically, I have come to the realization that I have been fooling myself about the way that I feel about you. It is apparent to me that the way that I respond to certain things that you say or do is because I am still very much in love with you. I also now understand that if I continue to deceive myself I am in jeopardy of losing someone who is very important to me.*
>
> *I apologize that in coming to terms with my feelings toward you that I have caused you great heartache. It is my intention to hopefully start bringing some joy to your life.*
>
> *Sheila, I really would like to begin the process of making you a significant part of my life again. I understand that words are not enough, but I just wanted to share these thoughts with you. I have every intention of letting my actions take the place of these words.*
>
> *I am not going out of town this weekend and at your convenience, I would love to elaborate on the above thoughts.*
>
> *Love, Greg*

I called my friend Susan and read her The Letter. I told her I wasn't sure what to do; I thought I might still be in love with Greg and was thinking of going back to him. It seemed after so many years of flip-flopping, he had finally come around.

"Don't be stupid," Susan said. "Don't take that chance. You're with X [The Original Asshole] now. He knows what he wants, he seems to be really into you, and it looks like you two could have a future. Greg? You seem to be forgetting what a flake he was all that time."

"But this letter," I said. "He really sounds sincere." I couldn't just let it go. Greg was always so nonchalant and reserved, acting as if nothing ever bothered him. I knew it must have been hard for him to write his feelings and was convinced he meant every word. It was what I had always wanted. What I had been pining for ever since our trip to the South of France.

"But there is one hitch—although I'm not sure if I should be concerned about it or not."

"What do you mean there's 'one hitch'? Fess up!"

"Well, in his letter he says he isn't going out of town for the weekend but when I just spoke to him on the phone he told me he had decided to go to D.C., after all."

"All right, so what's the big deal whether or not he goes away for the weekend? I'm sure you already have plans with X [The Original Asshole], anyway."

"The problem is he said he's going to visit his friend Helen."

"Who the hell is Helen?"

"Exactly. Some chick he used to sleep with. She's supposedly 'just a friend,' but I suspect it's more like a 'friend with benefits.'"

"Oh my God—you've got to be kidding. First he says he's going to D.C.— gotta drop off that love note, it's urgent! Then he's not; now he is again? Do you need me to remind you he's back to that same old wishy-washy bullshit?"

Susan was right. Even though what Greg wrote had the ring of truth, it didn't jibe with his behavior. Points for honesty, yes, but where exactly did the weekend jaunt fit in with his exquisitely worded profession of love and serious intent to bring me joy? So the plan was to be with me in the long term, but someone else for the next few days?

Susan reminded me that I had been to see Zena the Clairvoyant on Bleecker Street in the West Village in July. Zena read my tarot cards and asked me if the name X [The Original Asshole] meant anything to me. I told her no. She told me that I was going to marry a man named X [The Original Asshole] and own multiple homes. I was going to travel around the world. I was in my twenties and still gullible enough to trust magazine horoscopes, Ouija boards, and tarot card readers more than I did my own feelings. When I told my college friend Derek about my budding relationship with The Original Asshole, about The Letter from Greg and about my confusion, he advised me to be very careful.

Derek was a guy. He recognized the game. He could be an asshole, too.

"This guy [The Original Asshole] sounds too good to be true," he said.

I told Greg I was sorry but I planned to stay in my current relationship with The Original Asshole. And The Original Asshole played the role of concerned yet supportive new boyfriend, reassuring me, "Your heart is safe in my hands." As quickly as our relationship began, though, it started to fall apart. The Original Asshole was suddenly trying to convince me that, despite wearing a Brooks Brothers suit, toting a leather briefcase, and working at an investment bank, he was "down for the cause." I was unclear exactly what "the cause" was, but he was stressed out enough about it that he started to smoke more than usual. Maybe it wasn't "the cause," but his job at Salomon that was stressing him so much. He told me he needed to "decompress." I didn't smoke, but I tried to be supportive and empathize about how tough it must be as a black man with such a big job working long hours at such an important place.

Most nights after I finished my schoolwork and "roach patrol" in my own apartment, I would run over to his place, putting on one of his Black Panther XXL T-shirts he had had printed. They were white cotton, with an image of a grimacing black panther on the front and the words "Watch out" on the back. Then I predictably climbed into his big, fluffy bed with the 3,000-thread count Egyptian cotton sheets and goose-down pillows, folding into his strong arms. I didn't complain when he insisted that we sleep with the bedside reading light on and with his work documents, beeper, and masonry brick–sized cellular phone in the bed, just in case his boss called.

As usual, I ignored the red flags. The most obvious one was hidden under his black Calvin Klein biker briefs. It was a big green dollar sign tattooed in his crotch, not far from his penis. He told me it was to remind him of "necessary reparations" and "the importance of the economic empowerment of black people." Soon, all of our conversations became one-sided cryptic dissertations on "our need for readiness." Apparently I hadn't listened attentively enough, since I was definitely not ready for what happened next.

The leaves had changed color and fallen off the trees in Prospect Park. It was getting cold outside. The asshole started shucking his "deal slippers" (his pet name for work shoes) for black combat boots and donning a black beret, Che Guevara-style. Maybe he was planning to start a revolution. The white boys at Salomon had no idea whom they were *really* dealing with. He may have been an investment banker by day, but by night he was the pigeon-toed Huey Newton of Park Slope, and he was all mine.

The Original Asshole broke up with me, citing the usual story about needing some space. This didn't make me happy, but ultimately I was fine with it. I was actually more upset about how I had fucked things up with Greg. Despite his flakiness he was the only man I had ever been in love with. Soon, it all unraveled into a theater of the absurd. I was sick with the flu *and* in the midst of finals at school. But I needed to meet with my one and only client couple to discuss our new contract. They were finally ready to sign, and as I was having trouble keeping up with my rent, this was potentially a big financial relief. Since they had introduced me to The Original Asshole, I guess they felt compelled to talk me through what had really happened. They sat me down at their breakfast table. The Original Asshole hadn't offered me much in the way of an explanation about why we were breaking up, other than to say he was "confused." Now, I was grateful I'd finally be getting some real insight. Closure, perhaps.

"Please try not to take this too personally, but people just don't get you."

Bam. There it was. Right there on the table.

"What do you mean they don't get me?"

The husband was doing the talking. "They don't get your style. The way you look. Your whole deal." I was a full-time student, so my sense of personal style was pretty nonexistent. My outfits consisted of jeans and some colorful bohemian tops. I wore a nice tank watch with an alligator band my parents had bought for me at Bailey Banks & Biddle. My hair was wild, like Chaka Khan's. Minimal makeup, if any. That was about it.

"High-powered men like X [The Original Asshole] need to be with women that are slammin' and jammin'. You should make it want to pop! You are such an attractive girl, but you need to play up your looks. You need to wear more makeup and tighter clothes. How often do you go to the gym?"

I nearly fell off the chair. I was on a shoestring budget. I had planned on joining a gym, but hadn't gotten around to it yet. I ran, played tennis, and cycled in Prospect Park, but apparently not enough. More makeup? Tighter clothes? He had to be kidding. I glanced at his wife. Surely she would take my side. She had graduated from Yale and Harvard Law School, and seemed so smart and cool in a laid-back way. But she was hardly any style icon herself, opting for colored contact lenses, baggy sweats or jeans just about every time we met. He had obviously married her for her brains, not her beauty. Her hair was always standing up at the back, like the Heat Miser. My ex-roommate Pat even had a name for it. She called it "picky," because it was so dry and over-processed it looked like a bird had picked at it. My client had picky hair, and her husband was overweight and had bad breath. I looked over at her, waiting, hoping—through our sisterhood—she would save me.

Instead, she threw me under the bus. "And your hair, Sheila. We have to talk about your hair. I mean, what's up with *that?*" She waved her hands around the back of her head. "Have you considered relaxing or straightening it? Honestly. You need to do something. You need to look more professional. You *cannot* expect to date successful black men if you are going to keep up with this look. It's too...I don't even know how to describe it...*understated?* Basically, no one gets it. No one gets you."

She went on and on until I couldn't listen to it any more.

"Wait a second," I interrupted. "The men I date *like* my sense of style. I don't *want* everyone to 'get it.' That's the whole point. Everyone *gets* a tight black mini and stiletto heels. That's not me. I mean, it's not like I misrepresented myself. When I met X, I was wearing jeans and a T-shirt. My hair was exactly the way it is today. It's not like I *used* to wear tight miniskirts, tube tops, and a lot of makeup, then suddenly pulled a bait-and-switch the minute we started dating. Just because I wear holey jeans and a tank top at home doesn't mean I would ever go to a wedding or a business dinner dressed like that."

"Trust me," she said. "Men who tell you they like your hair or the way you dress are lying to you. X lied to you. So did Y and Z. All men, but black men in particular, want to be with women other men want to be with. Women who are put together and more...more...more...." Her husband found the word before she could.

"Trophyesque!"

"Exactly. Trophyesque."

Huh? What the fuck was that? Was it even a word?

"Trust us," she said. She smiled, and I caught her practically winking at her husband. "We're doing you a favor telling you this. If you want to date high-powered black men like X you really need to pull it together, and you can start by getting your hair relaxed."

Instead of letting me take the elevator down from their penthouse apartment, they should have just stuffed me in a big black Hefty bag and shoved me down the garbage chute, which would have been easy enough, since it was located right outside their back door. When I emerged on Park Avenue, I looked for a pay phone so I could call The Original Asshole at his office. He answered. I told him what had happened and burst into tears. He told me to calm down and not listen to them. He told me to "stop being so emotional," reminding me in a hushed tone that he was at the office. "Listen," he said, "I've got a work dinner tonight, but I can come over right after and we can talk things over. Sort all this out."

"OK, fine."

I said goodbye, hung up the phone and walked to the subway station to catch my train back to Brooklyn. The word "trophyesque" followed me down the stairs and onto the platform. It even had the nerve to sit next to me on the Downtown Number 2 Train. The Original Asshole never did show up at my apartment that night, or any other night, to explain what was true and what wasn't. It didn't really matter. I already knew the truth. I had mistaken his intensity for sincerity, misinterpreted his words to hold significance they didn't. His gifts had been disingenuous, just like he was, hand-wrapped with guilt and guile. I called my brother and told him the story. He said The Original Asshole sounded like more of a coward than an asshole, which he believed was far worse.

A couple of weeks passed before I called my clients to give them a piece of my mind. I had five final exams and two crits to tackle first. I told the wife I found their "pep talk" hurtful rather than helpful. I wasn't sure I wanted to work with them, regardless of our signed contract. It seemed strange they were paying me for my sense of style but belittling it at the same time. We had been working together for several months, and they couldn't seem to make a single aesthetic decision without me. They wouldn't buy so much as a bath towel or a dinner plate without checking with me first. I had taught them all about antiques, and my design sense was imprinted on nearly every room of their home. The wife apologized profusely on behalf of both of them. She said she realized after I left their apartment that they had "made a terrible mistake."

"I know it's impossible to forget everything we said, but you should just say fuck it. You were right. The Original Asshole was just confused—that's it. It didn't have anything to do with your hair or clothes. We are truly sorry, Sheila." I didn't believe her or her husband or The Original Asshole. Too much had been said already. It was obvious The Original Asshole had called them in the meantime, angry they told me what he really thought. None of it mattered anymore. The damage was already done. If nothing else, that day I learned my first important lesson about doing business: Don't mistake friendly clients for true friends. I moved on, graduated from Parsons, and started establishing my credentials with clients who would judge me on my professional skills, not on how I dressed or did my hair.

Some time after that, the husband of this client couple tried to sell me an antique wall clock. It wasn't just any ordinary clock: It was one of a kind. But I wouldn't touch it. The problem was, it was the same clock I had bought for The Original Asshole as a gift, the previous Christmas. Not one in the same style, not something similar. *The very same clock*. I had negotiated for it at a flea market and paid in cash, so I recognized it right away. Somehow my carefully considered Christmas gift to The Original Asshole made its way all the way from his beautiful brownstone duplex in Brooklyn to my clients' penthouse apartment on the Upper East Side in less than a year. I can't remember now if The Original Asshole gave it or sold it to them. I didn't bother to write that part down in my journal. It didn't matter. Either way, he should have just dumped the damn thing overboard in the Vineyard Sound when he gunned his speedboat, while heading to his family's place in Oak Bluffs.

CONDÉ NAST

House&Garden

HOW TO
WORK WITH

pattern
and **color**

LONDON NEWS
Winners from
the **Chelsea
Flower Show**

Where to find
the **Hot Shops**

20 COOL IDEAS
for your
Kids' Rooms

OCTOBER 1997
U.S. $2.95

CHAPTER 6

FLUFFY CLOUDS

I'm convinced half the world secretly wants to be a decorator. How do I know? Because of the crowds I draw when I tell strangers what I do for a living. Because of the way people dote on me at cocktail parties. While the lawyers, bankers, and corporate executives talk shop amongst themselves, I am the one cornered by the powder room, held conversational hostage by the woman with too much Kabuki makeup, picking my brain about Farrow & Ball paint colors.

The reason everyone covets my job? Because they have absolutely no idea what I *actually* do for a living. I suspect most people, including many of my own friends, are convinced that what I really do, between popping delicious bon-bons into my mouth while watching Oprah on TV, is buy expensive things with rich people's money. Perhaps they see me as like Daryl Hannah's character Darien Taylor (Gordon Gekko's interior decorator and mistress) in the movie *Wall Street*. Her famous line to Bud Fox, played by Charlie Sheen: "You got it. Great spender of *other* people's money." That pretty much summed up the breadth and depth of how most people regarded my career.

Many people imagine my days spent leisurely shopping for the perfect floral chintz-covered sofa to go in the living room of Mrs. Hardwick's classic prewar Park Avenue six. I wait patiently for its delivery and make sure it's perfectly positioned across from her matching club chairs. I'm a white-gloved lady-in-waiting, carefully attending to this magnificent piece of furniture like it's a high-ranking noblewoman at the royal court. I do my best Bruce Lee imitation on its goose-down pillows and seat cushions, shaking, fluffing, and karate-chopping, arranging and meticulously rearranging until everything is just so. Then, to complement Mrs. Hardwick's gorgeous new furniture acquisition, I'm allowed to borrow a fabulous Tracy Reese brocade dress and get professionally made-up by the glam squad to be photographed posing seductively against the piece for a national magazine, earning loads of undeserved attention.

I wish. If most people had a clue about what a typical day in this (or any other) working designer's life was like, I'd wager all bets would be off regarding their interior decorating career fantasies.

In our business, interior design is the science, and interior decoration is the

House & Garden of October 1997, was my first shelter magazine cover. As a designer, I like nothing better than having a project on the cover of a national magazine.

While I didn't really like to wear dresses as a child, this one was a favorite. The red and white gingham check is a classic, and became the inspiration for the upholstery for a client's dining room chairs.

art. To do them well requires you to engage both the left and right sides of your brain equally. Make no mistake: The guts of the biz is the design, and the glamour—what people notice, flipping through the pages of the glossy shelter magazines—is the decoration. What captures your full attention, taking your breath away when you walk into a room you absolutely love—or hate—is a clever combination of the two.

It's a blessing I keep farmer's hours, getting up and out of bed by five. I don't mean just rubbing the sleep from my eyes or hitting the snooze button. I mean dressed, fully coherent, teeth brushed and flossed, bed made, juice glass rinsed and put in the dishwasher. My first waking hour is usually spent working on anything that requires full concentration without interruption. The early morning is radiantly, magnificently, spectacularly silent: There is no phone ringing, no intercom buzzing, no client meetings, no anxious staff asking questions and needing immediate answers. Typically, I'll check shop drawings and floor plans; make changes to work orders; and create the day's punch lists for my staff. By 5:45 a.m., my brain is already streaming a matrix, an archival client-information system supported by a series of flowcharts and spreadsheets that can track anything and everything from conception through delivery at any moment of the day.

By 6:10 a.m., I'm in Central Park and already running late, having made my way past the drug dealers between 111th and 113th streets, acknowledging them with a firm nod, and the crackheads, already strung out, eyes glazed over, hustling to the corner bodega for a can of Ensure, no doubt the only calories they'll ingest for the day. I dodge waves of obnoxious cyclists in their full-on rainbow regalia—red and yellow skintight spandex shirts, black, butt-padded shorts, and aerodynamic helmets—whirring past on their Cannondale road bikes. *"On your left!"* they yell. I heed the warning, pulling Dolby's leash in tight and moving quickly to the right. Invariably, 20 seconds later I'm nearly mowed down by another pack. *"On your right!"* they shout. We make it to the Great Hill without getting sideswiped. I can finally let Dolby off his leash.

Once I feel confident Dolby's burned off enough of his manic Jack Russell energy and has done all his morning business, we head home, this time walking against the traffic pattern of Lance Armstrong look-alike cyclists, runners, in-line skaters, and power-walkers. After dropping Dolby back at the apartment, I head to the gym and onto the treadmill for my morning jog to nowhere. I run 5 miles, which now takes me nearly 50 minutes since I can no longer keep up an 8-minute pace because, despite what Demi Moore says, 30 is not the new 20, but

When I designed a powder room for one of my clients, we used hand-screened wallpaper
in blue and yellow by Pintura Studio, and a marble and nickel sink from Waterworks.

the same old tired-ass 30 it has always been. I quickly lift some free weights and
do some core training exercises with an inflatable red ball and something resembling a gigantic blue diaphragm called a Bosu. By the time I shower and
dress, it's nearly eight. I finish sending out punch lists to my staff, along with a
bunch of other emails.

Soon I'm headed downtown, lugging a heavy canvas L.L. Bean tote bag, the
only truly portable yet acceptably stylish container sturdy enough to withstand
the weight of the marble, tile, and wood-flooring samples I'm carrying. My bags
also contain assorted fabric memos in different color schemes, and one roll of
toilet tissue. I arrive at the Garrison job site on East 15th Street and am immediately informed there is a problem with the powder room: The Waterworks pedestal sink I specified won't fit. Somehow, the measurements are off by 2 ¼ inches.

"It's gotta fit. Make it fit. I don't care if you have to take out the entire wall."
I take a deep breath; it's too early to be barking at the crew. "Hold on. Where
are the drawings? Let me take a look at the drawings." I know I checked and
re-checked all the measurements eight times before the job went out to bid.

"Does anybody have a tape handy?" Mine is buried deep beneath stone in my tote bag. Giuseppe the carpenter hands me a tape measure but it's only in metric. The width of the space comes up 57.15 millimeters short. I rack my brain, doing a quick conversion. Sure enough, it's just about 2 ¼ inches. I double-check our drawings and they are indeed accurate. Someone screwed up. Thank God it wasn't me or my staff.

"You guys need to figure this out and find the additional two and a quarter inches." I'm interrupted by my phone ringing. It's one of my design assistants, Christian. He's at the home of an entertainment client, trying to get into the master bedroom for a rug delivery and installation. Christian whispers into the phone that he can't because our client's baby-mama is still passed out drunk from Mary J. Blige's party the night before. "How do you know *that*?" I ask Christian. He tells me the uniformed housekeeper volunteered the information on her way to the dry cleaner. The guys from Stark Carpet are waiting impatiently to install the rug, but more urgently, the baby-mama's 4-year-old daughter by another rapper is clinging to Christian, crying and hungry. I tell Christian to "look in the cabinet and pour the girl some Sugar Pops or whatever cereal you find."

"I found a box of Raisin Bran, but the milk in the fridge is curdled."

"Do you see any bread in there? Make her some toast with peanut butter and jelly. On second thought, better make it just jelly. The kid could have a peanut allergy." I don't need to create baby-mama drama or get sued by the baby-daddy because the starving child went into anaphylactic shock. Christian dutifully follows my instructions then asks, "What about the rug?"

"Leave it in the hallway outside the bedroom door with a note explaining that we'll reschedule the installation for tomorrow afternoon. See if you can make it for four. But hurry up, you've got to get downtown to the flower market then over to meet the truckers at the Hillmans'." We have a delivery of twelve pieces of George Smith upholstered furniture arriving at their place on the Upper East Side, and Mrs. Hillman has made a specific request for pale pink peonies. She is hosting a late afternoon tea to celebrate her daughter Kelly's recent engagement, and the clock is ticking.

Just as I am about to walk out the door, our 15th Street client shows up, eager to check on the progress of her renovation.

"Can we do a walk-through?" she asks.

"Sure," I say, well aware I was due at another client meeting across town on West 57th Street 15 minutes ago. I do the walk-through with my client and show her some cerused oak samples for her kitchen cabinets. We are standing atop a pile of lathe and plaster rubble in what used to be a kitchen. Right now, it's a void, with nothing but metal framing and wires protruding down from the ceiling like tentacles. In response to her wide-eyed expression of apparent concern, I explain, "Everything always gets worse before it gets better. We still expect to have you in here by Thanksgiving."

"Are you sure?" She looks around.

"Yes," I assure her, even though I'm not really sure myself. Part of what people pay me for is to make sure their projects get done on time and within budget.

"Is there a working toilet here?" she asks. There is, but I'm afraid for her. The entire crew has been using it for more than a month now, and it has never seen a scrub brush nor met a can of Lysol. I can attest from personal experience that it's far worse than any public Port-a-Potty. I reach in my bag and, with an apologetic half-smile, hand her my roll of Charmin.

As soon as I hit the back seat of the cab on the way up to 57th Street, my phone rings. It's Lisa, one of my administrative assistants, calling from the office.

"There's a problem with our container coming from London," she says. "The crates are stuck in Customs because the bill of lading says they contain mantels."

"They *do* contain mantels," I explain. "Two custom-made ones we purchased from a dealer in England. So what's the problem?"

"I don't know. It's confusing. Something about restrictions and taxes on foreign clothing imports."

I tell Lisa to get the paperwork from the client's file and fax it over to the folks in Customs. I hang up.

Ten minutes later, I get a call back from Lisa: "Customs insists on speaking to you because your name is on the paperwork."

"Fine. Give me the phone number and the guy's name. I'll call them right away."

"Sheila, by the way, ahh, I forgot to ask but… do you mind if I take next Thursday and Friday off? My best friend Nicole is getting married in Bermuda and I'm her maid of honor."

I pause to let this sink in. "So let me get this straight: You're the maid of honor, the wedding's in Bermuda, and it's been planned for how long?"

There's an embarrassed silence on the other end of the line. So I eventually weigh in: "Lisa, I need to check the calendar when I get back to the office. I don't think it's going to be a problem, but I still need to check." I hang up, thinking *I should really hire an office manager to deal with this stupid shit.*

ABOVE For the living room of a client's townhouse in downtown Manhattan, I chose a paint that
I love—Farrow & Ball's Yellow Ground.
OPPOSITE I brought the colors of New York's Central Park indoors to the dressing room with a hand-
painted wallpaper from Stark.
OVERLEAF I used striped draperies in grey and red in the paneled library.

I call Lisa right back. "Will you please go into my office and look on the right side of my desk? There should be a light blue envelope addressed to my Mother. Take the stamp off, put it in a FedEx envelope, and make sure it goes out overnight. No signature required." Lisa springing her Bermuda trip on me somehow leads to the sudden realization that my Mother's birthday is Saturday and there's no way my card will arrive in time unless it goes via Paul Revere or FedEx.

I hang up, but before I have a chance to dial Customs, my phone rings again. It's a carpenter from 15th Street calling to say he's found the missing 2 ¼ inches in the powder room. Great. I finally reach Jim Giardi in Customs at JFK Airport and spend the rest of the cab ride explaining to him the difference between the stone mantelpiece for a fireplace and the mantle—as in a shawl-type of cloak—that King Henry VIII or a Pope John Paul II would wear. I assure Mr. Giardi we're not trying to smuggle foreign garments into the U.S. without paying the requisite taxes or duties. I invite him and his associates to open the crates and see for themselves.

Now I'm stuck in traffic heading up Third Avenue, which gives me time to switch shoes, substituting a pair of Prada sandals for my leather barn clogs, which also double as construction boots. I shove the clogs into my bag, under the fabric samples.

On my way into the Franks' building, I'm stopped by the newish doorman who doesn't recognize me. "Good morning. May I help you?"

"Yes—I'm here for the Franks in 14E. My name is Sheila Bridges and I'm their interior designer."

"Are they expecting you?"

"Yes. But I also have keys."

Riding up to the 14th floor, I brush plaster dust from my jacket and put on some lip gloss. I no longer own any clothes that require ironing. Everything I buy is wrinkle-free. I ring the bell and there's no answer. I ring again; no answer again. Surprising, since the doorman has surely called up by now. Oh, well. I'll ring just one more time, then use my key.

I open the door, hesitantly, with my key. "Hello, hello. Jeffrey? Elaine? Are you here? Is anyone home?" I hear a door to one of the bedrooms slam and start to walk toward the sound. "Hello?"

It's not Mr. Franks but rather a woman, who is not Mrs. Franks, either. I realize it's his mistress. I've seen her from time to time, usually sneaking out the back door by the butler's pantry. I say a polite hello as she grabs her bag and scurries past without making eye contact.

Mr. Franks pads down the hallway barefoot, wearing a white terrycloth bathrobe. I apologize for being late. He's ready to talk about his bathroom renovation. I show him some marble samples and he narrows it down to three: Thassos, the whitest of them all; Carrara, which has a lot of grey mixed in; and Calacutta, which has some beige streaks. When he decides he likes the Thassos best, I warn him about its porous nature. I caution that it will stain quickly—as soon as anybody leaves a bar of yellow soap on the vanity. *Or,* I think to myself, *the first time Mrs. Franks spills a glass of wine on it, which is inevitable since she's an alcoholic with a strong penchant for Pinot Noir.*

Do they want the stone for the vanity top and tub surround to be polished or honed? Tiles laid straight or staggered? Subway or square shape? A backsplash? Sinks under-mounted or over-mounted? Kohler bathroom fittings and hardware in polished nickel, brushed nickel, unlacquered brass, stainless steel, polished brass, chrome, or oil-rubbed bronze? What do *I* think?

Go with the satin nickel.

"Can we do a niche in the shower for shampoo and shaving cream?"

"Yes, of course." I dig for my measuring tape, which has worked its way up from under the stone samples to become wedged between two fabric memos. I take measurements and jot down a few notes. The corners should be mitered. The niche has to be tall and wide enough to accommodate the Franks' shampoo bottles as well as their L'Occitane shower gels and body cleansers.

"Oh, and by the way, can we make the shower enclosure frameless? Did I mention my wife needs a seat in the corner so she can sit down to shave her legs? And I might want to put a TV over on the wall by the tub so that I can watch the game on Sundays. And what about the floors? Will they have radiant heat? Are we still going with the herringbone pattern in blue and white? Or should we go for that basket weave instead?"

"I have four flooring samples right here if you want to take a look." I dig them out, feeling a twinge in my right side, which reminds me why it's not such a great idea to carry around 20 pounds of stone on my shoulder all day.

We go over the Toto toilet seat ("Yes, it's heated and elongated and, no, the temperature will not exceed 104 degrees Fahrenheit"), the bidet I've ordered ("Yes, it's exactly the one Elaine picked out"), and the color of both ("Colonial White").

"Is it possible to make the medicine cabinet surface-mounted?"

"Well, yes, but we bought the recessed one you wanted a month ago," I remind him, pointing to the 24-by-26-inch hole in the wall where it's intended to go.

"Would it be a problem to return it?"

"It might be. There will definitely be a restocking charge. The one you picked out was really nice. Are you sure you want to change it?"

"Yes. We were on vacation in Venice last week and Elaine fell in love with one she saw there. You can get the name of the store from the concierge at the hotel. We were staying at The Gritti Palace. Then you can follow up and let us know what you think."

What I *really* think? *You are a lying, cheating pain-in-the-ass, and had you taken a closer look in that same Venetian medicine cabinet mirror you would have seen you are way too old to be sleeping with your best friend's daughter-turned-mistress who is clearly just using you to get back at her father.* That's exactly what I'm thinking as I give Mr. Franks a wan smile. He reminds me he has a flight to Berlin by looking at his wrist, which does not feature a watch. I assume it's his way of telling me our meeting is over.

"Right, I know you have to get to the airport. No problem. Have a safe trip and just email me with any questions you have about the bathroom or anything else."

I load the marble and tile samples back into my bag and switch shoulders: Maybe if I let them yank on my left side long enough it will balance out my newly acquired case of scoliosis. Heading back uptown, I get a call from Christian. He's at the Hillmans' and the furniture has arrived.

"How's it going? How does everything look?"

"We have a problem."

"What's wrong?"

"The sofa won't fit in the elevator. It's too long."

"What?! You've got to be fucking kidding me. Can they take it up the stairs?"

"Yeah, but it's 32 flights, and they say they have to charge us for every floor."

I know this is a charge I will inevitably have to eat. It's my fault someone in my office didn't double-check the length of the sofa and the height of the elevator cab. This is exactly why I'm constantly riding my assistants' backs about details and dimensions. When avoidable mistakes are made, it costs me money.

"Do you want me to see if we can get a crane to hoist it and bring it through the living-room window?"

"No way. Too complicated and risky. Plus, it would be even more expensive. Just stay there until they bring it up the stairs. Did you get the flowers?"

"Not yet. What color are the peonies supposed to be again—white?"

"No. Pink! Pale pink—definitely not that bright Pepto Bismol or cotton-candy color. Think dusty. Soft. Blush. Remember—she wants the flowers to match with her Limoges dessert plates."

"Right. OK. Got it."

I zoom back uptown in a cab. It's time for Dolby's midday walk. I swig some orange juice from the bottle, staring into my nearly empty fridge. I grab an overripe banana. I haven't had time to go grocery shopping so I eat a handful of stale Carr's Table Water Crackers as a chaser. This will have to hold me until I can get a real meal.

After Dolby's walk, I hail a gypsy cab and rush back to the office where I'm handed a stack of mail and enough phone messages to wallpaper the bathroom. I also have 89 new emails in my inbox, many flagged *urgent*. Some are from friends and clients, but most are the typical business solicitations I'm bombarded with daily. There's one about a new rug showroom specializing in colorful cotton flat-weaves, one from a Canadian company making hand-painted acoustic panels, and another from a store selling rubberized floor tiles made from recycled bicycle tires. I quickly go through close to half of them but I have to move on. It's time to finish the reflected ceiling plan and lighting schedule for the Conrads' apartment on Fifth Avenue.

The intercom buzzes. My friend Karen is on the line.

"Do you know of an inexpensive upholsterer in New Jersey who can fix my desk chair?"

"Not offhand, but let me think about it and get back to you."

I finally return the phone call from Larry, my wood finisher, who is about to start a job at a project on Central Park South. There's a problem: Section A-4 on page 18 of the co-op's alteration agreement, under "Work Restrictions," reads *All cabinetry and finished trim components shall be fabricated off-site. The application of spray finishes is not permitted in the building.* That's exactly what we were planning to do and it was in the original estimate. Shit.

"How much would it be for a brushed lacquer finish instead of sprayed?"

"It's a lot more labor. At least another ten grand."

"And how much longer will it take?"

"Probably two or three weeks." Damn. We were already on a tight schedule.

"Let me talk to the client and get back to you."

The intercom buzzes again.

"Sheila, it's Christian on line three."

"Hey, how's it going? Is all the furniture in place? How does it look?"

"Well, the good news is the sofa made it up the stairs. The bad news is they can't make the turn in the hallway to actually get it into the apartment."

OPPOSITE AND ABOVE The basic color scheme of this client's living room is red, white, and blue, but I used accents of yellow to make it appear a bit less patriotic.

I used patterned Moroccan cement tiles to pave the floor of this rooftop garden. The walls of cedar trellis

are used for both privacy and protection. All-weather, woven outdoor furniture is arranged to ensure that the amazing view of the Empire State Building is unobstructed.

"Jesus Christ."

"Also, it took a lot longer than we thought because they had to take their lunch break right as we hit the 24th floor."

The intercom buzzes.

"Hold on a second, Christian. Yes—what is it?"

"There's a Mr. Jerry Allen on line two. He says it's urgent. Apparently he's left you four messages in the past two days and really needs to speak with you. He mentioned he was referred by our client, Mr. Franks."

"OK. Tell him I'm on another call, I'll be right with him." *Who is this guy and why does he keep calling?*

"Christian, I've got to take this call but here's what I want you to do," I say, picturing the Hillmans' new, $18,000 sofa stuck in the hallway. "Just tell the guys to carefully unwrap it, remove all of the cushions and flip it the other way so the arms are facing the door. If that doesn't work, call me back and we can talk about maybe taking off the rear legs. Let me know what happens."

I pick up Mr. Allen on line three, apologizing for not calling him back.

"I know you're busy, Sheila, so I'll be brief: I would like to set up a meeting to show you the latest in central vac technology. It's really great stuff and I'm sure your clients would have a need."

Actually I disagree. I don't think any of them "would have a need."

Mr. Allen starts telling me about retractable hoses and attachment kits. I pretend to be mildly interested but I know it won't be long before I'm nodding off. I'm tired, as usual, my life requiring me to be constantly at the wheel driving 120 mph on only four hours of sleep and no time to even glance in the rearview mirror. I try to deflect with small talk: "So, how do you know Jeffrey Franks?"

Turns out he's married to the sister-in-law of Mr. Franks' third cousin's step-nephew on his mother's side from West Bumfuck, Nebraska, and her family has been in the vacuum business for forty-something years. Gotcha. Makes sense. He steers our conversation back in the direction of hoses. "So, I think you'll be very impressed by all the options and versatility of our systems. Can we take a look at our calendars, Sheila?"

Time to move on. "Mr. Allen, of course I'm well aware of central vac and I appreciate everything it has to offer, but believe it or not almost all of our clients prefer to stick with traditional vacuum cleaners. My schedule is just too crazy for the next few weeks, so unfortunately I can't set up a meeting. If you'd like to mail us some information, we'll certainly keep it on file. Thanks for being in touch. Sorry, but I have to take this other call."

It's my brother. "Hey, what's up?"

"I pulled my left hamstring playing basketball last night. I can barely walk." So what else is new? Every week it's a different sports injury. A week ago it was his right rotator cuff. He tells me he's thinking of going to Aspen with his girl-friend for New Year's but money's tight and the airfare is pricey.

"Consider it done. It'll be your Christmas gift."

Lisa buzzes from the common area up front, informing me that all of my staffs' desktops are frozen. "Sorry, Sidney, I've got to go. Apparently we are having some computer issues here at the office and, on top of everything else, now I'm friggin' Ms. IT, Miss Tech Support. I'll talk to you later."

I check my computer. It's working fine and there's no indication of any prob-lem with the network. I head up front and can see everybody else's screens are static, with their cursors spinning. I roll back the desk chairs, climb under the shared worktable, move their handbags, and get caught in the octopus of wires and cables underneath. I spend 10 minutes trying to troubleshoot, then end up simply unplugging everything—router, modem, ethernet cable—and plugging it all back in to reboot. My staff stands around watching me. Maybe next time, they'll remember how to do it themselves.

"If this doesn't work, please call Evan at Digital Society right away and get him up here as soon as you can." Crawling out from under the desk, I bang my head and walk back to my office seeing stars.

There's a call from a client in L.A. on line three. It's about their son's bathroom. *What now?* I thought we already signed off on everything. Demolition starts on Monday at 8 a.m. Please don't tell me they've changed their minds—*again.*

"We want to change the layout of Ryan's bathroom." Ryan is their 10-year-old son.

"What do you mean?"

"We want a shower only—no tub."

"I thought we were doing a shower *and* a tub."

"Yes, but we think it may be best to eliminate the tub."

After much back and forth, alternately playing the roles of designer, child psychologist, and family therapist, I finally get to the bottom of it. They are worried if Ryan has a tub it will encourage him to masturbate. It will make it too easy, they say. *As if Ryan couldn't figure out how to masturbate standing up in the shower.* It's not really my place to tell people what they should already know. My job is to offer creative solutions, explaining the options and costs, to let my clients make their own decisions and then to execute them efficiently. Ryan's father says he'll think about it and get back to me by the end of the day.

I check back in with Christian and he gives me the full report: The Hillmans' sofa made the turn and is now sitting in the living room where it was intended. All the furniture has been arranged, the pale pink peonies are positioned on the table next to the stack of Limoges dessert plates. The caterer has arrived and is setting up, and the first guests are expected shortly.

It's nearly 5 o'clock and I've finally finished the Franks' paint schedule and sent it to Mark, our painter. I really need to get back uptown to walk Dolby, but first I have to stop by the cocktail party at 200 Lexington to honor Vanessa Smythe, the new editor-in-chief of *Victoria* magazine. I received a hand-written note on the invitation from the publisher, so I have no choice—especially if I ever want one of my projects to grace the pages of their magazine again. I can't afford to hire a publicist so I handle my own P.R., which means loads of phone calls, drop-bys, appearances, and all the aforementioned schmoozing, none of it directly related to my actual client work.

On my way downtown, I'm on the phone with Sotheby's confirming an absentee bid for a pair of antique Danish, neo-classical giltwood mirrors, meant to go above those two fireplace mantels that were stuck in Customs. A call from my Mother interrupts.

"Hold on a second Mom. I'm just finishing up a call."

It's her third call of the day. "I never heard back from you," she says.

"I'm busy, working. You know it's much better if you call me in the evening, after work." I want to say, *You don't ever call Sidney in the middle of the day while he's teaching, do you?* "Hang on." I finish up quickly with Sotheby's.

"What's up?"

"Are you going to be at Aunt Olga's for Thanksgiving? Will you be coming home for Christmas?"

"I'm pretty sure it's yes to both." I'm thrilled Thanksgiving dinner will be at Olga's this year, since it's only a five-minute cab ride from my apartment. I rifle through my mental calendar. I know I have to work on Friday the 25th, the day after Thanksgiving. And I will definitely be going home for Christmas, although I'll probably drive down to Philly on Christmas Day. Too much traffic otherwise. My Father has a rule I'm starting to despise. We *must* be home at Christmas. No matter what. No excuses, no exceptions. It was fine when I was in college but now that I'm a grown woman in my thirties, with my own life and commitments, it seems ridiculous. I'd rather be in St. Barts.

"Mom, I'll let you know for sure closer to the holidays. Sorry, I've got to go.

I'm late for a cocktail party and I have a dinner after that."

I do a quick drive-by at *Victoria,* making meaningful eye contact and wishing congrats before rushing off to my friend Charles' birthday dinner.

I don't have time to stay for the actual meal but wanted to at least stop by to bring a card and gift. After the birthday toast I rush out onto the street to catch a cab. During the ride uptown, I think about how rare it is I actually see another person of color at any of the cocktail parties, dinners, or professional functions I attend. Once in a while, if I strain hard enough, I might spy a familiar face from across the crowded room. But as I move through the sea of attractive white faces I soon realize it's that cute black waiter again rather than another interior designer. "Seared filet with Roquefort cream?" he asks, extending a smile along with a silver tray and paper cocktail napkin.

"Yes, thanks." I reply, shoveling the tasty hors d'oeuvre in my mouth.

By the time I get home, it's 9 o'clock and I can feel Dolby's weight against the door as I push it open. No doubt the poor little guy has been crossing his legs, needing to pee, for the past eight hours. I throw down my stuff and grab his leash. He goes straight to the first tree and lets out enough water to put out a small brush fire. I look down and realize he's stepping on an assortment of little bottles and red, blue, and yellow tops—used crack vials (the nineties drug of choice, uptown). We move down the street. The next tree has a half-eaten bar-becue chicken wing and a crab claw. He immediately lunges for them.

"Leave it! Leave it!" I yell. I realize I'm really hungry, too. Toward the end of our walk, I remember I need to move my car. Tomorrow's Friday; alternate side parking will be in effect. I get in and Dolby hops into the back seat. I drive around the block a few times and luckily find a space. We head back to my apartment, where I feed Dolby, then try to decide how to feed myself. One of the problems with living in Harlem is when you get hungry there are only three options: soul food, Chinese, or pizza. Sylvia's is closed by now. Chinese is too greasy. Looks like it'll be pizza by default. I run across the street to Wine Liquor and Lotto and buy a bottle of cheap chardonnay. Then I order a slice.

"Make that two, please."

I get back to my building only to find the elevator is out of order. How could that be? It was working ten minutes ago! I hoof it up eight flights of stairs. I figure it's my second (unofficial) workout of the day. Just think *Stairmaster.*

I begin to dismantle the stack of papers on my desk, trying not to spill tomato sauce on any important documents. I answer 24 hours' worth of email messages, and I start to organize the upcoming day. I review a few architectural drawings, sign paychecks, write a memo to a contractor, and compose a thoughtful reply to a teenager who wants to become a designer when she grows up. By the time my head hits the pillow, it's nearly midnight.

I fall asleep immediately but am awoken not long after when my cell phone, which I have forgotten to turn off, rings. My heart leaps. I glance at the clock on my nightstand. It's 2:16 a.m. Who could possibly be calling at this hour? I hope my parents and Sidney are OK. But it's not them. It's my client, Jiggy Earle, which of course is not his real name. Most MCs, hip-hop, and rap artists stay away from their given names and come up with something that has more flavor, which is why they call themselves Biggie, Jay-Z, LL Cool J (Ladies Love Cool James), Ice Cube, and Busta. If you do decide to use your real name, maybe you incorporate a prefix like "Lil" as in Lil Wayne, Lil' Cease, Lil Jon, or Lil' Kim. There's music pumping in the background. I recognize the voice. It's the Human Beat Box, Doug E. Fresh. I can tell Jiggy's in a car. He starts right in, "Big Willie Style."

"Yo, shorty…Why wasn't the carpet installed in my bedroom like you said it would be?"

"I'm sorry but it was scheduled for this morning at 9 o'clock. Candi was there and she wouldn't let us in. We tried knocking on the bedroom door several times but she must have been sound asleep. We rescheduled for tomorrow at four in the afternoon. That way, there's less chance of disturbing her again."

But Jiggy's already past his carpet and onto the next thing. I forgot about his ADD. Maybe smoke a couple of blunts, mix in a few uppers and a bottle or two of Cristal. Either way he's jumping around like a flea, probably in the back of his blinged-out Bentley with the spinning platinum rims. He interrupts my explanation before it's done:

"You know, Sheila, I just don't like those clouds you had painted on the ceiling of Versace's nursery. They aren't fluffy enough. They need to be much more fluffier."

"OK," I say, knowing that Dana, my decorative painter, is going to flip. She already needs a neck brace to ease the soreness from countless hours of painstakingly fashioning cumulus clouds with the sensitive touch of Michelangelo, and blue skies with the subtle nuance of Raphael on the ceiling of Jiggy's baby nursery.

"I want Versace's clouds repainted by tomorrow morning."

"What? It already *is* tomorrow morning."

"Yeah, that's right. Just get it done. I want to see fluffy clouds on her ceiling by the time I get up in the morning." I take another look at my clock. It's now 2:30.

"Look. There's nothing I can do about Versace's ceiling until after 8 a.m. I

From Michelangelo to René Magritte, fluffy clouds have always been a popular theme among artists, including myself. My mixed-medium Crayola crayon and colored pencil drawing was rendered at the age of eight.

don't know what the painter's schedule is but I will contact her and do my very best to get her back there as soon as possible. It might take a couple of days."

"Couple of days? Fuck that. I want those clouds fixed now!!"

I've had enough. I'm way past the tipping point. I'm livid. It's after 2:30 in the goddamned morning. All day, I've given service with a smile and without flubbing my lines once. But now it is service with an attitude. Total negritude. Jiggy's no longer got the professional designer whose Gramercy Park townhouse project was just on the cover of *House and Garden*, but the sistah from Philly who's ready to ram his "fluffy clouds," along with the phone, down his motherfucking throat.

Right, Jiggy, fuck that, I'm thinking as I hang up the phone.

I'm so riled up I have a hard time falling back asleep. These celebrity entertainment clients are killing me. They want everything *now* and they want it for free. It's a baby's nursery, for God's sake, not the Sistine Chapel. I finally nod off, but am awakened by a pulsating roar. It's a police chopper, hovering low overhead, circling the roofs of my Harlem neighborhood, on a search mission. Maybe it's a drug bust or somebody got shot. New Jack City. Since I live on the top floor, the beams of their floodlights shine right into my bedroom window. I get out of bed to a few tired sighs from Dolby and draw the Roman shades. I look at my cell phone. It's 4 a.m. I might as well get up since I have to be up by five, anyway.

This was my very first Christmas at our family home in Philadelphia. Every year that I can remember, we celebrated the holidays with a Douglas fir in our sun porch.

CHAPTER 7

MERRY CHRISTMAS

'Tis the festive season! *Christmastime in New York City.* Every year, just after Thanksgiving, it starts to build—the kind of genuine excitement and merriment only the holidays can usher in. Fraught with breathless anticipation, it features those charitable events and celebrations indigenous and exclusive to The Big Apple: The tree-lighting ceremony at Rockefeller Center; impending bonuses on Wall Street; Secret Santa office parties; ice skating at Wollman Rink; and the long-awaited window decorations at Barneys. When the colored lights atop the Empire State Building switch from white to red-and-green, just about everyone adjusts their attitude. Then, inevitably, by the end of the third week of December, all that contagious and overabundant holiday cheer is somehow rationed and re-gifted; the spirited sentimentality seducing tourists into dashing through the snow in their one-horse open carriages suddenly grinds to a halt, and the entire city regains its usual impatient edge.

As I opened the door to my local U.S. post office on 116th Street, I could have sworn some of those same angelic voices I heard singing Yuletide carols in my Harlem neighborhood were now back to revealing their truer natures, complaining and snarling in protest. No swans a-swimming or geese a-laying—just sixty people a-waiting in a line longer than the Triboro Bridge and snaking almost all the way out the door. Whoever had the bright idea to schedule an abbreviated staff of two to service the onslaught of holiday procrastinators—everybody who waited until the last possible moment to mail their cards, gifts, and money orders—ought to be fired. *Immediately.*

I took a deep breath, joining my fellow uptown denizens in line. After about twenty minutes, I was making steady progress—there were only 27 people ahead of me—when an argument erupted after an elderly amputee in a wheelchair tried to cut in. "I don't care how many legs you have," the guy behind him shouted. "You gotta wait your turn like everyone else!"

Another scuffle broke out when a woman waited until she got to the window to assemble her cardboard Express Mail box. She hadn't bothered to fill out the required delivery form, either. "Do you have any packing tape or a pen?" she dared to ask the postal worker behind the bulletproof glass. Her question was met with dirty looks, frustrated sighs, a lot of teeth-sucking, eye-rolling, and several catcalls from the line. I decided this was taking way too long. It wasn't worth it; I could buy stamps another day. I stepped out of line and headed out the door to go back to work.

'Twas the night before Christmas, and it was signaled by the reemergence of a steely December wind and a starless wintry sky, accompanied by *the* attitude and *the* rudeness for which we New Yorkers were so world-renowned. As a designer, it meant this was *Crunch Time*. Everyone needed everything. Yesterday.

"I'm hosting a Christmas dinner for 30 and I need those dining chairs delivered before noon tomorrow. Also, can you get my living-room carpet cleaned?"

"Stephanie and Robert will be home from college for the holidays so their bedrooms absolutely must be done by the 23rd. I realize it's already the 21st but do you foresee any problem getting their bookcases refinished before we leave for Telluride?"

"Will the painters be out by Friday? And what about the hand-screened silk wallpaper from the U.K. for Dan's study? After the installers finish, can you get someone to re-hang the paintings? If the art handler's not available, can you do it yourself?"

While I fully acknowledged that nobody had twisted my arm to work in a luxury service business, I was still shocked at how many of my clients couldn't be bothered to say thanks, no matter how many Christmas wreaths I jumped through on their behalf. *Forget about "pretty please." Whatever happened to just plain ole' please?*

In addition to The Miracle on 34th Street, I was expected to perform one on Park Avenue, another on the Upper West Side, and yet another on Lower Fifth Avenue. This was the time of the year when my job switched from Ivy-educated professional designer to glorified Gal Friday, handyman, and housekeeper, with my office elves handling the mundane tasks of hanging your drapes, fixing your toilet, and even trimming your tree if that's what you needed. If I was at your home and you were completely frazzled and overwhelmed, I had been known to toss a load or two of laundry into your stainless, stackable Miele washer-dryer before walking Max, your standard poodle, because Gabrielle the dog walker had stood you up.

"Sheila, I know your office is closing this afternoon for the holidays, but do you think you might be able to get me four calling birds, three French hens, and two turtle doves by this evening?"

"Sure. No problem."

What the heck. I certainly didn't mind performing last-minute holiday tasks, especially if they were for the common good of the household. It was how I earned the glamorous title of interior designer—not to mention a pretty good living. I was the one entrusted with turning your house into the happiest of holiday homes. And I was the *only* one ready, willing, and able to do almost anything to achieve that goal.

Finally, I had gotten around to wrapping my own gifts, loading up my car and hitting the road. The good thing about driving home to Philadelphia on Christmas Day was there was rarely any traffic. Santa and his reindeer had already flown back to the North Pole and most folks were already at their holiday destinations. Weren't parents around the globe watching gleefully as their pajama-clad children excitedly tore off ribbons and gift-wrap to get to their new SpongeBob SquarePants video, Beanie Babies, and Lego construction sets? Weren't girlfriends all over America grinning from ear to ear as they lay romantically by the roaring fireplace, opening the little gift box from Kay Jewelers with the diamond-heart–pendant necklace or engagement ring? Spouses blindfolded and giddy, jumping up and down on the blacktop in front of their two-car garage, exclaiming with joy as they opened their eyes and saw a shiny new silver Lexus wrapped in a big red bow?

My Christmas ambition was far humbler than the rest of the nation: It was simply to get home safely, in one piece. The challenge was to drive nearly 80 miles down the hairy, smelly armpit of a highway better known as The New Jersey Turnpike in a little over an hour. It was the swampy, sprawling suburban landfill of a Garden State that separated my new life in cultured, sophisticated Manhattan from my cozy upbringing in the historic City of Brotherly Love.

White-knuckled, my speedometer inching toward 85, I braved the dangerous three-lane obstacle course, slowing only for toll booths or to swerve around the odd plastic highchair or runaway hubcap. Dolby, on the other hand, slept soundly, sprawled out on the back seat, comfortably oblivious to it all. As usual, the highway was littered with truck retreads and miscellaneous other shrapnel from blowouts and accidents.

In between dodging debris, I focused on all the signs whizzing by, keeping me on my toes as I held the pedal to the metal:

NO TRUCKS OR BUSES IN LEFT LANE. So why did I keep having to pass them on the right?

LANE SHIFT. Okay, I'm ready for that, I can handle it.

LANES NARROW. How narrow? Am I gonna fit through?

REMAIN WITH DISABLED VEHICLE. What—as if I would try my luck on foot?

NO STOPPING EXCEPT FOR REPAIRS. Duh. Like there would be any other reason to stop? How about counting those picturesque power lines and fuel-storage tanks or sitting and sniffing that rotten-egg smoke billowing out of the oil refineries lining the road between Rahway and Elizabeth?

MOLLY PITCHER SERVICE AREA. I could use a stop to refuel—"Fifteen gallons of Sunoco unleaded, please"—and treat myself to a Cinnabon while I'm at it. Don't think so. The tank was still half full and anyway I needed to hurry up and get home to see my family. The clock was ticking. It was already mid-morning.

EXIT 6 PENNSYLVANIA TURNPIKE ROUTE 276 WEST 2 MILES. I spotted the sign for my turnoff and felt a familiar sense of relief. It wasn't far now. I tuned my car radio to 105.3 WDAS, the Philly R&B station I had listened to growing up. They were playing Donny Hathaway's "This Christmas," one of the few holiday songs I actually liked. So I sang along.

And as we trim the tree, how much fun it's gonna be together.
This Christmas.
Fireside blazing bright
We're caroling through the night
And this Christmas will be
A very special Christmas for me.

I passed City Hall, recalling the days when there was a gentleman's agreement not to build anything higher than William Penn's hat; now he was overshadowed by granite, glass, and steel skyscrapers. From the overpass, I spotted Hahnemann University Hospital, where I was born; then the Philadelphia Museum of Art; and Boathouse Row, as I prepared to exit the Schuylkill Expressway onto Montgomery Drive. Almost home. Signs for The Horticulture Center; The Japanese House and Garden; and The Mann Music Center, where as a teenager I ushered for Philadelphia Orchestra concerts.

Finally, after a little more than an hour and a half, I pulled into the driveway of our stately old stone house. These days, it always looked smaller than I remembered. My parents' cars were both parked in front of the carriage house. My Father's shiny black Porsche with the vanity plates had been replaced with a silver Ford Aerostar minivan, and my Mom's navy Fiat Spider convertible with the beige leather interior had been traded in for some kind of generic two-door Oldsmobile whose name I couldn't remember. The tall Norway Spruce next to the rhododendrons was lit up with colorful lights as it had always been since I was a child. Each window was aglow with a shining white candelabra. Holly garlands wrapped the outdoor lamppost by the red brick sidewalk and a wreath hung on the front door. It was the perfect picture of Christmas bliss. Welcome home for the holidays.

My Father greeted me exactly as he always did, opening the front door, stepping onto the porch, taking my bags from my hands, turning, and carrying them into the house. He set them down by the staircase, gave me a peck on the cheek, and we exchanged the usual pleasantries.

"How was traffic?"

"Not too bad."

"How about the weather up there in New York?"

"Okay, I guess. Cold and a bit windy. It rained yesterday. Other than that, it's been fine."

My Mother emerged from the kitchen wearing her apron. She was obviously very busy preparing dinner, but stopped to give me a big warm hug and a wet kiss, smearing her Chanel lipstick on my cheek. Dolby trotted in behind me and she exclaimed, "Oh, Sid, look who's here! My favorite grand-pup! Come here, come to Grandma!" Dolby ran to her, shoving his wet nose against her pant leg. He relished the attention.

"Joyce, why do you insist on calling him that?" my Father said. "It's ridiculous."

"Forget you, Sid! Leave me and Dolby alone. We're going to go get things ready for dinner. Isn't that right, Dolby?"

"So, who's coming to dinner, Mom?" I asked hesitantly.

"It's just going to be the four of us this year."

"Really? That's it?"

"Yep."

I was disappointed. It was always better when we had guests, like we did almost every holiday when I was growing up. The dinner table was always safer—more of a No-Fly-Zone, so to speak—with my aunts, uncles, friends, and other buffers around to shield us from the dangerous projectiles we regularly launched at one another if left unchaperoned.

"Oh. So where's Sidney?"

"Upstairs in the guest bedroom, I think. You're going to need to set the table after he moves his things." It was my brother's habit during the holidays to use our large glass dining-room table as a desk, filling it with stacks of his papers and folders.

"His things—you mean all those little blue exam books?" This time of year,

he'd be grading his students' first semester finals.

"I don't know. You'll have to ask him or go see for yourself. Anyway, you must be so tired. Why don't you go lie down and take a nap?"

"Does the dog need to go out?" my Father chimed in. He was always worried about a potential accident on his precious wall-to-wall carpeting.

"No, Dad, he's fine. He just went, right after I let him out of the car."

"C'mon Dolby—come with me. Come with your Grandmom to the kitchen. I have a special treat for you."

"Mom, please, no table scraps. I have his dog food right here in my bag. I don't want him to get sick later."

"Of course not. I wouldn't give him any scraps. Just a little gift I bought for him at the supermarket." She paused, then whispered behind the back of her hand with a wink: "*A turkey-basted rawhide candy cane.*"

Dolby followed my Mother into the kitchen, trotting happily behind her, his stumpy tail wagging.

I started up the three flights of carpeted stairs, stopping on the second floor to say hello to my brother.

"Hey, Sidney. What's up?"

"Not much."

"When did you get in town?"

"A couple days ago."

"When did vacation start?"

"Well, *technically,* the kids got out of school on the 18th. But it's not really a vacation for me."

I thought, Here we go again with Sidney's *"technically* I'm not on vacation" routine. It made me crazy. "Aren't you off for the next two weeks, till after New Year's?"

"*Technically*, yes, but I've got a lot of work to do."

My brother was the only teacher I knew who had Fall and Spring breaks, Thanksgiving, Christmas vacation, Jewish holidays, and all federal holidays, not to mention the entire summer off, but was never "technically" on vacation. I hadn't "technically" had a day off in three years, but okay, whatever you say Sidney...I went along with it, as usual: "Wow, that's too bad. You must be

---

PREVIOUS PAGES When I was ten years old, I decided that a photograph of my family's old stone house in Philadelphia would look better if I added colorful Christmas balls to the black-and-white image.
OPPOSITE These snapshots were taken by my Dad on Christmas morning when I was around three years old. I was thrilled to get my hobby horse!

really swamped with all those papers and exams to grade. By the way, how's your hamstring? Are you still in a lot of pain?"

"It still hurts."

"Have you seen a doctor or at least been taking some Advil?"

"Both."

"Well, hopefully, it'll be better soon, and you'll be back on the court making your 'statement shots.' My week was nuts, too. I'm going to head upstairs and lie down. See you in a while."

Sidney cracked a smile and shook his head as if to say, "Some things never change." He knew full well that whenever I was home, I spent most of my time holed up in my tiny third-floor bedroom—just like when I was a teenager. It was the only place in our house where I could have complete privacy. I still slept better in my old twin bed than on any of the expensive mattresses I had ever owned as an adult. I unplugged the white rotary phone in my room, turned off my cell, threw my jeans on the floor, and crawled into bed under my favorite kitty-cat print sheets with the rest of my clothes still on. I was exhausted. Just as I was getting to the good part—drooling on my pillowcase as the sugarplum fairies danced the Macarena in my head—I was woken by the shrill sound of my Mother's voice.

"Sheila! SHEILA!"

"What?" I sat up, startled.

"Sheila! SHEILA!"

"What?! What do you want, Mom?!"

"Get down here. It's time to decorate the Christmas tree."

"What?!"

"You heard me. Get down here. Time to decorate the tree...now!"

I got out of bed and went out to the third-floor landing. "Mom, I was lying down, trying to take a nap!" By now I was screaming at the top of my lungs, but she couldn't hear me. My Father, who was already blasting Rachmaninoff's *Piano Concerto No. 2* from the stereo, had started vacuuming the sea of blue carpet that ran continuously from the first-floor hallway to the dining room and into the living room. I was completely drowned out. I would have to throw my jeans back on and go downstairs. I looked in the mirror: I had creases on my face and my hair was a mess. I pulled a hat from my tote bag and put it on before heading downstairs. I stood in the kitchen doorway pouting. Dolby was following my Mother around in there. He looked up at me, cocked his head to the side, then immediately put his nose back down to the floor, sniffing around like a hound who was onto a hare.

Dolby was captured eating a rawhide candy cane, his Christmas gift from my Mother.

"Mom, I was trying to take a nap. Couldn't the tree wait an hour or two? I have had a really rough week. I'm exhausted."

"Well, Sheila, I'm tired, too, but there's a lot to do. You're the decorator, so go on and do your thing on that tree."

"What tree? I haven't seen any tree around here."

"Your Father just brought it in. It's been leaning on the side of the house in a bucket for the past week. He put it in the sun porch. You know where the ornaments are: The back closet upstairs, behind your room. I *asked* you to bring them down."

"Mom, I couldn't hear you—between Dad blasting his music and running the vacuum—while I was trying to sleep. And since when do I have to trim the tree all by myself? Shouldn't we be breaking out some eggnog or something, and doing it together as a family?"

"Look Sheila, you can see I'm busy trying to get the dinner ready here. I don't have time for any of this other nonsense. Could you just *please* go and do that tree—now?" Several cookbooks were splayed open on the counter; there was food piled in various dishes, some of it splattered around on the yellow Formica and the stovetop. The regular oven was on instead of the microwave. I didn't dare ask what was on the menu, but I suspected it might be French—and complicated. I climbed back upstairs, stepping over my Father, who was fully focused on sucking up pine needles with the crevice attachment of his brand new state-of-the-art Electrolux.

"Is Dolby shedding?" he asked.

"No, why?"

"You see all these white hairs I'm picking up?"

"Dad, those are dead needles from the tree, not dog fur. Dolby's been in the kitchen ever since we got here. Maybe if you had your bifocals on..."
He looked up suddenly, frowning: "Huh?"

"Never mind. Forget it," I said, holding up a hand to keep the peace. It wasn't worth getting prickly or starting an argument. I trudged back upstairs in a funk to fetch the ornaments as I had been told. No matter how old I was, whenever I came back home I was treated as if I were 12. Climbing over my Mother's off-season collection of designer shoes and handbags encased in clear zipper bags with mothballs, I located the boxes of Christmas tree ornaments, then made a show of huffing and puffing, dragging and bumping them downstairs, just in case anybody failed to register my annoyance.

Sidney poked his head out from the guest bedroom as I reached the second-floor landing. There was an unwritten rule that my brother would always stay there whenever he was home because he hated the bouncy trampoline of a mattress in his old bedroom. Besides, he was like the visiting tenured professor from Harvard who needed tonier accommodations than I did—his slovenly younger and less distinguished colleague from the local community college, with no workload and plenty of vacation time.

"Sheila, what's going on? What's with all the noise? Between the yelling, the music, the vacuum cleaner...how's anybody supposed to get any work done around here?"

"I don't know, Sidney. But I could use some help trimming the tree."

"I can't. I'm trying to dig out from under. I've got a ton of stuff—exams and essays to grade, college recommendations to write...You know how it is." He closed the bedroom door.

I made my way out to the sun porch with the stack of ornament boxes. I was on my own with our tree—a small, misshapen Douglas Fir that was drying up and losing its needles. Not quite as bad as Charlie's Brown's tree, but close. I spent the next half hour untangling a mass of lights from one of the boxes and carefully entwining them around the tree. When I plugged the lights in, nothing happened. *Shit.* I pulled the lights off the tree, trudged back upstairs, and found another set of multi-colored bulbs. Back downstairs, I wrestled with them till I got them wrapped around the tree, twinkling on and off, without further incident—other than about a dozen needle pricks on the underside of my right forearm, and a few sticky blobs of pine sap gunking up my hat and hair.

Next, I did a half-assed job with the trimming, throwing on several piles of old tinsel and handfuls of stale, cracked candy canes we'd used ever since I was a kid. *Ah, Christmas.* I remembered how much fun it was ripping open all that shiny silver paper to get at my new Slinky, my Etch-a-Sketch, the Lincoln Logs, and the rocking horse. The excitement and anticipation were almost more than I could bear. My Santa Claus fantasies didn't last long, though. Sidney told me it was all a big fat lie invented by our parents. So by the age of four, I no longer believed in Santa. He explained it was "Daddy" who had eaten all those Entenmann's and Stella D'oro holiday cookies my Mother had so lovingly baked and left out on a plate with a glass of milk on the fireplace mantel just above where our four hand-knit woolen Christmas stockings hung. That sour note still didn't dampen a wave of nostalgia from welling up as I dug for the antique mercury glass star that, every year without fail, went on the very top of our tree. Then my Mother started yelling again.

"Sheila!"

"What, Mom?!"

"SHEILA!"

"Mom, I'm not deaf: WHAT DO YOU WANT?!" I barked back.

"Where are you?"

"I'm right in here decorating the tree—just like you asked."

"I need you to set the table now. Go upstairs and get the silverware. Look in the small room behind Sidney's bedroom. It's in that old green dresser you used to take to overnight camp. We need four place settings."

"Okay Mom."

"And don't forget the serving utensils."

"*Okay*, already," I said, plopping down the felt ornament I was admiring in the palm of my hand. I remembered making it in fourth grade; not a bad effort for a 10-year-old.

On the way back upstairs in search of the flatware, I envisioned Martha Stewart standing in her kitchen at Turkey Hill, decorating dozens of delicious homemade sugar cookies, making scores of perfect snowflake stencils, and stringing hundreds of cranberries on a thread while basting her cornbread and pecan-stuffed, herb-rubbed, farm-raised turkey. I fantasized about spending Christmas with Martha, drinking spicy wassail punch, roasting chestnuts on the open fire while she whispered in my ear her secrets of how I might transform my passion for decorating and design into a zillion-dollar empire.

Back down in the kitchen, I handed my Mother four silversmith-cloth blue bags full of utensils. She checked inside the first one. "Sheila, this is not what I wanted. This is your grandmother Nanna's set. I was looking for the gold bamboo-style ones I bought at John Wanamaker. You know what I'm talking about—it matches with the King Tut porcelain dinner plates I got at Saks."

I let out a big sigh, turned, and headed back upstairs; I felt my blood simmering as I scaled the steps one more time. I found the correct flatware and brought it back down to Mom.

"Great, thanks," she said. "Now you can go set the table. Use the green placemats and red linen napkins. They're in the third drawer on the right side of the china cabinet." I went into the dining room and took a look around. It was the most tastefully appointed room in our entire house, the only one done by a professional decorator. The only problem was that the entire table was still stacked full of Sidney's stuff, including all those papers and exams he was so nervous about catching up on while he was *technically* not on vacation.

This was bullshit. I was fed up. First I get woken up from my nap, then I have to trim the tree all by myself, and now this. I was sick and tired of having to pick up the slack for my brother. My Mother liked to call him "The Absent-Minded Professor," and both of our parents were obviously so impressed by all his important work that whenever he came home he was constantly coddled. *Leave poor Sidney alone, he has so much on his plate. He doesn't ever get a real vacation.*

"*Dammit,*" I said, for the benefit of anyone within earshot. "How the hell am I supposed to set the table with all this crap on it? Why can't he use a desk like normal people? I don't care *how* busy he is. He can get off his ass and move his stuff."

Mom clamored out of the kitchen, stood at the bottom of the stairs and yelled. "Sidney! SIDNEY! I need you to get down here and move your things out of the dining room. Your sister is trying to set the table!"

My brother took his sweet time, eventually emerging from his upstairs "office" and slowly descending to collect his belongings in silence. I stood and watched, taking inventory: Five stacks of books; at least ten piles of student essays, work papers and exam booklets; a laptop; three tennis racquets; and a pair of cross trainers. Sidney gathered it all up without saying a word, went back upstairs and closed the door behind him.

I got some Windex and a roll of paper towels and carefully wiped down the glass surface of my parents' Milo Baughman dining table. I set the table as per my Mother's instructions, dimmed the chandelier, lit two slender red wax candles with one of my Dad's Bic cigarette lighters and positioned them *just so* along the center line of the glass table top. As I stepped back to admire my work, the chef appeared in the doorway to issue further orders:

"Sheila, now I need you to go in the kitchen and watch the oven. Make sure nothing burns. I have to go up, take my insulin, and get dressed. I should be back down in a few minutes." My Mother, in addition to suffering from hypertension since she turned 21, also had Type II Diabetes, just like my grandmother had had.

"Okay, Mom. Whatever you say." I added a two-fingered salute after she turned to go upstairs. Then I went to the kitchen and checked in the oven. My Mother had made our childhood favorites; sweet potatoes with fluffy marsh-mallows for Sidney and, bubbling with butter in the Pyrex dish right alongside, macaroni and cheese for me. It was my grandmother's recipe and it was already golden brown on top. *Yum.* But where was the turkey? Uh-oh: I spotted her copy of Time Life's *The Cooking of Provincial France* cookbook still open on the counter next to the oven mitts. There were two lidded stainless steel pots on the front burners; she hadn't said anything about tending those, so I wasn't inclined to check inside. Anyway, the burners looked to be safely on low. I was more concerned about the open cans of B & B mushrooms and the big pile of celery stalks lying on the wood cutting-board. The celery, along with iceberg lettuce, was one of the rare fresh vegetables to be found in the plastic bin at the bottom of our fridge. Normally, it just stayed there, though.

I kept one eye on the oven while I poured Dolby's kibble into his bowl from a green Iams bag. He looked up at me, went over to the bowl, sniffed it, and walked away. Clearly whatever scraps he had been foraging off the linoleum floor were far more interesting than the official dinner I had just served him. I checked on top of our Amana refrigerator. There they were, the real evidence that Christmas was officially here. Stacks and stacks of colorful round metal tins in an assortment of sizes. Fruitcakes. Under no conditions were they to be touched or (God forbid) opened by me or Sidney: They belonged exclusively to my Father. He was the only person I know to this day who absolutely, unabashedly, loved those giant doughnut-shaped bricks of densely packed wet brown cake dotted with assorted nuts and bittersweet cubes of candied fruit resembling Jujubes. I figured nearly every patient visiting his office during the month of December brought him at least one. For the entire winter holiday season and beyond, my Father used this stash to indulge in one of his favorite rituals—slowly relishing a chunky two-inch-thick slice with his black coffee for breakfast, as he read the morning newspaper.

At Christmas dinner in 1973, my Dad and brother wore their favorite bow ties.
I sat there with a bad attitude and random hair.

When we finally started to assemble at the table, I noticed the men were proudly dressed in their Christmas finest. My brother inherited our Father's whimsical yet practical love of sweater vests; he donned his over a striped button-down Etro dress shirt that was neatly tucked beneath the belt of his pleated wool trousers. This year, he had ditched his usual bright-colored professorial bowtie in favor of one of my Dad's turtleneck Dickies. I wondered what would possess him to want to wear either, then reminded myself how the pine cone must not fall far from the Christmas tree. Sidney's black leather shoes were carefully polished and he was freshly shaven, looking handsome and oh-so-proper, as always. My only question was, *How the hell did he afford all these expensive threads on a teacher's salary?*

My Father, who grew up decades before the advent of work "Casual Fridays," still felt most comfortable in silk neckties, even on the weekends. For this special occasion, he had chosen an abstract, subtly muted yet snazzy pattern that nicely complimented his tasteful powder-blue cotton shirt, beige cashmere button-down vest and dress slacks. He, too, was meticulously shaven and groomed.

When he sat down, I caught a whiff of thyme and clove, which could only mean one thing: He was wearing Aramis, his favorite cologne and chosen fragrance since the sixties. As kids, my brother and I had probably given him close to 40 bottles of the stuff over the years.

"Mommy, Mommy, what should we get Daddy for Christmas?" we would chime as we skipped through the aisles of the men's department on the first floor of Lord & Taylor. Her answer was invariably, "Get him some Aramis!" as she handed us each a ten-dollar bill to pay for it. Nowadays, if you checked his medicine cabinet, you would quickly discover he was overstocked with almost thirty Aramis items—spray bottles of Eau de Toilette, after-shave lotion, soap-on-a-rope...you name it. I had to admit, the scent did coordinate nicely with my Dad's magnificent head of hair, which was still thick and shiny as ever, thanks to just the right touches of Rogaine and Groom & Clean.

My Mother had yet to make her entrance, but we could tell from all the rummaging through drawers and slamming doors coming from upstairs that she was on to her final preparations. I tried to guess which theme it would be this year. I recalled her American Flag Phase, when I was a sophomore in high school, when all her Adrienne Vittadini sweaters and jackets had big shoulder pads and striped or starred patterns—right down to her patriotic bright red Ferragamo shoes. Another of my favorites was her Bumble Bee wardrobe, consisting exclusively of fuzzy-textured yellow-and-black outfits, which she sported the weekend of my college graduation.

Dad got up and went over to the bottom of the staircase. "JOYCE! What's going on up there? What are you *doing?*"

"I'll be right down! Why don't you put on some music and pour the wine?" While my Father went into the kitchen to get the wine, Sidney finally volunteered to help out by fetching his favorite holiday dinner CD from my Father's stereo cabinet, George Winston's *December. Oh God. Please, not that again*, I thought. The same way I never tired of my Mother's mac and cheese, my brother just couldn't seem to get enough of Winston's stirring classical-style piano solos. As far as I was concerned, it was far worse than listening to elevator Muzak. By the time we got to the seventh track, entitled *Night Part I: Snow* (only to be followed by *Part II: Midnight* and *Part III: Minstrels*), I felt like I was about to lose my mind. It was so relentlessly ephemeral and slavishly haunting that it quickly turned to a depressing drone—the kind of music you could easily imagine, if you played it enough times, over and over again, would surely drive you to park your car in the garage, close the automatic door tightly behind you, and sit and wait until you were overcome by carbon monoxide. It was perfect for the soundtrack of an Ingmar Bergman film set in Sweden in the darkest depths of winter...but home for the holidays in Philly? I should think not.

My Mother finally descended, ensconced in a fashionable St. John knit ensemble of crimson red and Kelly green—right down to her earrings and jeweled brooch. Her outfit featured a long, flowing linen holiday apron decorated with the image of a large, magnificently decorated Christmas tree. Her makeup, hair, and nails were impeccable, as always. She looked lovely. My Mom went into the kitchen to bring out the first course. Dolby followed her in and lay under the large glass table, content to gnaw on his new rawhide Christmas gift.

"Surprise; this year we're starting with escargots!" she exclaimed as she laid the tray on the table. I had seen those funny round, white dishes with the holes in them and those weird utensils resembling eyelash curlers in the kitchen on other special occasions; now my suspicions were confirmed. I passed the bread to my Father on my right.

"Sheila, will you please go turn the microwave on for 3 minutes and 40 seconds. The vegetables are already in there. All you have to do is press the button. I made your favorite—string beans with slivered almonds."

I pushed back my chair, careful not to disturb Dolby, who was blissfully concentrating all his energy on tearing apart his treat piece by piece, and did as I was told. My Mother was convinced she knew what I did and didn't like. She insisted on serving those frozen Birds Eye string beans with shards of nuts year after year, even though they were one of my *least* favorite foods. She had no clue I ate only fresh vegetables now.

"Hurry back, Sheila. I just realized we never said Grace. Sid—why don't you say something for a change?!"

Sidney and I exchanged glances across the table. *Say something? Like what?*

We all knew my Father was an atheist. Sunday mornings when Mom went to church and bible study, my Father was always busy elsewhere, usually fertilizing the lawn or wielding his hedge-clippers, connected to a long yellow power cord, shearing the thick green privet that surrounded all four sides of our property. If you couldn't find him working outdoors, planting Burpee tomato seeds in his garden bed, or repairing the cedar fence in our backyard, he would most likely be serving up a third set at Riverside, the local indoor tennis facility, with his doctor friends.

"Ah, Mom..." Sidney mumbled, shifting in his chair. "I think that's your department."

Dad remained solemn and stone-faced, looking straight ahead as the three of us bowed our heads and Mom rattled off something resembling "Thank you Lord for this food which we are about to receive for the nourishment of our bodies for Chrissakes. Amen."

"That would be, 'For *Christ's sake.*'" Sidney corrected her, carefully over-enunciating. An awkward silence followed. I noticed my brother was staring at me; ignoring him, I focused on pulling a garlicky snail, dripping with melted butter, out of its slippery shell.

Sidney kept staring at me and eventually said, "Sheila, what are you wearing?"

"What do you mean, '*What am I wearing?*' What does it look like I'm wearing?" I was still dressed in my worn jeans and black sweater covered in lint and stray pine needles, and I had on a green and yellow snowboarding cap smeared with sap. At least my socks were clean.

"You really should take off that hat."

"I have it on for a reason."

"Take it off. It's not appropriate to wear a *hat* at the dinner table," he chided. "Especially a ratty one like that."

My Mom jumped in: "Sidney—stop it. Leave your sister alone."

We were about to go back at it, like we were ten and seven again and gearing up for a fight over an Erector Set we were supposed to be sharing. At least now, I wouldn't end up getting rushed to the ER with a broken pinky finger, a black eye or in need of a tetanus shot like that time when our game of hide-and-seek went terribly awry.

"Okay," Sidney continued, "but this is Christmas and she's dressed like—"

"For your information, I have this hat on because my hair is a mess and I didn't have time to do it because *I* was helping Mom get dinner ready. Why don't you mind your own business and eat your escargots!"

"Just take the hat off."

I shot back. "You know what, Sidney, I'm sick of you trying to tell me what to do. I'm not one of your stupid little eighth graders. And just because you need to get all dolled up for Christmas doesn't mean I have to." *How dare my brother scold me like that at the table*, I thought. *I already had one strict father.*

My Mother tried her best to ignore our bickering, busying herself clearing the table, running back and forth to the kitchen.

"Mom, why are you rushing everything? I haven't even finished my escargots!"

"We're just about ready for the main course," she said, proudly. "It's *Coquilles Saint-Jacques à La Parisienne*, which is French for scallops."

Coquilles Saint-Jacques à la Parisienne
SCALLOPS WITH MUSHROOMS IN WHITE WINE SAUCE

To serve 6

1½ cups thoroughly degreased
   fresh or canned chicken
   stock, or water
1½ cups dry white wine
3 sliced shallots or scallions
3 celery tops with leaves, cut in

2-inch pieces
4 parsley sprigs
1 bay leaf
10 whole peppercorns
2 pounds whole bay scallops, or sea
   scallops cut into ½-inch slices
¾ pound fresh mushrooms, sliced

Preheat the oven to 375°. In a heavy 3- to 4-quart saucepan, bring the stock, wine, shallots, celery, parsley, bay leaf and peppercorns to a boil over high heat. Reduce the heat, and simmer uncovered for 20 minutes. Strain this court bouillon through a sieve into a 10- to 12-inch enameled or stainless-steel skillet. Add the scallops and mushrooms, cover and simmer for 5 minutes. Transfer the scallops and mushrooms to a large mixing bowl. Quickly boil the remaining court bouillon down to 1 cup.

SAUCE PARISIENNE
4 tablespoons butter
5 tablespoons flour
¾ cup milk
2 egg yolks

¼ to ½ cup heavy cream
A few drops of lemon juice
1 teaspoon salt
White pepper
¼ cup grated imported Swiss cheese

SAUCE PARISIENNE: In a 2- to 3-quart enameled or stainless-steel saucepan, melt 4 tablespoons of butter over moderate heat. When the foam subsides, lift the pan from the heat and stir in the flour. Return to low heat and cook, stirring constantly, for a minute or two. Do not let this *roux* brown. Remove the pan from the heat and slowly pour in the reduced poaching liquid and the milk, whisking constantly. Then return to high heat and cook, stirring the sauce with a whisk. When it thickens and comes to a boil, reduce the heat and let it simmer slowly for 1 minute. Mix the egg yolks and ¼ cup cream together in a small bowl, and stir into it 2 tablespoons of the hot sauce. Add 2 more tablespoons of sauce, then whisk the now-heated egg-yolk-and-cream mixture back into the remaining sauce in the pan. Over moderate heat bring the sauce to a boil, stirring constantly, and boil for 30 seconds. Remove from heat and season with lemon juice, salt and pepper. The sauce should coat a spoon fairly thickly; if it is too thick, thin it with more cream.

With a bulb baster, draw up and discard any juices that may have accumulated under the scallops and mushrooms. Then pour in about ⅔ of the *sauce parisienne* and stir together gently. Butter 6 scallop shells set on a baking

One of my Mother's favorite dishes was *Coquilles Saint-Jacques*, or scallops.

Recipes: The Cooking of Provincial France

Foods of the World

TIME LIFE BOOKS

This recipe was published in a Time Life series of cookbooks in 1972.

"Of course it is," I said, dismissively. What I really wanted to know was how she came up with the idea of serving a fancy French dish of scallops, cream, and mushrooms along with macaroni and cheese and sweet potatoes with marshmallows. I was about to say, "What's your culinary theme, Mom: *Parisienne-Negro fusion?*" But I decided to keep any more snarky wisecracks to myself.

"Well, I don't happen to like turkey very much so I thought we might try something different for a change," my Mother said. "Your Father loves French food—Don't you, Sid? In fact he's the person who introduced me to it, which was after he lived in the part of France named after the mustard. Didn't you, Sid?"

My Father had been a Captain in the Air Force after dental school in the fifties, and was stationed at the USAF Airbase in Chaumont, France, which was not far from Dijon. We had heard the stories of his travels all over France, Italy, Germany, Denmark, and Morocco a thousand times before. Characteristically quiet at the table, he seemed even more brooding today than usual. Maybe he was bored with the same old routines and dull conversation, as I was. Or maybe he just didn't like having snails for dinner. Finally, he put down his glass of chardonnay and said, "Yes, Joyce."

My Mother watched me dunk my bread into the leftover garlic butter and said, "Sheila, if you don't like the scallops…just don't eat them."

"You know I *love* scallops about as much as I love escargots."

Sidney gallantly came to our Mother's defense. "Sheila, that's enough of your sarcasm. First you show up looking a mess, with your hair stuffed in a baseball cap; then you get on Mom's case about the dinner she's been slaving over for hours. This is just not appropriate. It's inappropriate *and* disrespectful."

"Sidney, I told you, you should mind your own business and stop lecturing me like I'm 12."

My Mom tried to intervene as she sometimes did when I was little and couldn't defend myself against my brother's bullying. "Sidney, please," she said. "Please leave your sister alone." Then her voice quivered and she began to cry. A couple of tears plopped into the oversized scallop shell filled with cream sauce on her plate, at which point my Father put his foot down. Instead of directing his anger toward Sidney, though, he glared at me, raising his voice—something he rarely did.

"Now look, Sheila. Look what you've done. You've gone and upset your Mother and ruined her Christmas dinner. Every time you come home, there's some kind of problem like this. Every time. If that's the way it's got to be, then we're just going to have to say you're not welcome here at all!"

I was dumbfounded. Did I hear him correctly? I was no longer *"welcome here at all"*? And what the hell was he talking about, *"every time you come home"*? I knew my Dad could be tough, but this seemed extreme, even for him. I remembered how much it stung when he scolded me as a kid or meted out punishments, such as not being allowed to ride my bike. But this sounded harsh, severe, truly hurtful. Other than our silly spat over Christmas dinner attire and menu selections, there had to be some other deeper resentment setting him off here. What was eating at my Dad that caused him to blow up at me like this?

While sometimes I still felt like the same shy, sensitive child in my Father's presence, I was no longer intimidated by him. Our relationship remained complicated, but the financial umbilical cord attaching me to him was cut when I graduated from college. My older brother, whom I had idolized since the day I was old enough to mispronounce his name, seemed to be trying to emulate my Father. Sadly, though, in my estimation, he fell far short, especially since he was still on the dole, even as a grown man. From my perspective, one of the beautiful truths born out of my teenage desire to become a completely self-sufficient adult was that I no longer had to kowtow to my family. I didn't feel the same need to walk on eggshells; I had learned how to extricate myself from uncomfortable situations entirely, simply by choosing to. When things went wrong, when I got scolded for my supposed shenanigans, I didn't have to hide in my childhood bedroom anymore. I could speak up for myself. Or I could just walk away. Which is exactly what I did at our Parisienne-Negro Fusion Christmas dinner. I stood up from the table and threw my crumpled linen napkin down on my chair.

"Fine. You're absolutely right. It's obvious I'm not welcome here. Most parents are happy to have their children home for the holidays, but all you and Sidney seem to care about is what I'm wearing and what I look like. To be honest, I don't feel comfortable here *at all* and I don't want to be here *at all*. So I'll *just leave*."

Everyone looked stunned.

I marched up the carpeted stairs, gathered my belongings and threw them into my bag. All I wanted was to get back to my apartment in Harlem—my *own* place—as soon as possible. I took a quick look around. It was hard to believe this was the very same room my parents had brought me to when I came home from the hospital, the same spot where I had laid my head nearly every night for the first 18 years of my life. My comfortable little bedroom was still exactly the same, complete with its shiny brass headboard and white furniture with matching trim.

My favorite animal stickers were still stuck on the white, paneled closet doors and my bookshelf in the hallway was packed with books I'd collected from elementary through high school: Dr. Seuss's *Green Eggs and Ham*, Nancy Drew's *The Secret at Shadow Ranch*, J.D. Salinger's *The Catcher in the Rye*, and Joseph Conrad's *Heart of Darkness*. I was surrounded by the same abstract floral wallpaper I had begged my parents for and helped my Father put up. It was only just now beginning to peel away from the walls.

I checked in my dresser to make sure I wasn't forgetting anything, even though I hadn't been home long enough to unpack. My drawers were still full of all my stuff, packed with cotton bohemian T-shirts from high school I had bought from Urban Outfitters—years before it became a retail giant. I sifted through gold charm bracelets, curling irons, a Le Sport Sac purse, a pair of Jordache jeans, two pairs of Ray-Ban Wayfarer sunglasses, a Sony Walkman, TDK cassette tapes purchased at Sam Goody, and some of the albums I had saved my allowance to buy: Rose Royce, Al Jarreau, LTD featuring Jeffrey Osborne, KC and The Sunshine Band, and the Jackson Five's long-playing single "Dancing Machine." My best friend Nancy and I had nearly worn out that 12-inch vinyl record, spending hours practicing and perfecting our version of The Bump. Even my Texas Instruments calculator was exactly where I had left it.

Every crack in every wall, each creaky stair in this old house, felt intensely familiar. But the people in it no longer did. As I walked through the hallway on my way to the kitchen, heading toward the back door, I ran into my Mother.

"You mean you aren't even going to stay for dessert? Your Father baked a Joan Specter Candied Apple Walnut Deep-Dish Pie."

Joan Specter was a former Philadelphia city councilwoman and the wife of Arlen Specter, our Jewish, pro-choice, five-term Republican senator who was first elected when I was in high school. Despite the fact that he was considered a "moderate," I didn't really care much for his politics—or his wife's famous gourmet pies. When her pie company was sold to a Brooklyn-based outfit in 1989, my Father managed to get hold of the recipe and had been baking them ever since. It was yet another one of those cherished Bridges family holiday traditions.

"Thanks, Mom, but no—I really don't want to stay around for pie or anything else."

"All right, Sheila." My Mom let out a long sigh. "Please call me as soon as you get back. Just so we know you got home safe."

"Sure, no problem," I said, knowing I wouldn't.

I called Dolby, who scampered obediently out from underneath the dining room table, followed me out on my heels and jumped into the back of my truck. I backed out of the driveway and headed north on I-95, toward Manhattan.

Merging onto the Jersey Turnpike, I saw a sign that read FINES DOUBLED IN WORK AREAS. As I checked my speed, I kept thinking, *Am I missing something about the meaning of being home for Christmas?* Wasn't it supposed to be a welcoming place to gather—rooms filled with unconditional love, laughter, compassion, and trust? A time for reflection about the essential qualities that bind us together as a family? Why did I so easily buy into all the media hype of celebrating *the* perfect holiday with *the* perfect family, the family I wished would just allow me to shed my heavy New York armor, to be myself for a few days or hours without fear of judgment? Only now did I realize that when I shook the water in my glass snow globe, I was no longer entranced by the quiet softness of the falling flakes; each shake seemed to elicit a new bout of soul-searching and self-doubt. Instead of seeing a pretty picture of swirling snow accentuating a beautifully sculpted backdrop of pine trees and ice skaters, I saw myself: The disobedient rogue daughter and feral sister with the wayward hair, inappropriate hat, and disrespectful ways, ruining our family's joyous holiday celebration. Whoever coined the idiom "Home is where the heart is" was right, but now I knew mine was no longer anywhere remotely close to Philadelphia.

This vignette on the mantelpiece in my dining room in Harlem, New York, includes a decoupage plate by John Derian, hand-blown glass globes, and a vintage snow globe from Austria.

Snow

Now make a big ball of snow...
Push it! Push it!
See it go.
What a snowball!
See it grow!
See it grow!
And grow and grow!

What will I make?
I'll make a man!
I'll make the biggest
Man I can!
I will call the snowman Ned,
But first I have to make his head.

His head will have to have a hat,
His hat is on..just look at that!
He is so big, he is so tall,
He is the biggest snowman of all.

The sun! That sun! It came out so
    fast.
Do you think Ned is going to last?

Keep that sun away from Ned..
That sun is going to his head.

The biggest snowman of them all
Is very, very, very small.

Sheila Anne Bridges, 3-B

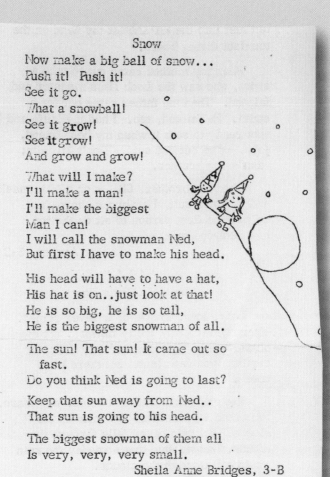

I was a poet and an artist (or so I thought) when I was nine years old.
My poem, entitled *Snow*, made the school magazine.

CHAPTER 8

THE LOOK

It wasn't hard to spot. In fact, you didn't even have to look for it. Walking the streets, stepping into an elevator, riding the subway, I saw it in just about every pair of eyes I made contact with. I had a name for it: *The Look*. It didn't matter whether you lived in a loft in the Meatpacking District or a doorman building on the Upper East Side, whether you waited tables or managed a billion-dollar hedge fund. Absolutely no one was exempt. It was that vacuous, vitamin D-deficient, somber, sullen, just plain old sick-and-tired-of-February (even at the beginning of February) look. And on this particular morning, I didn't need to glance in the mirror to know I was a prime candidate for regional spokesperson.

I rolled out of bed at 4 a.m. and straight into my grey sweatpants, not bothering to put on underwear, brush my teeth, or comb the tangled bird's nest on top of my head. I threw on my favorite black fleece hoodie, shoved my bare feet into a pair of fuzzy brown boots, and reached for my black wool fur-lined Helmut Lang coat. I had bought it the year before at a Barneys warehouse sale; now it was frayed on the bottom, its lining soiled, and half of its buttons either cracked or missing. The coat had taken a major beating this winter and I felt the same way.

Rummaging through my jam-packed closet, determined to properly accessorize *The Look*, I fished out my green down ski mittens and purple-and-white striped knit scarf. Looking like a wobbly Sherpa staggering back to base camp, I was ready to step out to walk Dolby and buy the paper. There was no time this morning for our usual Central Park outing or the gym. I had a plane to catch and was pressed for time.

"C'mon. C'mon…let's go!"

Dolby picked up on my impatience as I fastened the last two buttons on my coat and reached for his leash, which was buried in a pile of shoes under the mahogany table in my foyer. I was sick of the routine already: walking the dog morning and evening in perpetual darkness, bending down to pick up his poop in a Glad sandwich bag off the windswept, slippery, salt-encrusted sidewalk. The streets in our Harlem neighborhood were strewn with double-parked cars and garbage cans blown over by a bullying wind and sleet. Dolby was sick of it, too. He tugged at his leash, yanking me along, forging ahead like a husky running the Iditarod, doing his business in record time. We were back in from the bitter cold in 12 minutes flat, with no casualties except a soaked copy of the

New York Times and my black mini-umbrella, which had been decapitated, mangled, and rendered useless by a monstrous gust of wind that caught us by surprise on the uptown side of Lenox Avenue.

It was simple: I hated February. I hated it for all sorts of reasons. February brought out my Inner Scrooge. The days were short and my patience shorter. When I woke up it was dark. When I walked Dolby it was dark. When I came home from work it was still dark. When it wasn't dark the skies were dull and grey. Even when the sallow sun dared to show its face, it was still too cold to go outside.

February was also Black History Month. Whose bright idea was it to make the shortest, coldest month the one we cram all the positive contributions of black people into? Didn't they know how much we hated the cold? Why couldn't we celebrate Black History Month during August, which was three days longer and about seventy degrees warmer?

As far as I was concerned, February was the cruelest month, especially in a place like New York City. I had lived in Manhattan far too long to remember exactly what it was like in other places, but anywhere had to be better than here. All I wanted to do was crawl under my bedcovers and not come out. Which is why I sought sandier pastures whenever I desperately needed a change of scenery, an attitude adjustment, or quite simply a good thaw. This week I had lucked out: I had a television shoot in Miami and could tack on a couple extra days for myself. Not only did I get to fly business class and stay in an ocean-view room at the Delano Hotel without digging into my own wallet, but I could finally catch up on some much-needed sleep and essential beach time. Other than a little bottle of Ambien CR and a 28-day nap, it was the only antidote I could think of to the city that never sleeps at its ugliest time of year.

After I finished packing and pulling myself together, I gave Rebecca the dog sitter her final instructions, including the new code for my alarm and a reminder to go easy on the rawhide for Dolby. He had a knack for charming everyone out of tennis balls, pizza crusts, and rawhide bones. The last time I left him with her, Rebecca had unsuspectingly fallen under his spell, which meant I returned home from a weekend in Paris to what looked like *pain au chocolat* stains all over my brand new hand-knotted wool and silk Tibetan rug. I rubbed Dolby behind his brown left ear, told him goodbye, grabbed my bag, keys, and trusty fleece hoodie, and headed out the door.

One of the great perks of having a TV show was a car and driver whenever I was in production. Julien, who lived in Long Island City, was always on time, impeccably dressed in a button-down shirt and tie. His big black Mercedes sedan was so spotless you could see a mirror reflection of yourself in it from two feet away. My only complaint was that its plush beige interior smelled like Pine Sol instead of leather. This might have had something to do with Julien's insistence on hanging not one or two, but three pine-tree shaped and -scented air fresheners from the rearview mirror.

"Good morning, Miss Shay-la."

"Good morning, Julien. How are you?" I handed him my overstuffed canvas carry-on and slid into the back seat.

"We're going to La Guardia. Continental, I think. Let me check my ticket."

"Happy Valentine's Day, Miss Shay-la," he said as he carefully shut the door behind me.

With Julien, everything was always "Miss Shay-la." It made me a little crazy and I had tried several times to correct him, insisting he "just call me Sheila." Once I even resorted to phonetics, over-emphasizing the correct pronunciation—"Sheee-la." But it didn't work and I didn't have the heart to try again. Besides, it was Valentine's Day and I was in a rush to get to the airport. *Valentine's Day? Shit. How did I not know that?*

"Happy Valentine's Day to you, too, Julien."

I checked my phone. Sure enough, it was February 14th. And while the romantic side of me thought how nice it might be to receive a dozen long-stem roses, the galvanized side knew that given the questionable company I was keeping these days, there was a greater probability I would be served with a subpoena. I might even settle for a box of Whitman's Samplers, but I realized the best approach was to have low expectations. Even though I was dating someone, the day didn't hold much appeal. It was more of an excuse for people to wear goofy red sweaters and send Hallmark cards. I could never decide which was worse: Witnessing one of my employees running to the door proudly to claim a handful of helium-filled silver balloons that read "Be Mine" or watching one of my design assistants bite her cuticles all afternoon, silently praying for an FTD delivery.

In my office, February 14th started off in different ways, but it always ended up the same. There would be the teary phone call, followed up by the angry email, then *the argument*, and eventually the muffled sniffle-turned-sob and quick retreat to the ladies room to smuggle a roll of toilet tissue and hide it under the desk since the only office-designated box of Puffs had run out. What

---

OVERLEAF I saved these Valentine cards from some of my classmates, keeping them in a book called *The Nothing Book* that my parents gave me for my 11th birthday.

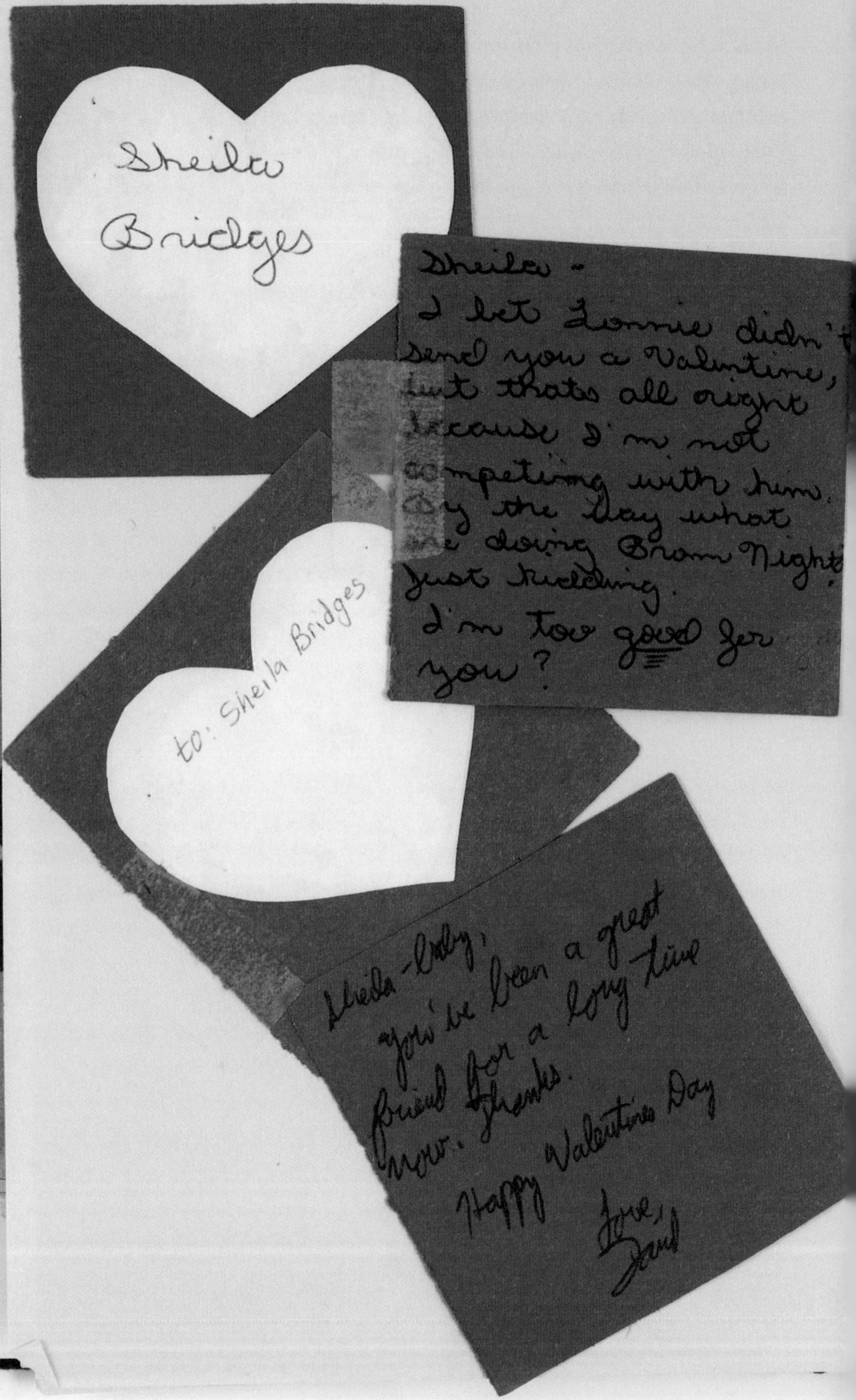

Sheila
Bridges

to: Sheila Bridges

Sheila —
I bet Lonnie didn't
send you a Valentine,
but thats all right
because I'm not
competing with him.
By the way what
are doing Prom Night?
Just kidding.
I'm too good for
you?

Sheila-baby,
you've been a great
friend for a long time
now. Thanks.
Happy Valentines Day
Love,
Paul

Sheila,
There's not much I can Day except for one thing, and that's that Floyd or whatever his name is isn't good enough for you. Why don't you follow in Lauren's footsteps

me) you can both come with me? It's a shame I can never be serious, anyway Happy Valentine's Day,
Love,
Tony

S-H-E-I-L-A! How you doing Sheila? That's nice. Well anyway Have a Happy Valentine's Day

Love,
Steve

Well Sheil,
It's been a long year so far. And you have to admit that I haven't bothered you lately. You're welcome!

Happy Valentines Day Sheila-Baby!
Love,
David

Valentine's Day hadn't cost me in bathroom supplies, it had most certainly cost in productivity: Forget about anybody meeting client deadlines on February 14th. With every delighted yelp of surprise, with every tearful sob I heard, I just wanted to roll my eyes. But I had learned to keep my own calloused feelings to myself, offering congratulations or condolences, hugs and tissues, depending on the whims of a few forgetful boyfriends and the arrival (or not) of a couple dozen carnations laced with baby's breath.

There was no denying it. Something was really bothering me, something beyond my immediate gripes about February and Valentine's Day. But instead of delving deeper, it was easier to just blame it all on New York. Had 15-plus years of living here changed me? Some days, it felt like the city was steadily chipping away at my youthful idealism, carving me into a hardened block of cynicism. Everything seemed different post-9/11, including me. On my short ride to the airport, I reflected back on Monday, September 10th, 2001, one of the proudest moments of my professional career. That morning the new issue of *Time* magazine hit the newsstands. It featured profiles of many notable professionals—including me—and I was named *America's Best Interior Designer*. CNN producers trailed me for two days in conjunction with the article, then ran a five-minute taped segment on me the night before. I celebrated by uncorking a bottle of Dom Perignon (a gift from a client) with a couple of friends. I couldn't have felt happier, as everything seemed to be falling perfectly into place.

All of the hard work and years of personal sacrifice had finally paid off. But the champagne bubbles barely had a chance to go to my head before everything fizzled and went flat. Instead of soaring, my career stalled, then plummeted in shrapnel and smoke, along with those four commercial airplanes and the World Trade Center the following morning. It was Tuesday, September 11th and *Time* magazine Volume 158, No. 11 was immediately replaced by Volume 158, No. 12—with a picture of the Twin Towers aflame. Within 24 hours, my momentary career high was replaced with an indescribable low as I joined millions of fellow New Yorkers in mourning the loss of colleagues, friends, family, and neighbors—and of our innocence. We would be forever bereft of the exuberance that was once endemic to the Big Apple in its heyday, long before the horrific attacks on that spectacularly sunny September day.

Now, years later, I was still left with a vague, nagging feeling of longing and loss: I simply missed the old New York—the one that didn't have a Starbucks on every other corner. Was I quickly becoming one of those smug longtime residents, wondering what had become of the city I once knew and loved?

These two photographs were published in *Time* in September 2001, but the timing couldn't have been any worse: Unfortunately, the magazine hit newsstands the day before the terrorist attacks on 9/11.

I spent most of my time on the tarmac putting out the usual client fires, answering emails and returning calls. That left the rest of the nearly two-and-a-half hour plane ride to read my scripts for the Miami shoot and stare intermittently out the window. Between preparing for my upcoming interview with French design guru, Philippe Starck, and Miami Beach real estate developer, Craig Robins, I fantasized about becoming Rip Van Winkle, taking that long winter nap and waking up when February was over. I unbuckled, climbed over the matronly-looking woman sleeping next to me and headed for the restroom in the cabin coach behind me. Normally, I avoided airplane lavatories but today I had made the mistake of drinking an entire liter of Poland Spring water I had snuck onboard, plus two complimentary mimosas. As I stood in the aisle waiting for the red OCCUPIED sign to change, I listened to three overly ripped, pumped-up guys, one in a neon-green track suit and the other two in shorts and muscle tees, discussing how they were going to "take Miami by the fucking balls" as soon as they landed. *I hope they aren't staying at my hotel* was all I could think. I looked away from the three stooges but made eye contact with a freckled redhead in an indigo-blue cardigan, quickly averting my eyes as soon as her gaze caught mine. While I strongly suspected *The Look* was exclusively found within the borders of New York City—not the airspace above it—I half expected to see it in her wide-set green eyes.

"Sheila? Sheila Bridges? Is that you?" said the redhead.

"Yes…ah…Hi…?" I was fumbling for a name. After a few awkward moments of silence, I said, "I'm sorry, you look very familiar, but I can't remember your name."

"It's Connie Levine, but you don't know me. I'm actually a huge fan of your work and I watch your TV show every week. If I miss it, I always TiVo it!"

"Oh, okay. Thanks for watching. So nice to meet you. I'm sorry—tell me your name again."

"Connie."

The moment I shook her hand, I heard the latch and saw the red OCCUPIED turn to a green VACANT. Perfect timing. I scooted around the grey-haired man with the horn-rimmed glasses who exited, waving goodbye to my middle-aged fan. I unbuttoned and unzipped my jeans and thought about Connie as I steadied myself to pee while standing. I wasn't exactly germophobic but there was no sense putting the seat down since I had a better chance of hitting the inside of the tiny metal bowl with it still up. This was definitely one of those moments when I did have to admit to penis envy.

On the way back to business class, I smiled and waved at Connie. I was a reluctant celebrity, always caught completely off-guard whenever someone recognized me. No matter how many times a week it happened, I just couldn't get used to it. Sometimes it had to do with the emergence of my own shyness and the predictable awkwardness of talking to total strangers. But most of the time it had to do with the fact that I wasn't a famous actor but instead a real-life designer playing a designer on TV. Some days I felt like my producers wanted me to dumb it down as much as possible, asking our guests the most obvious, pedantic questions—questions I already knew the answers to—and punctuating them with make-believe curiosity in place of the nagging ennui I was really feeling.

"Sandy, I've noticed your apartment feels so light and airy—almost loft-like. So tell us, how were you able to achieve that?"

"Well, Sheila, we have a lot of big windows and high ceilings. I painted the walls white and I didn't buy a lot of furniture. I think it makes the room seem more spacious."

"What a wonderful approach. It really does work. Your living space seems so open and inviting."

Despite the ditzy questions and predictable conversations, somehow my television show had gained momentum among decorating and lifestyle enthusiasts. Apparently, they really enjoyed watching me scour flea markets, check out homes or hotels, interview people about their lifestyles, and dole out free design advice. *Sheila Bridges Designer Living* aired in a coveted prime time slot, every Tuesday night at 8 p.m. And if you happened to be a junkie for it, but missed the original Tuesday night episode, you could catch a rerun weeknights at 3 a.m. or Sunday mornings at 11.

I was in the middle of shooting my fourth season and by all accounts everyone, from my agent to the production company to the network, seemed happy with the series—that is, everyone except me. Part of my ambivalence stemmed from the fact that I was just plain exhausted. No one had warned me about the enormous time commitment and tremendous workload, especially since I still had to juggle my full-time day job running my busy design firm. As fortunate as I felt about having my own television show—an opportunity many people around me seemed to covet—there were days when I wished I could just go back to my earlier simple life. I imagined what it would be like to live off the grid without hundreds of emails, phone messages, and huge stacks of snailmail stalking me everywhere I went: The pile on my desk at the production company, the mountain at my Madison Avenue office and at my retail store in Hudson, the stack in my box when I arrived home at my Harlem apartment and the heap shoved into my white metal mailbox across from the driveway at my country home—along with a note from my mailman to please stop by the post office to pick up the rest that couldn't fit.

I had dreamed of career success since the day I graduated from college, but now it was as though I had gotten tangled up in my own web, hemmed in by my own good fortune. It didn't help my feelings of indifference that even after all of the press and the accolades, I still couldn't seem to get any respect—often from the same people who had hired me for my professional expertise in the first place. It had been an especially rough week: One client left me a crazy voicemail message at one in the morning threatening to "come uptown and throw the fucking sofa through your goddamned window" because he didn't like the texture of the linen velvet fabric it was upholstered in, even though it was what he had insisted upon. Another was so bent out of shape at getting a "past due" notice on one of his unpaid invoices that he showed up at our office unannounced and threw $5,000 cash in hundred dollar bills in my assistant's face when she opened the door to greet him. Apparently, just because you were worldly enough to do your banking offshore didn't mean you had read Emily Post on etiquette or would bother to adhere to any of George Washington's *Rules of Civility*.

At least I was in good company—all my friends who were interior decorators, carpenters, textile designers, decorative painters, and architects catering to the upper echelon of Manhattan had similar stories. If we got together for dinner or cocktails after a professional function, the evening often turned into a forum for venting our frustrations at bad client behavior, each of us engaging in petty one-upmanship, trying to lend one another a supportive ear, as we shared the sordid details. It was a familiar scenario: We nearly broke our backs to please our most difficult clients, to ensure their homes were finished and furnished impeccably, all of their decorative accessories and personal accoutrements done in perfect taste, everything completed strictly in accordance with their laundry lists of specific wishes, while they hovered over us in distrust, micromanaging every step, changing their minds at a whim and blaming us for every reversal or delay. I didn't care about being an unsung hero of the home. In my Calgon, take-me-away moments, my fantasies were far simpler: that one day I'd have an entirely new roster of clients—every one of whom was gracious enough to let me do my job in peace.

Why am I killing myself for these ungrateful people? I thought as I stared out the airplane window. In my dreams at night, I used to see beautiful wild horses galloping past me; now, I was being trampled by them instead. Just thinking about it made me feel stressed-out and exhausted. Maybe it was the mimosas and the change in altitude. Either way, my coherent thoughts eventually got all jumbled up, turning to Jell-O as I periodically dozed off, until they were interrupted by a male voice making the tray-tables and seat-backs announcement.

As we descended slowly through a layer of white meringue-like clouds, I could see tiny patches of blue water peppered with little Monopoly boats far below. We were about to land in Miami. I settled back into my seat and closed my eyes again, still not able to pinpoint exactly what was at the root of my discontent. Whatever it was, at least I felt relieved to have escaped the icy grasp of the abominable snowman otherwise known as February in New York City.

Miami, one of my favorite winter escapes, is only a quick two-and-a-half hour flight from New York.

CHAPTER 9

MIAMI HEAT

My entire field of vision was taken up by a long row of oversized Pamela Anderson-style fake tits alternating with brightly colored thongs sandwiched between big brown buns. If I squinted hard, looking past the collection of glistening tanned body parts and white canvas umbrellas, I could make out the silhouettes of oil tankers and cruise ships lined up perfectly, like tiny toy replicas, evenly dotting the horizon line of the Atlantic Ocean. I leaned back on my chaise, placed my sunglasses back in my bag, and closed my eyes.

You couldn't have asked for a more perfect beach day. It was only 11 a.m., but already nearly 82 degrees: Sunny, not too humid and, more important, not a cloud in sight. I heard something about a "small-craft advisory" earlier on the news, but that was irrelevant since I wasn't planning on being in anybody's boat on anybody's ocean today. It was Friday, and I was determined to remain beach-bound, with one simple goal: I had 48 hours to change my skin's February jaundiced pallor to a more acceptable shade of brown.

After spending a few days shooting TV segments for my show, I could finally turn off my phone and relax. So there I lay, baking in the Miami heat, like a rotisserie chicken in an East Harlem carniceria window for all to see. I'd roll myself over intermittently, readjusting my beach towel on the cushion under me, remembering to reapply carefully selected grades and brands of sunscreen. I wanted to make sure I was evenly sizzled on all sides, like a slice of perfectly browned bacon. It was all in the numbers: Kiehl's SPF 15 on my face, Bain de Soleil 6 on my body, Banana Boat 30 balm on my lips to ensure they didn't burn and puff up like those fake wax ones I used to wear for Halloween as a kid.

Life was good and I felt happy. My hands and feet were meticulously manicured and I had even managed to tame the woolly mammoth that lived between my thighs with a Brazilian wax the day before. So far, the biggest stressor of the day was deciding whether to have the ahi tuna wrap or the shrimp BLT for lunch. Yucca fries or a side salad? A mojito or a glass of Veuve Clicquot?

I was thinking, *I could get into this South Beach lifestyle*. I'd often found myself wondering what it would be like to own a place here. The idea was intriguing enough that during my last visit, I'd scheduled half a day to look at apartments

---

OPPOSITE The Delano Hotel in Miami Beach, Florida, was one of my regular haunts during the late 1990s. I still love French designer Philippe Starck's whimsical and thoughtfully designed spaces.

with a broker. Even with shimmering ocean views, real estate was cheap compared to Manhattan. It could be a lot of fun working and hanging out here for a few months during the winter. I fantasized about designing a really minimalist space with an all-white interior. How cool would that be? And talk about a major departure from my classic Harlem six or my colonial house up the Hudson. I told my Mother about the idea and she said I needed another home about as much as I needed a hole in my head. She was right. The last thing I could use right now was more logistics and complications heaped onto my already full plate. I rolled out of my daydream and reached out to touch Stephen on the arm to make sure he was still there.

We had met in September at The Red Dot, a local restaurant near my country home upstate, and started dating right away. After so many summers in the Hamptons, I finally reasoned it was time to stop paying the big bucks to escape the very same city I paid the big bucks to live in. I got tired of the Hamptons grind, of bracing myself for gridlock on the LIE or the Northern State, for that lovely three-hour–plus drive out to Bridgehampton; sick of watching synthetic New York weekenders trying to jump the line at the Amagansett Farmers Market or beat each other to the last bag of Terra Chips at Sagg Main Store. So I decided to carve out a new niche for myself by heading north instead of east. I bought a small, white house with black shutters and a big front porch facing the Hudson River. It was on roughly 13 acres and set back from the road. I felt like there would be plenty of space to grow, as opposed to the Hamptons, where there seemed to be room only to resent. Upstate, there were enough crabgrass lawns littered with rusting cars, trampolines and double-wide trailers to call it the un-Hamptons. It also made me happy because it seemed far less clichéd.

While I wasn't big on picking up men at bars, I was lured by Stephen's boyish charm and Montgomery Clift-style cleft chin. It won him my business card, which in turn led to an email exchange the next morning, brunch at Brandow's the following day, and a relationship three days later. It was all a bit of an unexpected whirlwind but I was trying to just let go and see where it would take me.

"Hey," I said, stroking the hair on Stephen's left arm. "Are you awake?"

Stephen, or *Mr. Snuffaluffagus*, as I sometimes affectionately called him, was the hairiest man I had ever met; it was all over his arms, chest, and legs. I sometimes daydreamed about becoming a modern-day Delilah, bringing my blue Gillette razor to bed at night, shaving his furry back while he slept with his face planted unknowingly in the pillow. Stephen was also the whitest guy I had ever had a relationship with, which didn't mean a whole lot since he was also the first. Other than being set up on a blind date with Robert De Niro, who apparently decided I wasn't chocolatey enough, this was uncharted territory for me. I liked my men more like Snoop than Snoopy, which really meant white boys simply weren't on my social radar. All the ones I met in high school and college had beer breath and only seemed interested in getting their hands into some popular girl's bra or panties. After spending much of my adolescence watching their mediocrity blossom, I just couldn't imagine myself waking up in the arms of one. Call it harsh. Call it self-righteous. Call it whatever you like, but it seemed to me whenever things got rough, daddy made a phone call and everything got worked out.

They were accepted by the best schools, nailed the hottest girls, and landed the best jobs. Like most of my friends, I got tired of explaining that my presence in their spatial hemisphere wasn't some token gift thanks to the generosity of affirmative action. I grew bored with my rote answer: "No, actually I'm *not* here on scholarship." And God forbid I should elaborate. Then I would be accused of copping an attitude, having a chip on my shoulder, being uppity.

Stephen was born in Southampton but his family eventually relocated to upstate New York, which is where he grew up. He liked to describe them as "college-educated farmers," which led me to picture a bunch of fine, upstanding WASPs dressed in well-ironed plaid flannel shirts and overalls, driving tractors around town. Lineage was the only asset his family retained after generations of bad investments and broken marriages. Who needed money when you had good looks and a proper pedigree? He liked to remind me that his ancestors (both maternal and paternal) had arrived on the Mayflower. "The first ship, not the second," he would often add. I tried my best not to hold it against him.

I envied the ease with which Stephen seemed to navigate through life. He walked into every room with this sense of patrician confidence. Ruggedly handsome, square-jawed, and rough-hewn, he reminded me of the Marlboro Man, although he smelled more of entitlement than cigarettes. It was that very same attitude of remote confidence that had attracted me in the first place. I wondered what it must feel like to breathe that sort of rare air, believing—no, *knowing*—that you deserved a foot in the door wherever you went.

During every period of my life I watched entitlement in incubation. I had witnessed enough to write my own version of Langston Hughes' *The Ways of White Folks*.

My education and my job as a designer had given me a zoom lens into an at-times warped world I wouldn't have seen otherwise. I had often worked with clients who thought nothing of redoing a $25,000 paint job because little Austin had decided to make "art" with his magic markers all over the dining room wall. Or buying a *second* custom-made silk damask living room sofa for $15,000 because their darling Elliot had taken his scissors to the original. It made perfect sense: Let your sons know the world is theirs for the taking. Be it the glass coffee table they throw their sister through or the draperies they set ablaze. Childish gestures enabled, giving birth to an unparalleled confidence that is virtually impossible to rattle in adult life. No barriers, no glass ceilings. Boundaries? They were for all those *other* people, the ones whose ancestors didn't arrive at Plymouth Rock aboard the first ship. People like me.

"Stephen, are you awake?" I said, pulling back from his arm.

"I am now!"

"Oh, sorry. You must have been sound asleep. What do you want for lunch?" His eyes were closed. He was obviously still dozing, not thinking about food as I always was.

"I don't know. What time is it?"

"12:40."

"Why don't you ask for a menu?"

"Well, I don't need it but I can get one if you want to take a look." I realized Stephen hadn't known me long enough to understand I stayed at the Delano so often I had the entire beach and poolside dining menus—breakfast, lunch, snacks, and cocktails—memorized front to back. I wrestled my bikini top back on. I wasn't shy about going topless on the beach but my modesty resurfaced when food was involved. Somehow French fries with truffle oil and nipples coated in Hawaiian Tropic just didn't seem to mix. I waved to get the waiter's attention.

"Hey, do you want to go for a run later?" Stephen asked.

"Maybe before dinner if I have the energy." I had already worked out early in

TOP I was featured on the cover of *Fine Living* in the spring of 2002.

ABOVE LEFT The VHS videocassette is of *Sheila Bridges Designer Living*, the lifestyle show I hosted.

ABOVE RIGHT The cover of a *Fine Living* brochure.

At the request of the network (which no longer exists), all logos have been removed from the above promotional materials.

OPPOSITE These are two video stills from two episodes we shot in South Beach, Miami.

In 2002, I was fortunate enough to be chosen as part of a national advertising campaign for Millstone coffee.

the morning at the David Barton Gym with George, my local personal trainer. "Actually, the more I think about it—probably not. I was planning on having a cocktail or two with lunch."

"Where's dinner tonight, anyway?"

"I got us a reservation at Casa Tua but I'm happy to just stay here and eat if that's what you want."

It was the last day of the South Beach Food and Wine Festival and Stephen and I were planning to enjoy some of my TV host perks, which meant plenty of parties, free cocktails, and VIP treatment. I had flown down three days earlier to shoot my scheduled segments and Stephen had arrived from upstate in the morning. He was an independent carpenter/builder and had been divorced for 10 years; his two teenage daughters, Lindsay and Samantha, lived with him most of the time. By all accounts, he was a good dad. It was his ex-wife who was the deadbeat. Or at least that's what he told me. My crazy schedule rarely allowed me to spend much time together with Stephen and his girls. I liked it that way. I wasn't sure I wanted an instant family with a man who had a reputation for devouring younger women the same way Dolby feverishly chewed up his Milk Bones Biscuits, leaving crumbs all over the floor.

I was 10 years younger than Stephen but still a decade older than most of the women he usually dated. It was another milestone in my dating life, since I had always hooked up with guys whose ages hovered close to my own. Stephen loved to be in love, which meant it didn't take him long to lay his affection for me out like a plush shag rug. But it was so thick I often found myself tripping on it. I hated that clumsy, out-of-control feeling of falling; so, in an effort to keep my balance, I often held my feelings in check. Plus, I was skeptical of a Pilgrim who wore clogs and worked as a carpenter, had pedigree but no money, and drove a Porsche Boxster. Who wouldn't be?

By the time we had finished lunch and were onto our second bottle of champagne, Stephen wanted to talk television.

"So I have a great idea for a TV show," he said, wide awake and animated now.

"Yeah, what's that?" On my fourth glass of Veuve, I was just getting comfortable again in my chaise. The combination of champagne, food, and sun had gone to my head, and I felt myself dozing off.

"I've been thinking a lot about it and I'm really excited. It's called 'Carpentry Cuisine.'"

"'Carpentry Cuisine'?" I repeated. I had to admit it had a certain ring to it.

"Right. It's kind of like *This Old House* meets *Rachael Ray*. But without the women."

I couldn't help but chuckle. "Stephen, are you kidding? Why would you want to do anything even remotely resembling *Rachael Ray*?"

"No, really. Rachael Ray is incredibly popular. You may not like her show, but a lot of people do." I checked my watch: Time to reapply sunscreen. Stephen wanted my full attention. "Just hear me out," he said, reaching out to touch my hand.

"Okay, so this is the basic idea," he continued. "As a carpenter you don't need a deluxe Cuisinart or a $7,000 Viking range to make a great meal. All of the tools we work with every day can be used just like kitchen utensils to make all kinds of delicious dishes. We could get your TV crew to shoot me and a couple other guys working on a house in Rhinebeck. Picture this: We take our lunch break and we make Nail Gun Cedar Siding Salmon, Arugula Salad with Block Planer Shaved Parmesan, and Sawzall Fruit Cup for dessert."

"Sawzall Fruit Cup?" I laughed. Stephen had taught me that a Sawzall was to a carpenter what a Porsche 911 Turbo was to an investment banker. It was a big electric dick of a tool that could cut through anything including sheetrock, siding, and brick. Zero to 60 in 3.5 seconds. A scary weapon to most people, but a builder's best friend. Now Stephen wanted to go on TV and demonstrate how to cut up apples, oranges, and peaches with the thing. He was on a roll now: "We could set up a couple of saw horses and a half sheet of plywood as a table and sit on joint compound buckets as seats. We can use all kinds of other tools to make dishes, like a paint stirrer to mix the vinaigrette or an electric drill bit to knead the bread dough."

"Sounds interesting, but sweetie, seriously, why would you want to have a TV show?" I already knew the answer: He had a seemingly insatiable need for attention, something I wasn't very adept at providing, especially given my hectic schedule. Furthermore, I was still on the fence about how I felt toward him. Stephen was an acquired taste and, while I had grown to love him—thanks in part to his persistence—I just wasn't sure if we realistically had a future together.

"I don't know," he went on. "I just think it would be incredible. You have a TV show and you're no different or better than anyone else. So why shouldn't I have one?"

No different or better than anyone else? I wasn't sure exactly what he meant by that but I wasn't going to let it slide.

"Stephen, I never said anything about being different or better than anyone else. I have a TV show simply because I was offered one. I'm an interior designer and I host a show about design. Besides, what does my having a show have to do with you suddenly wanting one? What, are we like Frick and Frack now?" I was starting to sound just like my Mother.

"No, Sheila, we're not like Frick and Frack. I just think it would be really great. So what's wrong with that? You're a regular person just like me, but you live this charmed life. Everybody loves you and you get recognized everywhere we go. Hell, I mean you do all this cool stuff, travel all over, stay in expensive hotels, come to swanky places like this. No offense or anything, but

I have to ask myself what makes you so special?"

Suddenly, I felt myself thrown back to the second grade. I wanted to punch Stephen just like I had Keith Saltzman. Instead, I closed my eyes and inhaled deeply. It wasn't worth getting sent to the blue bench again. *Breathe, Sheila. Breathe. Let it go. Just let it go.*

Every man I dated nowadays seemed to have issues with my career. It was becoming a recurring theme in my romantic life. They started out enthusiastic enough about me having my own business, but the minute I started focusing my attention back on work, the relationships always seemed to crack and splinter. Maybe I didn't have time to bake Stephen a proper cheese soufflé, do a load of laundry, or pick his kids up from school. But I could certainly show some support by signing on board with his idea—even if it was slightly stupid and sexist. Perhaps getting on TV would help Stephen assert himself and get over his hidden insecurities, making him feel like more of a man instead of a eunuch. "Okay, so I think maybe your idea could work. Do me a favor and write it up when we get back home. I'll send it to my producer and my agent." I looked over at Stephen, who had grown quiet, pensive. So I went on, "But don't forget, the whole TV thing is a huge commitment. It looks all glamorous from the outside, but it's shit on the inside. It's a ton of work and the money isn't what you might think. Besides, who's going to run your jobs while you're off filming the show? Who's going to drive Lindsay and Samantha to school?"

He stood up, took off his Vuarnet sunglasses, and brushed the sand from the hair on his legs.

"Where are you going?" I asked.

"In the water. It's too hot. I can't sit here anymore."

I hoped I hadn't pissed him off. I just wanted things to be easy for a change. No bickering. No soap opera drama. I didn't want to compete with Stephen or any of my other boyfriends. Hadn't any of these guys played sports? Didn't they realize we were supposed to be on the same team?

I could see Stephen was beginning to burn. The deeply carved lines around his hazel eyes were tinged with red.

"Do you want to come in?" he asked.

"No thanks," I said as I rolled over onto my stomach. "I just want to lie here and be still for now." I watched as Stephen walked across the wide expanse of beach and into the ocean, his flat, spatula ass gradually disappearing into the water. I reached down to readjust the bikini bottom that was wedged in my big brown round one.

Sitting in the waiting room at my dermatologist's office, I found myself staring at the biggest pair of feet I had ever seen. Correction: The biggest feet I had ever seen on a woman. What got my attention was the cleavage. Décolletage wasn't particularly sexy when it was down there between your toes. Once it caught my eye though, there was no turning back. I fixated on those feet for what felt like 20 minutes. Each elephant trunk of a leg led down to a meaty shank of foot shoe-horned into a scuffed black leather pump at least one size too small. The beige-colored flesh spilled out like a well-done calzone stuffed with too much mozzarella and pepperoni. *What did they call that legendary creature who lived deep in the woods of the Pacific Northwest? Bigfoot. But the Native Americans had another name for it….*

My appointment was scheduled for two and it was already three. What I was hoping would be a routine in-and-out visit to Dr. Lewis was turning into an annoying test of the little patience I had, especially because I had forgotten to bring my laptop. I had already flipped through every outdated issue of *Newsweek, Sports Illustrated*, and *Entertainment Weekly* in the magazine rack. I had stared at the framed landscape on the wall until all the pointy treetops and tall wheat fields merged into one subtle, yet continuous brushstroke of green and gold. I had counted every single one of the squiggle patterns in the ho-hum nylon carpet. Out of distractions, I homed in on the huge feet planted next to mine. Had she ever seen a podiatrist about those bunions? I wondered what brought her here. *Sasquatch. That was it! My memory served me well.*

I had a thousand things to do, my assistant Darren had overbooked my entire afternoon, and the only thing I could think of was I needed to get out of here as quickly as possible and get back to work.

But I also needed to find out what was going on with my hair.

I hadn't noticed anything strange when I was in Miami two weeks earlier. Audrey, my hairdresser down there, hadn't said anything even though she did my hair three days in a row while we were taping. Stephen hadn't mentioned anything and Lord knows he was always playing with my hair.

Early the following week, though, my New York hairdresser Kyle had stopped suddenly in the middle of blowing my hair out for a black-tie dinner.

"Hey," he said. "I just noticed something weird. You have these two tiny bald patches at the back of your neck."

"You're kidding."

"No, seriously. Look at this." He turned off the blow dryer, put a big clip in my hair, spun me around in the chair, and held a mirror to the back of my head. There they were: Two perfectly round, symmetrical hairless spots, staring back at me like a pair of penny-sized doll eyes. My scalp looked as though it had been branded with two small coins. I had been preoccupied with them ever since. The flesh was clean and smooth like the underside of my forearm. I kept rubbing my index finger over the spots, expecting to feel stubble, but there wasn't any. What were they? Maybe I had ringworm—whatever that was. Or an allergic reaction to something I ate. Had I slept on something that pulled my hair out? It didn't make any sense that two identical spots would appear so suddenly. I had always been pretty adept at self-diagnosis, but this time I was stumped.

"Miss Bridges?" Dr. Lewis' assistant stood in the doorway of the reception area with a blue folder in one hand and a plastic clipboard in the other.

"That's me." I stood up, relieved it was finally my turn and I was going to get an answer about what was happening on the back of my head. The doctor would figure it out, write me a script and send me on my way. I was healthy and never made a habit of hanging around doctors' offices, except for regular annual checkups and the occasional trip to the dermatologist. I had always had sensitive skin. As a child I developed eczema, and as a teenager I became allergic to those fabric softener sheets like Bounce, which gave me an itchy fish scale-like rash. I liked to deal with whatever issues cropped up quickly and efficiently so I could get on with all the truly important stuff in my busy life.

I followed the white coat and dark ponytail down the long corridor to a small examining room.

"Have a seat. The doctor will be with you shortly. Feel free to hang your coat and bag over there," she said, motioning toward the metal hooks on the back of the door before leaving the room and closing the door quietly behind her. I hung up my coat and scarf but held onto my bag for security's sake. I wasn't really worried. Then again, anytime I went to the doctor, I did feel some apprehension. My blood pressure was normally 110/70. For checkups, it had a tendency to skyrocket and would have to be taken a second time at the end of the exam. I always blamed it on the sterile surroundings and continued to wonder why doctors never seemed to bother decorating to put their patients at ease. Surely they could afford to. Their offices were all the same—cookie-cutter spaces filled with human studies in composure waiting in the silent company of total strangers to pee in a waxed-paper cup—or worse. Some of us fidgeted like children in Sunday School; others sat still as a portrait model posing for a drawing class. Inside we all churned with stomach upset, chest pains, shortness of breath, or just plain numb worry. How about a few interesting patterns on the walls instead of flat and anemic paint colors? Or maybe some well-placed art photographs? It was all drab Benjamin Moore Decorator White, generic Impressionist posters, and viewless windows masked by cold aluminum mini-blinds.

A discreet knock on the door interrupted my decorator's reverie.

"Yes," I said.

"Good afternoon, Sheila," said Dr. Lewis, offering me a pleasant smile and striding over to the small stainless steel sink in the corner to wash his hands. So what brings you here today?"

"There's something strange going on at the back of my head. My hairdresser noticed it a few days ago. It's two identical bald patches right above my neck. I have no idea when they appeared or what could have caused them."

"Let's have a look," he said, rolling his stool closer to the examination chair. I reached back to hold the hair off my neck. I could feel his latex-gloved fingers gently probing my scalp. After less than 10 seconds, he rolled back toward the floating water lilies in the framed, fake Monet poster. He looked me in the eyes.

"It looks like *Alopecia areata*."

"Alo what?"

"Al-oh-pee-shah air-ee-ah-tah." He said it loud and clear as if I was deaf and had forgot to put in my hearing aids. Then he spelled it out: "A-L-O-P-E-C-I-A A-R-E-A-T-A. It's a common autoimmune disease of the skin that causes hair loss. Your immune system mistakes your hair follicles for foreign invaders and attacks them, stopping the hair from growing. Don't worry, it's not life-threatening."

"Are you sure? You only looked at my head for like two seconds." I wanted my money's worth. After waiting over an hour, surely I deserved a more thorough examination. Maybe I should get a second opinion.

Dr. Lewis smiled. "*Alopecia* is very easy to diagnose. The tell-tale sign is one or more small, smooth, bald patches, which is exactly what you have."

"Do a lot of people get this?"

"It affects about 2 percent of the general population. Onset is often in childhood, but it can strike at any age. In most people, the hair grows back but it can take months or even years."

"*Most* people?" I had never been like most people.

"*Alopecia can* result in total, permanent hair loss either on your scalp or your entire body. But that's very rare."

"So, wait a second, you're saying I could go from these two tiny bald patches on the back of my head to no hair on my whole body?"

"Yes, but only in the more extreme forms of the condition, called *Alopecia totalis* and *Alopecia universalis*. When we're done, I'll give you some pamphlets you can take home and read about it."

"I don't get it. I'm healthy, I'm almost 40...this is so out of the blue. Why would I have gotten this now?"

"Unfortunately, we don't really know what causes *Alopecia*. It's believed stress *could* be a contributing factor but that's never been proven. The disease doesn't discriminate. Men and women of all ages and races can get it, but if a family member had it you have an increased likelihood. Do you have any family history of baldness?"

I started to think back. My parents were well into their seventies but both had full heads of hair. So did my brother. I thought about my grandparents. My Mother's father died at age 54 from a stroke, leaving her fatherless when she was only 16. Her mother had died from complications of diabetes when I was in the third grade. And my Father's parents hadn't fared any better, both dying of heart attacks at relatively young ages. I had known them only in framed sepia photographs standing on my Dad's bedroom dresser.

"My Mother's father didn't have any hair, but I think that was just regular male baldness," I said, recalling those pictures. "I'll ask my parents, but I'm pretty sure we don't have any family history."

"Hmmm."

"So what can we do to about this?"

"There really isn't a proven cause or cure for *Alopecia*. As an autoimmune disease, it's tricky to treat because your own body is attacking itself."

"Great. So there's nothing I can do? Just wait and hope and pray it grows back on its own?" *Fuck*. My mind created a battle zone between my skull and scalp, with white blood cells carrying heavy artillery on one side, helpless hair follicles waving a white flag on the other, and me watching helplessly from the sidelines.

"In most cases, the follicles are still healthy, which means they can grow hair back at any time. In your case, the fact that you noticed it early is good. If we start to treat it aggressively right away, I can't imagine there will be any long term problem." Thus far he'd been pretty matter-of-fact, which left me wavering somewhere between mild panic at the prospect of losing my hair and relief that this thing wasn't going to kill me. Now, he was sounding a little more upbeat. Maybe I didn't have to worry.

"So what exactly do you mean by 'aggressively'?"

"The most aggressive form of treatment is cortisone injections. They stimulate your follicles and force them to begin hair production. You come back for shots about once a month for several months. We use tiny needles and give you multiple injections into your scalp. We can set up another appointment to do that or you can have your first treatment today if you'd like."

"Well, since I'm already here, we might as well start now. How long does it take? I have a meeting uptown at four." My schedule had become such a tight series of appointments that if I was late for just one meeting, it sent my entire life calendar into free fall.

Dr. Lewis checked his watch. "We'll have you out of here in time. I promise." He rolled back on his stool to the metal counter and buzzed his assistant to come back in and set up. I watched as she placed sterile cotton pads, gauze, alcohol towelettes and more than a dozen small needles on a tray. Never mind that I'd had an incredible fear of needles since I was a child. Back then at least I had gotten a root beer-flavored lollipop for being brave. Dr. Lewis pushed a button on the side of the examining chair and my upper body automatically reclined. I felt the bright white lights on my head. *Bring on the pain*.

"I'm going to need you to hold your hair over to the right," Dr. Lewis said focusing a look of intense concentration on the back of my head. I did as I was told, grabbing as much hair as I could in my right hand. It was thick and healthy and it felt soft as I swept it upward and to the side. I took a big handful and twisted it into a low knot on the back of my head. But my hair had always had a mind of its own, and some of it wriggled free. I could feel curly wisps fall back onto the nape of my neck. I twirled the loose hairs around my fingers. They took hold like vines clinging to a tree branch. I moved each of the wayward strands back toward the big knot, then tilted my head down and to the left. I barely caught a glimpse of the first syringe out of the corner of my right eye. It was the anticipation more than the needle itself that always made me wince.

"You'll feel a slight pinch when the needle goes in."

Yeah, right. Except I was about to get something like 15 of them in a row directly into the bald patches on my scalp. I couldn't believe that just 10 minutes earlier I had been fidgeting in the waiting room, bored, reading magazines, staring at the wall, trying to remember the name of Sasquatch.

I felt the first needle tip pricking my scalp then plunging in. *Please God. Please. Please don't let him pierce my brain.* The needles were small, but every time one went in I felt that pinch followed by a sharp pain ricocheting through my head. I felt it again and again until all of the syringes were finished. Dr. Lewis blotted the patches with a piece of sterile gauze and asked me to hold it against my scalp for a few minutes. There must have been some bleeding.

When he was done administering the shots, Dr. Lewis pushed the button again, raising me back to a sitting position. "I'm going to recommend some blood tests so we can rule out any other conditions like hypothyroidism, Lupus, or Addison's disease," he said. *Great. Just great. First it's no big deal, then we're talking about going bald, now it's some chronic, terminal illness. Well at least it wasn't cancer.*

"You also may need to see an endocrinologist, depending on the results of the blood work. I can refer you to someone." He pulled a pen in from the breast pocket of his lab coat and started writing on a small pad. "I'm going to give you a couple of prescriptions for topical minoxidil creams. You rub them into your scalp at night. They're a bit greasy but seem to be pretty effective, especially in conjunction with the cortisone injections. We'll see how things go for a few weeks. If the condition persists, I might recommend some oral steroids."

"Steroids? Don't they have all kinds of horrible side effects?"

"Yes, there are potential side effects. Some of them can be a bit challenging, like insomnia, fluid retention, weight gain, moon face, liver damage, and sometimes convulsions."

A bit challenging? That seemed awfully nonchalant, as if having liver damage or convulsions was akin to catching a common cold. And what about the "moon face?" *Fucking moon face?* Seriously? I had no idea what that was but I knew I didn't want it. The only moon face I had known in my lifetime was from 35 years ago, the friendly one that glowed in the starry sky with a wide smile full of Chiclet teeth. *Hey diddle diddle. The cat and the fiddle. The cow jumped over the moon. The little dog laughed to see such sport and the dish ran away with the spoon.* But this was no nursery rhyme. This was my real life and it was taking a bizarre turn. I wondered if Dolby would bark and then laugh at me when he saw me sporting a moon face.

"I'm going to pass on those oral steroids. I don't think the moon face or that weight gain will go over so well with my TV network or my boyfriend. I have enough trouble trying to swallow an aspirin so I'll stick with the shots for now, thank you very much."

Dr. Lewis smiled. "Don't worry, Sheila. I'm sure this will work out fine. By the way, I was on a Delta flight to Charlotte last month and I caught part of your TV show. You were someplace exotic like Tunisia. Casablanca, maybe?"

"Close. Marrakech, actually. That was the hour special on Morocco we shot last year," I said, handing him back the blood-speckled clump of gauze.

"Nice. I've never been. Well anyway, we'll deal with this as aggressively as we possibly can. My *Alopecia* patients have always had very good results with the cortisone." He handed me several small sheets of paper. "Get these filled, be sure to have your blood work done, and I'll let you know as soon as I have the results. You can pick up the rest of your paperwork and those pamphlets on your way out. I'll see you back here in a few weeks for another round of injections. Okay?" He smiled as he got up from his stool, turned, and headed out the door. Dr. Lewis was full of smiles today.

I shrugged my shoulders and muttered, "Okay." But I was thinking *I'm not okay at all.* I felt slightly dazed, blurry. When I went back to the waiting room to pay my bill and get my pamphlets, I looked around for something or someone familiar. Even though it was the same place where just fifteen minutes earlier I had been waiting for a routine visit to the dermatologist, the scene was unrecognizable. Suddenly everything faded to black. Sasquatch was gone and so were my hopes for a quick, easy fix. I would be seeing a lot more of the inside of this office—and of Dr. Lewis' needles—than I could ever have imagined.

Everyone in my Mother's family used to say that I got my hair color from my maternal grandfather, Edward Corbitt Winfrey, especially when they looked at his childhood photograph.

CHAPTER II

KENTUCKY FRIED CHICKEN

On my way home from work, I made a quick stop at the pharmacy to pick up my prescriptions. Once inside my apartment. I opened the white paper bag to find three large tubes, and read each of their labels slowly, one by one: Elidel cream (*Pimecrolimus topical*); Nystatin ointment (*Triamcinolone Acetonide*); and Clobetasol propionate ointment. All three had instructions to apply twice daily.

I was already confused. Did that mean I was supposed to apply all three at the same time twice a day or separately, which would be six applications in one day? Leave it to me to overthink every last detail, inevitably making life more complicated than it already was. In this case, though, I had to get it right, especially if it could mean the difference between keeping my hair and losing it. I would have to give Dr. Lewis' office a call in the morning. In the meantime, I was anxious to find out if baldness ran in my family. So I called my Mother.

"Hi, Mom. How are you doing?"

"Fine, but tired. Your Father and I just got home from Harriette and Hart's. They threw such a wonderful dinner party. It was catered. We had appetizers and a sit-down dinner with red snapper, wine, and dessert. We laughed and laughed. Boy did we laugh. And—"

I cut her short. "Sounds great. Listen, Mom, I went to the doctor this morning and apparently I have this autoimmune skin thing called *Alopecia areata*."

"Alo-what? You mean aloe, as in the plant?"

"No. Just listen," I said, enunciating extra loud and clear. "Alo-pe-cia a-re-a-ta. The name doesn't really matter. The point is that it can make your hair fall out. Anyway, what I need to know is do we have any history of baldness on either side of the family—yours or Dad's?"

"My father was bald."

"I already know that" I interjected. I had never met my maternal grandfather.

"But he was blond when he was young. You certainly didn't get your hair color from me. You really got it from your grandfather."

"Right, so what about—"

"Your hair looks just like his did, same color, texture, and everything."

My Mother wasn't listening to me, which wouldn't be the first time; she rambled on about her father: "When you were a little girl, everyone always said you looked just like my father, starting with the hair. Truly, I used to get that all the time: 'Oh, doesn't she look just like your father?'"

"Mom, I *know* that. What I'm talking about is baldness. Were there any men or women in your family who lost their hair when they were young?"

"No. Not that I remember. Why? What's the problem?"

"I just told you. I have this autoimmune disease called *Alopecia*."

"Autoimmune disease? Jesus Christ. What's that supposed to mean? Please don't tell me—you mean like HIV?!"

"No, Mom. Not like HIV. It's a skin disease. I went to the dermatologist today because I found these two little bald patches on the back of my head. Well, actually, Kyle my hairdresser found them. Remember, I told you about that black-tie dinner I had to go to last week?"

"The black-tie dinner—yes."

"Well, when Kyle was doing my hair for that he noticed these two weird hairless spots in the back of my head. So I went to the doctor to have them checked out."

"And what did he say they were?"

"I just told you what he said they were. They're a symptom of a condition called *Alopecia areata*."

"Sheila, I don't know about that, but I do know I've been telling you for years to stop washing your hair so much. I'm sure that's what caused this aloe vera or aloe-whatever-it-is, and why your hair is falling out. You've been wash-ing it way too much ever since you were in high school. Don't be so stubborn. When you were little, I never washed it more than once a month. That was it."

I was suddenly thrown back to my childhood.

One Saturday a month I would be summoned to the second floor bathroom I shared with my brother Sidney. My Mother would kneel over me, sleeves rolled up, armed with a big bottle of Johnson & Johnson's No More Tears shampoo, and wielding the hand-held shower head. I would slosh around in the big blue bathtub while waves of suds splashed onto the ceramic floor and up on the tiled walls. My Mother would lather and wrestle with the tangled mop atop my head, dousing it with cream rinse. I hated getting my hair washed. Why did it take so long? All that tugging and pulling on my head—it hurt. But that was nothing compared to what I would feel when it was finally dry and ready to be pressed.

My Mother, whose hair was quite fine and manageable compared to mine, could not deal with my thick, kinky curls beyond giving me a center part, then braiding them into two or three crooked plaits, one on each side and another at the back. Once my hair was thoroughly dry to the roots, which usually took a few days, our housekeeper, Mrs. Dutton, was paid to handle the rest.

My hair is finally manageable and under control, thanks to our strict housekeeper, Mrs. Dutton.
I was afraid of her when she held that hot comb in her hand!

"C'mon now. Sit still, Sheila. I'm not playing with you. I have stuff to do and your Mother will be home soon." She would slide me onto the yellow kitchen stool with one hand, while shoving a shallow Pyrex dish into the oven with the other. On the counter next to the stove sat a small white hand towel, a regular comb, and a large jar of Ultra Sheen hair grease. My grandmother's black cast-iron skillet, which normally occupied the front-left burner, would be moved to the back of the stove to make way for the straightening comb. Its fine metal teeth were ominous—blackened and tarnished from the heat like the iron tip of a fireplace tool used to stoke ashen-hot logs. Its brown wooden handle rested on the metal stovetop below the burner, worn smooth from years of strong, determined hands and layers of old grease.

This is what my hair looked like, most days, on its own. I always seemed to have a halo of frizz.

Back then I was simply frightened by the blazing-hot blue flame that hissed out of the square burner and heated the stiff teeth of the comb. Now I was deeply saddened by the whole idea of it: generations of black women led to believe that the straighter your hair was, the better you looked. Like a recessive family gene, the illusion was passed down from mothers to daughters and to their daughters. Every stroke of that searing comb, we were taught, could somehow burn away our enslaved past as plantation pickaninies; every greased, singed strand moving us closer to our round-hipped, full-lipped fantasies of white beauty and acceptance. As if flattening each individual nap might somehow quiet our beloved yet ornery female ancestors, voices rich with strength devalued, and natural beauty unappreciated.

I cringed as I felt the hot metal coming closer to my scalp. The comb sizzled and smoked when it first touched my virgin hair, smoldering gradually to a crispy quiet. My fragile curls crackled then collapsed obediently under the force of the heat, the chemistry of the Ultra Sheen, and the weight of history. When Mrs. Dutton peeked into the oven to check on our dinner, I flinched forward and quickly paid the price.

"OUCH!" I yelled, as I felt my right ear burning.

"Now what did I just tell you, Sheila Anne? That's what you get. I told you to keep still, didn't I?! Lord have mercy! Now hold still while I get to these grapes in your kitchen." This was the part I dreaded the most. The "kitchen" was the area at the back of my head, right below my ears, and the "grapes" were those tiny, naturally knotted curls at the base of my neck. My Mother and Mrs. Dutton were both adamant about getting rid of them.

By the time it was all over, I looked like a baby seal. My hair was slicked down as if it had been conked, shiny and smooth from the grease. My head was tender to the touch, with small burns on one ear and at the top of my neck. The kitchen smelled of Shake 'n Bake pork chops and burnt hair.

I spent the next 48 hours sidestepping my usual after-school routine of touch football in the street and Wiffle Ball on our front porch, for fear of being teased. My new "press and curl" put me at risk of losing my respected tomboy status on the block.

"Egghead! Look at Sheila the Egghead," Sidney taunted.

"She looks like a greaseball!" added Teddy Whitney, Sidney's friend from across the street. Three days later, it threatened rain, and my hair finally began to resemble its former self, its thickness and nap rising with the humidity and barometric pressure. By the end of the week, I was back to two or three thick Brillo plaits instead of one greasy straight one down my back. My halo of blond frizz also reappeared, leaving my Mother exasperated, as usual.

"Seriously, Sheila. I've told you over and over to stop washing your hair so much. It's not like those white girls' you went to school with. And I don't care how much conditioner you use. Black hair can't handle all that water."

"Okay, Mom, never mind. I've got to go. I'll talk to you later." I hung up the phone in frustration. My Mother's logic at times like this never ceased to amaze me. I knew my diagnosis had nothing to do with how much I washed my hair, but I still wasn't sure what it did have to do with. It just didn't seem to make sense. A week before, everything was normal. Then all of a sudden, these two bald patches show up and I'm being told I could lose all my hair. How could this be happening? There had to be a reason for it. I decided to call Jared.

Jared was my tall, handsome, "gay husband" (as my straight friends liked to call him) who lived next door to me, upstate, with his partner of 15 years. While he probably didn't know a whole lot about women's hair, he was an ER doctor and surely he could help me make some more sense of all this. We had bought our houses within a month of each other and became the oddities on our street, Orlich Lane, which was populated with an assortment of redneck conservatives and country bumpkins. We liked to joke about "there goes the neighborhood." *Well, it's a real nice place to raise your kids except for that colored woman with the TV show and those two homos living right next door. What a shame.* I left Jared a voicemail message, hoping he would get back to me soon with some reassuring medical wisdom.

I tried Stephen before I went to bed, but got his voicemail, too. Where was he on a Tuesday night at 10 p.m. that he couldn't answer his phone? Maybe already asleep. I went about my usual routine, walking the dog, ordering take-out, catching up on emails and paperwork. Around bedtime, I brought my bag of creams and ointments into my bedroom and put them on the nightstand. Dolby perked up when he heard the paper bag rustling.

"Sorry, no treat. Now go lie down." He cocked his head and smiled, unconvinced. "Dolby, it's not for you. Now go lie down!"

I stood in front of my big mirror with a small hand mirror in one hand and a tube of ointment in the other. My scalp was sore and there were tiny red scabs from all of Dr. Lewis' injections earlier in the day. My hair was as thick and curly as ever, though. Thank God for that, because even if these spots didn't go away, who would notice them under all that? Was it really possible this *Alopecia* thing could make it all fall out? I applied the three medications, taking great care to follow the instructions on each tube, rubbing each of them into my scalp.

I spent a sleepless night, tossing and turning, mulling over my diagnosis: Left leg out of the covers, right leg in. Then right leg out and left leg in. First, I was too hot, then too cold. I couldn't get comfortable, couldn't relax. I even kicked Dolby off his usual spot at the foot of the bed and onto the floor. In the morning, when I got up and started to make the bed, I noticed greasy stains all over my white cotton pillowcase and the upholstered silk headboard above it. It looked as though I had eaten a bucket of Kentucky Fried Chicken and smeared my hands across them both. I took a look in the mirror. My under-eye bags were there, as always, but my hair was more of a mess than usual. Normally, it looked kind of sexy in the morning—or at least that's what my men often told me. This morning, the front was all right but the back was matted at the roots, clumped and slimy from the cream and ointments. It looked like the Jheri curl fairy had paid me a surprise visit in the middle of the night. I couldn't help but think of the Eriq La Salle character, Darryl Jenks, in the eighties comedy, *Coming to America*. I looked like Darryl's little sister.

Funny how things could turn on a dime. Just two months earlier, when I was flying to L.A. for business, as I checked in, the airline attendant asked me if I was single. I told her yes and she kindly volunteered to try to seat me next to a single man. I remember thinking, *Wow, they can do things like that?*

Sure enough, there was a bunch of men traveling alone in business and first class, but how did she figure out which ones were single? Probably checked their ring fingers when they were at the counter. As I took my seat in the sixth row, I noticed a chubby black man with a greying moustache and receding hair-line three rows away. I sincerely hoped she wasn't trying to hook me up with him. He looked so familiar. Why couldn't I think of his name? Finally, I heard the guy next to him call him Ted. That was it! "Ted" Lange, otherwise known as Isaac from *The Love Boat*. Was *he* single?

After a while, Eriq La Salle, who, after *Coming to America* went on to star in *ER* on TV, sat down next to me. I noticed he wasn't wearing a ring, but he wasn't my type. And besides, I had just seen him with his fiancée in a magazine showcasing their beautiful home in L.A. Eriq was really pleasant and we chatted for much of the flight. Every time he leaned forward or got up from his seat, though, I couldn't help but check for a drip stain on his headrest. All I could think of was *Soul Glo*.

I was too rattled to go about my usual early morning routine of Central Park and the gym. How could I think about working out when all I wanted to do was get my dermatologist on the phone to make sure I was following the idiot-proof directions on my prescriptions correctly? I brushed my teeth, turned on the shower, and stepped in. After a moment's hesitation, I quickly hopped back out and started searching the medicine cabinet. Pushing everything else on the shelf aside, in the top right corner behind the little plastic bottle of Visine and the Ban antiperspirant, I found it. There it was: A small, square grey package with the Four Seasons logo embossed on it in white. I pulled out the hotel shower cap, nervously tucked my matted hair underneath, making sure every last strand was inside, and jumped back into the shower. Hey, you never knew when a mother's advice might come in handy. In this case, I decided not to take any chances.

My Self Portrait

My nickname at school in the first grade was Cookie Monster.
I still love cookies, with the exception of Oreos.

CHAPTER 12

THE TASTE OF BALDNESS

E.A.T. was my favorite place for breakfast in New York City. On top of its convenient location directly across the street from my Upper East Side townhouse office, they made the best scrambled eggs around. Not too runny, not too dense; not too wet or dry. Just *right*. My little routine there was one of my favorite guilty pleasures. I ordered by rote as soon as the waitress arrived: "No menu necessary, thank you. Scrambled eggs with salmon, no onions; toasted, buttered sesame-seed bagel; a glass of freshly squeezed grapefruit juice." The problem was, every time I got the check, I was floored. Thirty bucks for breakfast—not including tip! I tried substituting O.J. or some other type of bagel, but the message delivered on that little slip of paper was always the same: *Way* overpriced.

So I made my trips to E.A.T. a once-a-week treat. There I would sit, every Tuesday morning between 8:30 and 9, parked at the bistro table behind the large picture window, luxuriating in my perfectly fluffy scrambled eggs and salty smoked salmon, observing the Madison Avenue parade of Fendi and fur-clad Upper East Side ladies. Each week, as I reluctantly handed over my platinum American Express card at the end of my breakfast, I vowed this would be the last time. And every Tuesday morning, like clockwork, I would be back. No matter how hard I worked and no matter how much I tried to convince myself I deserved it, I always felt guilty about spending money on things of no inherent value. When it came to a fancy breakfast, though, I figured if I was willing to be extorted once a week, I might as well do it in style.

This morning, I had finished eating early. Instead of hustling up to the office, though, I sat at my usual table waiting for Audrey, my dark-haired, full-figured Mexican makeup artist, hair stylist, and confidante.

Each week while we were in production, she would arrive at my apartment promptly at the crack of dawn, her small black flight-attendant–style Tumi carry-on in tow. The ritual was always the same. First came the "Are you awake?" call on my cell phone and, very shortly thereafter, the screech of the door buzzer followed by Dolby's barking. Next came the chime of the doorbell, more barking, and, once I opened the door, the familiar rumble of Audrey's suitcase wheels punctuated by the purposeful click-clack of her three-inch heels on the hardwood floors as we made a beeline to my bathroom. Ignoring normal circadian rhythms with the same unwavering dedication as the manager at my local Dunkin' Donuts, never once complaining, Audrey managed to transform my big brown bags miraculously into lush brown eyes, using an artful combination of the magical brushes, potions, and lotions she kept in her rolling beauty shop.

Through the E.A.T. picture window, I spotted Audrey struggling to make her way up the sidewalk. She was caught in an upper Madison Avenue pedestrian jam, first squeezing her way past a row of nannies with double-parked strollers, then stuck behind an impeccably coiffed young blonde pushing a giant navy blue old-style pram, plus two perfectly groomed Cavalier King Charles Spaniels taking their uniformed housekeeper for her morning walk. I watched as Audrey finally pulled out of the right lane, passed the slow-moving pram on her left, then quickly swerved back to the right, scooted around the leashed twin pedigrees, and executed a sweeping turn into the front door of the restaurant. Moments later, she rounded the prepared foods section and arrived at my table in a flurry of woven textures, busy patterns, and flashy colors.

Before Audrey had even one arm out of her coat sleeve, she bent over to peer at the bare patches starting to widen between my hairs on my scalp. There was a fierce battle raging up there, a fight my hair was definitely starting to lose.

"Sheila, we haff got to buy you some hair," she announced, checking my head from various angles.

"Audrey," I hissed, scolding her like a 7 year old, "will you please sit down and stop that!" I didn't want her examining my scalp in public, let alone knocking one of my stray curls into somebody's omelet. Audrey finished taking off her coat and sat down. "Sorry, Sheila, but it's getting—"

"What exactly do you mean by 'buy me some hair'?" I interrupted, speaking barely above a whisper as I glanced around suspiciously. The last thing I wanted was the done-up, botoxed blonde at the next table to overhear us.

"I mean ezzackly what I say. We haff to start shopping for some hair for you. It's coming out so fass now we aren't going to be able to hide it moch longer." Audrey spoke fluently but with a fairly heavy Mexican accent, which I found to be one of her many endearing traits.

"I know, I know." She was right. I let out a deep sigh. "I just can't believe this shit is happening." Trying to run a successful business and host a weekly TV show was enough already. Now, on top of it all, *my fucking hair was falling out*. Handfuls of it were dropping from my head like dead leaves from a neglected houseplant. It made me sick to my stomach to even think about it. I wondered if the network suspected anything. They must. Otherwise, my agent wouldn't keep telling me to keep it quiet.

For the first few months after my initial diagnosis, the bald patches were small, barely noticeable. But now they seemed to move around my head with intention, cropping up here and there in steadily increasing numbers. It was as though they had a master plan for permanent occupation. My scalp was being taken over by a small army of strategically motivated squatters. Every time I washed my hair or looked closely in the mirror, I could expect another one to show up. On a Tuesday, I would spot one behind my right ear; the following Friday, another would appear on my crown.

To supplement my visits to the dermatologist—as an extra insurance policy—I had also started seeing a Dr. Lu, in Chinatown. He specialized in herbal remedies and acupuncture. A short, compact man, he spoke in clipped sentences as if he was in a hurry and had no time for prepositions. "Eat many vegetables," he would say, or "Wheat no good." Dr. Lu was duck-footed and wore a starched white coat and wire rim spectacles that hooked behind his tiny ears. They reminded me of the type my college boyfriend Kevin had worn. Maybe it was a doctor thing. Dr. Lu suggested I take so many stinky brown herbs and supplements that it was hard to keep track: Qi Bao Mei Ran Dan (concentrated), Wu Ling Pain (strengthening bladder function), Xue Fu Zhu Yu Pain (relieves blood stagnation since 1830 A.C.E.), Chaun Qiong Cha Tiao Wan (natural extractives), Imperial Qi (strengthening kidney function), Fuke Yang Rong Pian (supplement). Some were brewed like tea, from bags of powder or sticks and leaves; others were taken in pill form, with or without food. After a while, I was taking handfuls of eight pills three times a day. I had to create an Excel spreadsheet just to keep all the instructions and quantities straight.

Every appointment with Dr. Lu ended with tons of acupuncture needles sticking out of my hands and feet. I looked like a porcupine. He told me not to exercise. Then he told me not to drink any alcohol or eat any dairy products. His most recent instructions had been to rub freshly sliced ginger on my feet and sit in front of a space heater until my head began to sweat. While I certainly believed in the efficacy of alternative medicine, and had tremendous respect for Dr. Lu's ancient Chinese lore, none of his cures seemed to be working. And anyway, I'd nearly burnt the soles of my feet and had just about enough of his Asian tough love.

Some of my girlfriends had started sending me bottles of shampoo and conditioner their hairdressers had recommended. Others sent articles about hair loss, names of doctors or pills: "It's called Hair, Skin and Nails, and comes in a pink bottle. You can buy it at CVS." With each package came enthusiastic testimonials and endorsements. I felt like a lot of them also came with unspoken expectations. *It worked for so-and-so's friend or what's-her-name's colleague or cousin. Her hair grew back; she was cured.*

I knew everybody was trying to help, but oftentimes it only made me feel worse: I hated to disappoint people and was worried that if my hair didn't grow back, I would have fallen short, somehow let them down.

"So do you mean actual hair or a wig or what?" I asked Audrey.

"I mean everything, my love. Hair, wigs, weaves, whatever. I think we should look into az many options az possible."

Our conversation was interrupted by my favorite waitress, smiling broadly as she approached our table. Audrey cut the hair talk short, and ordered a decaf cappuccino and almond croissant, which I figured added at least another five, maybe ten, bucks to my bill.

"Also," Audrey continued, once our waitress was out of earshot, "if we can find some hair just like yours, I can even make you a toupee."

"A toupée?!"

"Yes, darling. That's right—a toupee."

I had to either laugh or cry, so I decided to laugh.

"Seriously, Sheila. I can make you one zo nobody will know the difference. I am very talented with all types of hair and will take care of abzolutely everything."

"Not to sound harsh, Audrey, but you're a stylist and make-up artist. Since when do you know anything about making a toupee?"

"Don't you worry, Principessa. My ex sister-in-law in California works for a wig company. They do beautiful toupees and hairpieces. I'll give her a call tonight and talk to her about making one for you."

By now Audrey was fully engaged in her almond croissant, taking it apart daintily, bit by bit, ensuring that not a single crumb dropped on the green marble tabletop. She left a ring of lipstick on the rim of her cappuccino cup, dabbed the corner of her plump, crimson lips with the starched white linen napkin, and gave me an earnest look. I couldn't believe we were actually talking toupees. I imagined myself as a black, blonde, female version of Howard Cosell. In other words, looking fairly ridiculous. I realized I didn't know the first thing about "buying hair."

"Do you need me to research some places that sell hair or do weaves or whatever?" I asked. Audrey was from Miami, had not spent much time in New York City, and was still finding her way around.

"I will look into it, darling. Like I told you, I have it all covered. But if you have zee time to make a few calls, ask for some recommendations, that would help."

"All right, I'll do that. I can think of at least two friends who had to wear wigs for a while. Let me get a couple names from them."

"Perfect!" Audrey said, as she folded her napkin, got up and put on her coat. She bent down to air-kiss me on both cheeks. "Sorry, Princess, but I haff to run. I have a photo shoot for Australian *Vogue* downtown at 10:30. Don't want to be late for *that*. Bye, love. We'll talk later."

Waiting for my $40 breakfast check, I gazed out the E.A.T. picture window as my voluptuous hairdresser, makeup artist, confidante—and surprise toupee-maker—turned the corner of Madison and 81st and disappeared down the block in a hurry. After overcoming my usual sticker shock and paying the check, I headed back out past the prepared foods and baked goods section. Eli Zabar, founder and proprietor of E.A.T., was no dummy; come to think of it, he had to be some kind of marketing genius, selling all these $18 omelets and $45 butter-cream frosted cakes. Sure enough, Eli had set up a deadly display of juicy latticed pies, seductive berry tarts, and exquisitely baked muffins practically blocking the exit. There was no way this uptown girl with a serious sweet tooth was going to escape without at least one of those luscious frosted cupcakes or a black-and-white cookie. Then a row of cute little gingerbread men with delicious-looking faces caught my eye. How about one of those?

Consumed with thoughts of weaves, wigs, and toupees, I bought two of the gingerbread men at eight bucks apiece, handing my money over to the cashier behind the glass case and heading back across the street to my office. The weekly stress of waiting and watching as my hair fell out was making an already bad sugar habit even worse. Dodging an oncoming car, I bit a chubby leg off the first gingerbread man. *Crunch.* Between the injections at the dermatologist and the needles at the acupuncturist, I was starting to feel like a human pincushion. What a nightmare. *Crunch. Crunch. Crunch.* Now his torso with the green buttons was half gone. *Crunch. Crunch.* Finishing off the torso, I almost got hit by the M2 Express bus as it changed lanes. *Crunch.* The idea of getting a toupee was giving me *agita. Crunch.* Now his arm. *Crunch.* Then his other leg. *Crunch.* And finally, I bit into the smiling, sugar-frosted face on his big brown hairless head, to find out what baldness really tasted like.

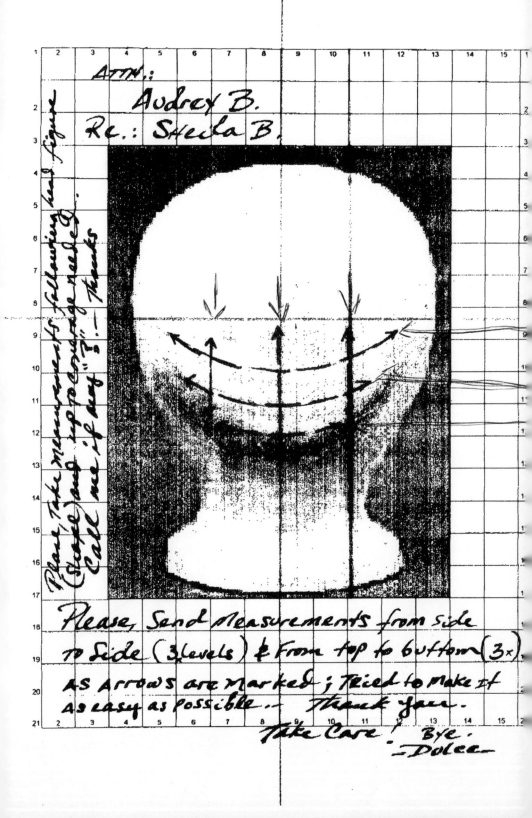

ATTN.:

Audrey B.

Re.: Sheila B.

Please Take measurements of following half figure (Stage) and to provide needle. Call me if any "?".— Thanks

Please, Send Measurements from side to Side (3 Levels) & from top to buttom (3x) As Arrows are Marked; Tried to Make it As easy as possible.— Thank you.

Take Care! Bye.
— Dolce

CHAPTER 13

WIG THEORIES

I arrived back at my office with the intention of returning phone calls and tackling the mountain of mail and client folders stacked on my desk. Instead, I spent the next 40 minutes on the phone with my friend Monica explaining what was going on with me. She gave me a weave tutorial and the 411 on the best wig and hair shops in New York, referring me to what she considered "the most reputable shop for genuine human hair" as well as "the best weave salon in New York City" where supposedly *absolutely everyone* went, including Christina Aguilera, Tyra Banks, and Beyoncé. Even Diana Ross was rumored to fly in from L.A. several times a year to have her weave tightened there.

"But aren't these weaves a pain in the ass to maintain?" I asked.

"Initially, yes. But you get used to it. Like anything else."

"And how does Anthony feel about it?"

"Well, first of all, I didn't really ask Anthony what he thought. It was my decision to get it. I was the one who had cancer and it was my hair that was falling out. And you know how these black men are. They probably care more about our hair than we do. So I'm sure he was fine with it."

I felt some relief after we hung up. Monica had gone a long way toward reassuring me that wearing one of these things wasn't so bad. She reminded me that she chose to keep her weave even when her own hair grew back post-chemo, and still wore it proudly, two years into remission. I had a few problems with the whole notion of wigs, weaves, and extensions. First of all, I didn't have cancer. Plus, I had never been a big fan of them to begin with. I had a hard time reconciling the idea of wearing someone else's hair. I had an inherent dislike of fakes and phonies—be they people, knock-off Louis Vuitton bags, boobs, or hair. Wigs were for Halloween costumes or women with something to hide. I had stuck firmly to wearing my hair curly despite all those pressures to do otherwise. Under these new circumstances, though, I was beginning to have a change of heart. It had less to do with personal hair politics and more to do with a basic desire to keep my job. The fact of the matter was, now I *did* have something to hide.

After replying to a bunch of emails and returning some calls, I reached Audrey on her cell. I had decided to shift my negative attitude into a more positive direction.

OPPOSITE This fax was sent to my office so that my hairdresser could take measurements to make a toupee for me. Needless to say, I was less than thrilled by the idea.

"*Hola*," she answered.

"Hey, Audrey, it's me, Sheila. Okay, so I never thought I'd say this, but maybe we should start with the weave place first. I got the name and number of supposedly the best one from my friend Monica. There must be some reason why all these women get weaves, right?"

"That's right. Yes, *mi amor*, you could look just *fabuloss* with the right weave!" Audrey said.

"Whatever," I said. My attitude adjustment had lasted less than ten seconds. It was obviously going to take some time for me to get used to the idea of a weave.

"Anyway, I'll set up an appointment and let you know when it is." I hung up.

Before picking up the phone again, I leaned back in my desk chair and thought about Audrey. She truly was a godsend. I had known her for less than four months, but in that short time she had given me the type of unconditional support you would only expect from family or close friends. She had called me a few months back to tell me she was coming up for Fashion Week; I told her I was thrilled. She said she would love to stay longer if I could help her find some additional styling work. She was fun to hang out with when I was working in Miami, so I was happy to give her some New York connections. And besides, we had recently fired my regular hairdresser/makeup artist, so the timing couldn't have been any better. "Things really do happen for a reason," my Mother always said, and in this case I had to admit she was right. The Universe had sent Audrey; someone must have been looking out for me.

I finally picked up the phone and dialed the Ashanti Salon. The receptionist grilled me with questions, making it very clear not just anybody could call up and expect to get an appointment *like that*. I did a little begging and some not-so-subtle name-dropping, finally securing a coveted appointment with none other than Ashanti herself, for Thursday morning at 10. Apparently they had just had a cancellation; I was made to feel very lucky.

"Your initial consultation will be for Ashanti to simply examine your hair and explain your options," the receptionist explained. "The cost is $450, regardless of whether you keep the appointment. Ashanti will give you a thorough assessment and following that we can discuss pricing with regard to moving forward. We accept Visa, Mastercard, and American Express, and full payment is due at this time."

Four hundred fifty bucks for a consultation and *then* we talk about pricing? Well, what did I expect? This was New York City. If I was willing to spend thirty bucks on scrambled eggs and juice, with a nice view of Madison Avenue thrown in, then shouldn't I be grateful to have my head examined by *the* weave guru of Manhattan for a mere $450 bucks? I buzzed my assistant.

"Darren, can you please put an appointment on the calendar: Thursday, 10 a.m., the Ashanti Salon, 295 Broadway, 2nd floor?"

"Sure, Sheila. Anything else?"

"No, that's it, thanks."

Darren buzzed back 10 seconds later. "Actually, you have a meeting already scheduled at 9:30 Thursday with Tony and Kathleen. Remember, they're due in town on the 8th."

"Shit, that's right. I totally forgot." My most important clients were flying in from the U.K. Oh well, we would just have to reschedule. "Can you call and see if they can do it later in the day?" I had practically promised my firstborn to get an appointment with *the* Ashanti of Ashanti Salon and it had been made very clear there was no way I would get my $450 back if I didn't show up.

I dialed Audrey's number, got her voicemail, and left a message about meeting me for the Ashanti consultation. In the meantime, I figured I should do some of my own preliminary research on the internet. When a new project or idea took over my brain, I developed an obsessive focus and had to find out everything I could right away. So instead of paying bills, reading scripts, or turning my attention to neglected client matters, I spent the rest of the morning eating Sour Patch Kids and staring at my computer screen as I Googled every hair-related keyword and phrase I could think of, starting with "wigs," "toupees," and "curly human hair." Following every search result, jumping from one website to the next, it was amazing what I came across. There were literally thousands of sites for wigs and hair. It was exciting at first, but I quickly started feeling overwhelmed. They offered solutions to every hair challenge and hair-loss problem imaginable. They sold everything from wigs to extensions to hairpieces, clip-ons, falls, and toupees, the full complement—you name it, they had it—made from either human or synthetic hair. There were other sites selling shampoos, vitamins, hair tonics, and pills promising to make your hair stop falling out, if that was your problem, or, if not, to make it grow longer, thicker, and faster than ever before.

Until that morning, I had no idea how many Hollywood celebrities and models were in the wig game. I perused the Raquel Welch Signature Collection. *Signature*—what did that mean? She autographed her wigs? I spent 10 minutes staring at Raquel's "Short Stuff " and "Dixie Pixie," comparing them, trying to figure out the difference between the two, which I never could. Eventually,

I concluded that since I had always admired Raquel Welch's figure way more than her hair and it wasn't her body that was for sale on wigs.com, it was time to move on. I spent another 20 minutes thoroughly investigating Eva Gabor's wigs before deciding I was way out of my element there. I would do much better sticking with Beverly Johnson's "Ebony Collection." But even that exercise ended in frustration: I found a few of Beverly's wigs whose texture suited me, but not one in the right color.

Two hours and three 20-ounce bags of Sour Patch Kids later, I finally decided to call it quits. My tongue was gnarly and my teeth felt like they were about to fall out. I glanced at my watch. I couldn't believe I had just spent the entire morning online without finding a single wig or hairpiece that truly matched what was falling out of my head. Well, maybe it hadn't been a total waste. So what if I hadn't found the perfect replacement hair? I *had* learned a lot and all this newfound knowledge resulted in the formulation of several groundbreaking wig theories. And what my theories lacked in supporting data, they more than made up for in creative methodology.

According to my research, most of the wigs made for black women were named after our relatives. Short, flirty ones were called "Kendra" and "Shakila." The more traditional, conservative styles were given names like "Bessie," "Hildreth," or "Carol." Most of the wigs marketed to white women, by contrast, were designated by active nouns: "Action," "Power," and "Charisma" were among the more common ones. No wonder us black women could never get ahead. Here we were with nothing but wigs named after our aunts and grandmothers when, instead, we should have been naming them with all the qualities we wanted to possess. I had just formulated *Wig Theory Number One.*

Wig Theory Number Two was based on the power of suggestion, and related to the principle of osmosis. Its premise was quite simple. If you wore a wig named *Charisma* at least eight hours a day, you would become more charismatic. Placing *Charisma* on your head, enveloping your brain with it for so many hours per week, would guarantee it would permeate your scalp, inspire charismatic thoughts, and empower you to become more charismatic. It made sense to me.

Wig Theory Number Three was personality-based. My research indicated that most of the large wig manufacturers had gone to great lengths to provide elaborate descriptions of their products' distinctive character traits, which they enclosed in the packaging. Apparently they were banking on the notion that if you chose to wear a wig, not only did you need help in the hair department but also in the personality department. *Irresistible!* "A friendly, gently curled little hair helper with distinct femininity and flirtatious charm, this lively yet classic cut combines sporty attitude with a fashionable silhouette that can be styled tousled or tame!" I couldn't decide if reading this made me want to buy her and wear her or take her out on a date.

Clearly the refined sugar in the Sour Patch Kids had gone to my head. I needed a break. Thank God my cell phone rang, interrupting the formulation of *Wig Theory Number Four*. It was Audrey confirming she could meet me at the Ashanti Salon on Thursday. In the meantime, she suggested we check out a place called "Stylish Strands," which specialized in all types of human hair for weaves and toupees. Audrey gave me the address and I told her I was on my way. Two minutes later, I ran out of the office to the unforgiving stares of my employees, hopped in a cab, and headed downtown.

This is one of the many wigs I wore to hide the fact that I was rapidly losing my hair while taping the fourth season of my television show.

CHAPTER 14

THE HAIR DELICATESSEN

"West 21st Street, please. Just off Fifth Avenue," I said, jumping in and slamming the yellow cab door shut. As soon as we started moving, I felt my coat pocket vibrate. It was Audrey, calling on my cell.

"Hi, my love...I'm going to be a few minutes late, so go ahead inside. I'll see you in about fifteen...."

"Okay. Hurry. Bye."

I would have preferred to wait on the street so we could go up together, but it was way too cold and windy for that. I had been outside for a only minute and I could already feel the frigid air swirling every little hair on my head, lifting them up and off my scalp. It was shaping up to be a rough winter. Regardless of whether I ended up with a wig or a weave, I would definitely need to invest in some warm hats.

I took the elevator up to the eighth floor, solo. As I pushed open the heavy glass door to Stylish Strands, my first thought was, *Who decorated this place?* Or rather, who didn't? It was a cavernous rectangular room that looked way over-due for a new paint job. Most of the floor space was taken up by rows of beige fiberglass chairs packed tightly together. Almost every seat was occupied by a woman, and they came in all shapes and sizes. Someone needed to replace the big fluorescent lights that appeared as though they had been randomly shoved up against the dingy white ceiling. As a designer, I never understood why peo-ple couldn't be bothered to create spaces that were at least moderately pleasant. It didn't have to cost a lot. The principle was really quite simple: What made it look like you cared was that you actually *did* care.

This space was entirely devoid of color or character. It lacked any distin-guishable feature other than how it made me feel, which was like I had just walked into the waiting room of a free women's clinic in the South Bronx.

The room was packed. I made my way around, scanning up and down the rows for a place to sit. Most of the women were flipping through magazines or talking on their cell phones. I finally joined the ranks, finding an empty seat near the door, which was good because that way Audrey would spot me as soon as she walked in. As I sat down, I kept thinking, I'm not exactly sure who or

---

OPPOSITE Don't ask me why, but this vintage photograph of a delicatessen counter reminded me of shopping for hair extensions.

what these other women are waiting for, but I'm waiting for Audrey.

A voice with what sounded like a heavy Spanish accent—it was hard to tell—boomed from the loudspeaker.

"Number 21. Ten ounces of Swedish Blonde. Number 21. Ten ounces of Swedish Blonde."

The announcements, replete with static, were deafening. It was like listening to the conductor on the subway; half the time, you had no idea what he or she had said. Either the announcer was putting her mouth too close to the mic or yelling, or both.

"Number 21. Ten ounces of Swedish Blonde. *Please step up!*" I covered my ears and watched as a tall, lanky blonde unfolded her thigh-high black leather boots from underneath her chair and hustled up to the counter.

At the very front of the room, above the large avocado-green Formica counter, a large LED display flashed the number 21 in red.

Other than that, there were no clear signs or indications of what all these women were doing here. I had to remind myself that they weren't nervously awaiting the results of a pregnancy test or scheduled for an appointment to have an abortion. Then I noticed a small young woman with mousy brown hair pop up behind the countertop and speak into a microphone. So, *she* was the one making all that noise.

"Number 22. Four ounces of Black Straight Asian! Number 22."

I watched as a petite Japanese-looking woman in my row stood up abruptly and rushed to the front. Perhaps I'd been too quick to judge: Maybe it was less like a free medical clinic in the Bronx and more like the counter at the Carnegie Deli on 55th Street at the height of the lunch-hour rush.

"Number 23. Five ounces of Blonde Curly Perm! Number 23. Five ounces of Blonde Curly Perm!"

I sat immobilized, transfixed by the constant back-and-forth between the waiting area and the counter. The announcements came so fast and furious, and they had everybody jumping so quickly to respond, I could hardly keep up.

"Number 24. Eight ounces of Black Nubian Princess!" the girl barked into the mic. The striking black woman in tight jeans sitting next to me put down her copy of *US Weekly*, got up, and strode briskly to the front, the rubber soles of her boots squeaking on the faux marble tiles as she went.

Just then, Audrey walked in. She had enough sense to pull a ticket from the large white metal dispenser with the "Take a number" sign affixed to the wall next to the door. "How long have you been here, Sheila?" she asked, as she took the Black Nubian Princess' empty seat.

"Just a couple minutes."

"You didn't get a number?"

"Uh...oops, sorry. I guess I forgot." Paralyzed by the combination of harsh fluorescent lighting and all the commotion, it was all the excuse I could muster. Apparently, Audrey had failed to recognize that the ambiance of this place was seriously compromising my sensitive aesthetic nature.

"Well, now we have one, lovie," she said, giving me a reassuring pat on my pant leg and pressing the little red ticket into my hand, "and less hope iss not too long of a wait."

I settled down and took a good look around at my fellow human-hair shoppers. Apparently it wasn't just sisters who wore weaves nowadays. Nearly every New York City socioethnic group you could imagine was represented, each one holding her ticket, waiting for her number to be called, exhibiting varying degrees of patience. The woman to my right had to work on Wall Street. Wearing a charcoal grey pin-stripe suit and reading *The Financial Times*, she had a slightly stiff but confident look about her. Surely her coworkers at Morgan Stanley had no idea she wore hair extensions. Then there was the hip, spiky haired chick in a black leather bomber jacket, camouflage cargo pants, and yellow-and-black Puma sneakers. Was she here for herself or shopping for a magazine shoot? And there, three seats to my left, sat the biggest surprise of them all: The straight-laced, blonde-haired, blue-eyed, WASPy-looking suburban housewife dressed in pleated khakis, Gucci loafers, and a white cotton button-down blouse with a Peter Pan collar. Everything about her screamed Greenwich, Connecticut. *What the hell was she doing here?* I wasn't close enough to be sure, but I was willing to bet those were cultured pearl earrings she was wearing. Audrey caught me craning my neck and nudged me back to reality with a poke of her elbow.

"Sheila, let's go. They called our number." I hadn't even heard it. We stood up in unison and Audrey led me to the counter, her heels tapping out their usual purposeful click-clack on the worn linoleum. *Boy, I hoped no one recognized me. I could have used a pair of those oversized tortoiseshell sunglasses celebrities always use for red carpet events—or when they are suspected of DUI and being taken away in handcuffs.*

An Hispanic girl who couldn't have been more than eighteen looked up at us from a half-eaten chicken caesar salad in a white styrofoam take-out container. She was wearing an orange cardigan the color of Tang. "Number 37?" she asked.

Sensing I was too overwhelmed to say anything, Audrey yanked the red paper ticket out of my hand and handed it to her.

"Hello, my name is Audrey. I am a hairdresser and stylist."

"How can I help you ladies?"

"And this is my client, Sheila. We are looking for hair to make her either a weave or a toupee. We need to see what types you have available."

Suddenly, this familiar feeling took over the pit of my stomach. Just like the time my Mother took me shopping for my first bra, even though my boobs were still the size of bee stings. I had absolutely no need or desire for what she called a "brassiere." I was totally embarrassed. All I wanted was to bolt out of there and disappear. But my Mom stuck with her firm determination and bought me one anyway. The whole scenario was...*humiliating.*

Now it felt like Audrey was taking exactly the same approach. Deep down, I didn't really want anything to do with this hair-buying business, but she was being so adamant about it. Maybe she didn't believe in miracles the way I did.

Meanwhile, I found myself grasping for hopes of "recovery." Part of me knew if I wished and prayed hard enough, my condition would reverse itself and my hair would miraculously grow back. I fantasized about my new head of hair. This time I'd be less irreverent. No more complaining about its unruliness when it rained. No more comparisons to Richard Simmons when it got humid. *I promise.*

The girl at the counter nonchalantly motioned to a chart on the wall behind her with the white plastic fork in her right hand. She didn't seem at all bothered by the fact that there was still a crouton stuck on the end of it. The wall chart had dozens of photographs of women with all kinds of different hairdos.

"You can see we have over 100 types and styles," she said, waving her crouton-pointer in the direction of the chart. "You're gonna have to be more specific." She crunched down on the crouton. The fork had resumed its previous role as an eating utensil. Now she was using it to play with a piece of wilted romaine lettuce.

Audrey reached in her bag and pulled out a large pink folder. It contained an assortment of 8-by-10 headshots of me with my thick head of hair. As the consummate professional, Audrey had come fully prepared—of course. Nevertheless, I was impressed. I, on the other hand, felt like nothing but a lame sidekick, just dragged along for the ride.

"Like this," she said emphatically, tapping my head in the top photograph with her right index finger. "This is exactly the texture and color we need."

Crouton Girl put down her plastic fork, reached out and took the photos

OPPOSITE My hairdresser kept these photographs of me in her "hair file." She demonstrated what I looked like with my mane intact, showing it to "hair people" when we went hair shopping.

from Audrey. She flipped through them, with a slightly puzzled expression as if she couldn't identify the face in the mug shots, then plopped them on the counter and slid them back toward Audrey. She picked up her fork again and attacked what was left of her chicken caesar, stabbing several wilted leaves in quick succession while addressing us:

"Yeah, we've got hair like this. You're gonna need either Blonde Spanish Wave or Light Brown French Curl. How much you want?"

"Enough for a shoulder-length toupee."

"Okay, so that's about eight or nine ounces. Take a seat and wait till we call your number again." She handed the ticket back to Audrey.

We headed back to our places, but found they had been taken by a plumpish woman with braids, and a teenager wearing a green baseball cap. I wondered what type of hair they were waiting for. We eventually found another pair of seats smack in the middle of the room. Audrey flipped through an issue of *InStyle* while I quietly pretended to read an article about global warming in *Newsweek*. All I could really think about, though, was my hair. Now that I was beginning to lose it, it was always on my mind. I had never devoted so much time to thinking about it before.

Ironically, my hair was one of the few physical attributes I really liked. At 5'4", I felt two inches too short. My butt was far too flabby and, no matter how many hours I spent at the gym, I could never get my triceps toned exactly the way I wanted. My breasts were perky enough, but I really would have preferred a C cup to the B I had. My hair, on the other hand, was unique. It was slightly unmanageable and unpredictable, like I was. I liked its unkempt nature, its distinctive color. It was such an unexpected combination of gingery brown layers, and alternating straight, curly, and nappy textures that people almost always assumed I had either spent countless hours at the beach spraying lemon juice on my head or shelled out a thousand bucks at Bumble and Bumble for expensive styling and highlights. Okay, so maybe some days it didn't look all *that* great, but it was still indisputably mine. Perfectly imperfect and definitively me: *My* hair, *my* look. I had never seen anyone else with anything like it.

"Number 37. Eight Ounces of Blonde Spanish Wave and eight ounces of Light Brown French Curl! Number 37."

I was still in a dense fog and once again didn't hear our number being called. I sat frozen in my chair, lost in my hair reverie, staring at the dirty, cracked patch of flooring under my favorite brown suede boots.

"C'mon Sheila, that's us." Audrey grabbed hold of my arm and, with a chorus of *excuse me*'s and *pardon me*'s, we edged our way out of the row and back up to the counter. I was relieved to see that homegirl had finished her salad and closed up its styrofoam container. No sense getting grated Parmesan and crouton crumbs on my new hair if you don't have to.

"This here is the Spanish Wave and this one is the French Curl," she said, carefully removing the hair from their cellophane wrappers and holding them out to us in her hands. Audrey took them one at a time and held them up to the light. I wanted to reach out and touch them, but before I even had a chance, with a decisive "We'll take the Blonde Spanish Wave," Audrey handed them back to the girl, who slid them back into their bags.

"Great," she said, punching the jumbo-sized keys on her Casio calculator with the same gusto she had demonstrated forking her romaine lettuce.

"That will be $295 plus tax. How would you like to pay?"

Well, I'll be damned. Who knew human hair was taxable in New York State? Audrey glanced over at me, hoping I'd finally break my silence so we could wrap up this transaction and get the hell out of there.

"Uh…Do you take credit cards?" I muttered, reaching in my bag for my wallet. Two hundred ninety-five bucks for half a pound of hair. I had no idea it would be so expensive.

"Yes."

"American Express?"

"Yep. Amex is fine."

I took my corporate card out of my wallet and handed it to her. "Here you go."

This wasn't exactly the equivalent of buying a carton of paper clips or printer-ink cartridges at Staples, but it was definitely a legitimate company expense. I needed hair for work. There was no way I was going to show up to client meetings or magazine or TV shoots without it. No hair, no work. Besides, I was racking up 295 valuable membership points that I could redeem later. Right? *Right.* I couldn't wait to explain this logic to my bookkeeper.

The Caesar Salad Girl swiped my credit card, wrote "non-returnable" in black letters across the top of the charge slip, and handed it to me along with a ballpoint pen for signing. *Done.* Almost as easy as walking into my favorite deli and ordering a ham and cheese on rye with spicy brown mustard—only the wait was a bit longer. I took back my American Express card, the yellow receipt, and the small pink plastic bag containing my eight ounces of Blonde Spanish Wave. Audrey followed me out to the elevator. As I punched the down button, I turned to her and smiled. *Damn,* I thought. *I forgot to ask for a pickle.*

I didn't know the first thing about buying human hair until my hair started falling out.
I bought this piece for $39.99 at a local wig and hair shop.

CHAPTER 15

WEAVE ETIQUETTE

"That'll be nine dollars and 25 cents," the cabbie said, making eye contact through his rearview mirror. "You want the receipt?"

"No, thanks," I said, handing him a ten. "Keep the change." I jumped out, headed over to the door of 295 Broadway, a classic grey, cast-iron Soho loft building, and hit buzzer No. 2 for Ashanti Salon.

A disembodied voice answered: "Yes."

"It's Sheila Bridges. I have an appointment with Ashanti." I got buzzed in and clambered up a steep flight of creaky wooden stairs. On the second floor landing, I leaned in to shove open the heavy metal door, which revealed an attractive young black woman sitting at a curved metal and glass reception desk. Her skin was golden brown, the color of butterscotch—my favorite ice cream sundae topping.

"May I help you?" she asked, not bothering to look up from her magazine. I thought I recognized her squeaky voice from the phone call earlier in the week.

"Yes, I'm Sheila Bridges and I have a 10 o'clock appointment with Ashanti." I couldn't help but notice her hair. It was perfect. Too perfect, in fact. It hung from her crown in glossy, straight columns, thicker and shinier than a Mattel doll's. It had to be either a wig or a weave. She looked up and gave me the once over, suddenly ratcheting up my self-consciousness. I was wearing a navy bubble goose-down vest, simple crewneck sweater, and jeans on top of brown and green leather cowboy boots. Okay, so maybe I didn't have on enough makeup. I didn't know you were supposed to dress up for a weave consultation; Monica should have warned me.

"You have a consultation with *Ashanti?*" the receptionist asked. I was thinking maybe this girl's hair tracks were simply sewn in too tight, interfering with her ability to hear. I decided to give her the benefit of the doubt and repeat myself—again.

"That's right: It's Sheila Bridges, 10 o'clock, with Ashanti," I said, searching for the perfect combination of words to mollify Malibu Black Barbie's attitude. "I called to set it up earlier this week. You had a cancellation. You charged my credit card $450. Or maybe it wasn't you I spoke to."

"Oh, yes, here it is," she said, closing her magazine and glancing at the date book next to it. "Please have a seat." She motioned to a shiny black pleather loveseat with sequined, pewter-colored toss cushions. They looked like remnants from a cocktail dress somebody had chopped up, the kind of fussy embellishments I couldn't stand. "And please feel free to look through some of those hair books," she added, indicating the metal magazine rack by the loveseat, which contained several large leather-bound volumes. "Ashanti will be with you shortly. She's just finishing up with a client."

Audrey made her entrance just as I picked up the second hair book and propped it on my lap. She was wearing one of her many signature Diane von Furstenberg jersey wrap dresses, with geometric patterns and Popsicle colors on top of sashaying hips and full-on décolletage. As she had already reminded me several times since we met, she was over-the-moon proud not to have missed a DVF sample sale in more than a year.

"*Hola, mi amor.* How are you?" As always, she pronounced the "you" more like "joo."

"Fine. Have a seat." I scooted over to make room. "What's in the bag?"

"Oh, just a little some-sing I picked up for myself on the way over here." Audrey pulled a pumpkin-colored knit top out of her brown shopping bag. "You like it?"

"Very nice. Where's mine?" Audrey chuckled and shrugged. "Anyway, Ashanti should be with us in a few minutes. Meanwhile, I'm checking out these hair books."

As she slid closer to me on the little sofa to peer over my shoulder, I was engulfed in a cloud of her flowery perfume. Almost all of the pictures in the portfolios were of glamorous-looking women with shoulder-length, shiny, straight hair. There were very few with long, curly locks; clearly the weave choice du jour was straight.

"How do you think I would look with straight hair down to my waist?" I asked, running my index finger down the clear plastic sleeve to trace the thick, chestnut-brown mane on a light-skinned beauty. *Pocahontas,* I thought, as she stared back up at us.

"Stunning, Sheila. And with the right weave, you can style it however you want—straight or wavy or curly."

"Excuse me, ladies," the receptionist interrupted, "Ashanti will see you now. Please follow me."

I put the hair binder down on the glass coffee table in front of us. Our receptionist waited as we dislodged ourselves from the slippery black pleather then turned to lead us down a long, narrow corridor. Along the way, we passed a tall, slender black woman wearing oversized shades and a baseball cap. Despite the disguise, I recognized her as one of the supermodels I had just seen at Bryant Park during Fashion Week. I had even gone to her 30th birthday party in TriBeCa at El Teddy's a few years back. I tried to play it off and not stare.

"Hey, wasn't that V—"

"Yes," Audrey snapped before I could spit out the name. Clearly, proper weave etiquette did *not* include outing supermodels at the salon.

The corridor opened up to a large, open space with big double-hung windows and exposed brick walls. The room was flooded with cool morning light.

"Hi. I'm Ashanti. Have a seat."

She motioned to the large black, raised stylist's chair in front of her. I shook her tiny bird-like hand and climbed into the chair. She shook out a black nylon smock before fastening the snaps behind my neck. Ashanti was thin and wiry— her body looked tight and sinewy like a runner's—but it was diminished by her long, thick Milli Vanilli–style dark braids, which were swept up into a loose bun. What were the lyrics to that song my roommate Patricia and I loved to sing, back in the day? *Ooh ooh ooh, girl you know it's true!*

"Very nice to meet you. I'm Sheila and this is my hair stylist, Audrey. She does my hair whenever we're taping my TV show so I figured it made sense to have her here." What I didn't add was that Audrey had become more or less my permanent escort ever since this *Alopecia* ordeal had begun. She was the only person I trusted to help me navigate the complicated hair maze I felt trapped in. Our recent expedition to Stylish Strands had finally slapped me back to reality.

Making a purchase at the human hair deli was a wake-up call. I decided it was time for me to take control, speak up, and become more of an active participant—and less of a passive observer—in the whole process. After all, it was about *my* head and *my* hair.

"Fine, no problem," Ashanti said, glancing at Audrey. "Please have a seat, Audrey." She pointed with her comb to a second stylist's chair next to mine. Once I settled into Ashanti's big chair, she began running her hands through my thinning mop. Checking in the mirrored wall in front of me, I caught a look of disappointment flashing across her face.

"So tell me," she said. "What's going on with your hair?"

"I was recently diagnosed with an autoimmune skin condition called *Alopecia*. Maybe you've heard of it?"

"Yes, of course."

"As you can tell, it's really thin in the back, especially at the nape of the neck, and behind the ears." I would have given anything for all those grapes in my kitchen now.

"I see," she said, gathering my hair with both hands and pushing it upward until I resembled a giant used Q-tip.

"Do you think you'll keep losing it or is this it?"

"Uh, well, hopefully this is it. But there's really no way to tell. I mean, I could lose more. The doctors just don't know. It's been pretty predictable up 'til now, but lately it's been coming out in bigger clumps."

Ashanti looked at me skeptically. "Okay," she said, "the front area seems to be much thicker. We could do a weave there and try not to disturb things too much down in the back." She used the end of a wide-toothed black comb to part my hair near my forehead and crown. "We can braid what's left up here, but we'll need to be extremely careful not to make it too tight. Otherwise it could start falling out faster."

Falling out faster. Falling out faster. I repeated the words in my mind. *Thanks Ashanti*, I thought, *just what I don't want to think about right now.* Without saying a word, I shot Audrey a sideways glance that shouted, "Save me, please!" She didn't miss a beat, stepping right in:

"Can you please tell us how much hair we would need in order for Sheila to have a full, curly, natural look?" she asked, digging into her oversized Marc Jacobs satchel for the large pink folder that contained my headshots. Lately, she had been showing them around town more than her own I.D.

Ashanti took a good look at the pictures of the original me, the pre-hair loss Sheila Bridges.

"Hmm. You had a really beautiful thick head of hair."

"Yes, she did," Audrey chimed in.

"Was that your natural color?"

"Yes, it was," I mustered, "I mean is. Some of those were probably shot in the summer. It would always get a lot lighter in the sun." Damn: I had to get over this habit of talking about my hair in the past tense.

"Wow. Nice. Really nice. I love the color. For a weave, you're going to need about 15 ounces of hair. I would suggest either Crowning Glory on 16th Street, Stylish Strands on 21st, or Adorable Hair-Do on 24th."

"We've been to Stylish Strands already," Audrey said.

"Oh?" Ashanti replied, with seemingly newfound respect. "What type did you buy?"

"Blonde Spanish Wave. Enough for a toupee anyway."

"That sounds about right. Either that or French Curl."

Ashanti certainly knew her human hair. I was briefly impressed. But as usual, I needed to know much more.

"Can you tell me a little bit about the maintenance of a weave? I mean, how often do I have to get it done and how long does it take you to put the actual hair extensions in?"

"You get it redone every other month and it takes about four hours. Most of our clients come in weekly—or at least every other week—for a styling."

"How much is that? I mean how much to get it done each week?"

"It's $100 for a basic wash, blow-dry, and style. The weave itself is around $750, depending on the hairstyle you want and how much cutting of the weave we need to do."

"Can you use the same hair over again or do we have to buy new every time?"

"You have to buy new hair. We take out the old and completely start over for each new weave."

Jesus Christ. This was going to be expensive. Who had time for putting in extensions every other month, shopping for new human hair every time, not to mention trips to the hairdresser at least every other week? I had friends who spent their Saturdays sitting around the beauty shop getting their hair washed and set. Some of them even slept in pink sponge rollers at night to keep their hairstyles just so. Talk about a turn-off to men, at least any of the ones I knew. All this hair coiffing was not for me. I had loads of better things to do in my free time, starting with spending more time at my place in the country, riding my quarter horse, Red, or my Burton snowboard. Thinking back, maybe my aversion to the hairdresser stemmed from all those years being dragged to the Jean Madeline Salon by my Mother for her weekly appointments. When it came to my beauty regimen, low maintenance was the key.

There was just no way I was going to be running around buying hair and spending upwards of a thousand bucks every other month for hair that wasn't even mine.

"And what about washing it? Do I have to do anything special? I'm pretty active. I run or work out almost every morning. It gets really sweaty so I wash it a lot. ... And in the summer I like to swim."

I might as well have uttered a dirty word. Ashanti cut me a look that almost knocked me back in the chair. "*Swim?*" she said.

"Yes, swim." There. I said it again. *Swim, swim, swim.* I loved the beach, I loved to swim in the ocean, and I had recently put in a beautiful new gunite pool at my property upstate. "I love to swim."

"I wouldn't advise it. I mean, you can swim, but just don't get your hair wet."

"Well that does tend to happen when I go in the water. I actually get my entire head, hair, and body wet." The smart alec in me emerged. I was even going to tell her about how I liked to host the occasional underwater tea party in my pool.

"Most people with weaves make sure *not* to get their hair wet when they swim." *Dumbass,* she probably wanted to add. "Besides, as you might imagine, chlorine is terrible for your hair."

Yeah sure, but how could it be all that bad doing a few laps, as long as you rinsed off and showered afterwards, which I did religiously? I refused to believe there would be any permanent damage from that. Now this was getting a little annoying.

"Well, I can't imagine it's any worse than all the toxic chemicals you people use for coloring or straightening. Believe me, I've noticed how all colorists and hairdressers wear latex gloves…"

"All I'm saying is I highly recommend you wear a bathing cap if you're going to dunk your head under water."

What the hell was it with black women and water? I couldn't recall having seen a single African-American woman competing for the U.S. swim team at the Summer Olympic Games. I did remember Debi Thomas, the black figure skater. She was the 1986 world champ and 1988 Winter Olympics bronze medalist. But that didn't count: It was frozen water. Come to think of it, there were hardly any African-American figure skaters either. There was Debi and that little French girl and nobody else. What was that all about? Were we scared we might botch a triple axel, fall down, slide on the ice, and get our hair wet? I looked down at my watch and noticed it was already going on 11 o'clock. We had been here for almost an hour.

"Thank you very much, Ashanti," I said, forcing a smile. "Actually, I have a meeting at 11:45 all the way up in Harlem, so I need to get going. This has been really helpful, though. I guess I have a lot to think about."

"All right, then. Do you want to schedule an appointment now? We're generally booked three to four weeks in advance, but we could always give you a call if there's a cancellation."

"Well, thanks, but actually I'd like to think about my options for a bit, so I'll probably just call when I'm ready. Can I get your card?"

"Sure; they're out front by the desk. You can grab one on your way out."

"Great. Will do. Thanks again." I said, climbing down from the chair.

Audrey and I said our goodbyes and I led the way out, marching past the receptionist, and forgetting to take a business card. Halfway down the stairs, Audrey stopped me.

"My goodness, Principessa, what's with the big rush to get out of there?"

"Well, we were there for an hour and I do have a meeting uptown. Honestly, though, when I think about it, this whole weave thing is just not me. I mean, it's… it's just…" I started to chuckle uncomfortably. "For me, it's kind of ridiculous. Do you actually think I would spend all that time and money every month on buying human hair, sitting up there getting weaves, and going to all those maintenance appointments? I mean it's more than my mortgage payments, for God's sake, and what do I get for all that? Hair I can't even get wet in a swimming pool? To tell you the truth, I think I'd just rather be bald!"

"Just calm down, *mi amor*," Audrey said, laying a hand on my shoulder. "I understand. I get it, Sheila. I really do. The weave is not for you. I think the wig or the toupee is really the way to go. That way, we can still see what *your* hair is doing. Ashanti was right in what she said about zee weave: It would pull on your scalp and make it come out faster. We don't want zat. No way. I'm going to call my ex sister-in-law tonight so I can start working on zat toupee for you."

"Okay, I totally agree. Anyway, thanks for coming along. I've really got to run. Can't be late for this meeting. Important client. I'll call you later." I kissed Audrey on the left cheek and ran out to Broadway to hail a cab. I spent most of the ride uptown making calls on my cell phone. It was getting harder and harder to keep pace in the midst of all this hair stuff. What a complete mess. With my regular work demands, social obligations, the TV production schedule, doctors' appointments, lab tests, acupuncture sessions, hair and wig shopping, and now this weave consultation, I was beginning to feel like I was being held hostage by my scalp. Meanwhile, everything else—including a few of my close friendships and my relationship with Stephen in particular—seemed to be quickly unraveling.

The distance between Stephen and me had widened over the past several months, and now I was in that familiar head space I had experienced so many times before: Wondering why I could never seem to resuscitate these relationships once they flatlined. While I couldn't put my finger on exactly what had caused us to fall apart in the first place, Stephen and I were at odds nowadays about pretty much everything. You name it, we fought about it. His only solu-

MAINTENANCE

The followings are general washing instructions of your HUMAN HAIR PRODUCT. The specific weave or braid procedure will determine actual hair maintenance requirements, so ask your hair stylist for specific washing and maintenance instruction.

1. Detangle hair from ends to roots before washing.

2. Carefully wash with lukewarm water and a mild shampoo.
Do not rub or twist the hair.
Follow with conditioner.

3. Gently squeeze out the excess water and pat dry with towel.
Do not roll or rub the hair into the towel.

4. Dry and Style hair as recommended by the hair stylist. For bonded hair, do not blow dry or apply heat over adhesives.

Hair-care instructions came enclosed with my first purchase of human hair.

tion for my increasingly humiliating hair situation was to nag me about having more sex and maybe even a baby. I pointed out that this made no sense, especially since he had already had a vasectomy when he was still married.

"I'm willing to have it reversed," he offered.

"Not necessary," I maintained.

"Come on. You'd be such a good mom, being so organized and all. Just imagine how cute it would be. Our own little cocoa puff." That was his nickname for a biracial child—"cocoa puff." Nice, eh?

"No, Stephen. I am not prepared to have a baby right now. I'm not sure I'll ever be. Besides, you're too old to have any more kids. You'd be in your seventies when they were in college."

I was nearing the big 4-0, and he was already pushing 50 and constantly complaining about the rheumatoid arthritis that was beginning to settle in his right hip. The only cocoa puffs I wanted with Stephen were the kind you poured from a cardboard box into your breakfast bowl. Pass the skim milk, please.

I was almost at my destination, which was the Columbia University campus, where I had a meeting with the president to go over the floor plans for his new office in The Low Memorial Library. Think positive, Sheila. *You are not going to lose all your hair. You are not going to lose all your hair.* It wasn't working. So I decided to play one of those imaginary kids' games. If you see somebody walking their dog on the street before you get to 116th and Broadway, you won't lose your hair. I started staring intently out the cab window. Buildings, trees, and cars whizzed by. We stopped at a light and pedestrians hurried across the avenue. I saw women with strollers, bike messengers, an ambulance, and two police cars. A brown UPS truck, a white Con Edison van with its blue trim, dozens of yellow cabs, but nobody walking a dog.

My thoughts accelerated. Come on, Sheila, pull it together. Stay positive. This is a big meeting. You need to focus on it. But I was rapt with thoughts of baldness. I liked to be in control and hated that my own immune system had betrayed me. Now it was calling the shots, and this whole hair thing was threatening to take over my life. Then out of the corner of my eye I caught a glimpse of him. His long, stiff grey tail was thumping on the sidewalk. He was wearing a metal-studded collar and had a yellow ball gripped firmly in his teeth. He (or she—no, on second thought, it had to be "he," because who would put a collar like that on a female?) appeared to be some kind of a pit bull mix. He waited patiently alongside his owner for the light to change. They were probably headed over to the dog run in Riverside Park. What I wouldn't give right now to be in the park, tossing a tennis ball to Dolby. It was 11:47, I was 2 minutes late for my most important meeting of the week, and there was no more time to think about losing control—or the rest of my hair.

CHAPTER 16

MERMAID SCHOOL

"You *must* be kidding," I said, frowning in the direction of the gigantic fish tank that formed the entire back wall behind the long wooden bar, making a rather impressive backdrop for rows upon rows of bottles, wine glasses, and tumblers—definitely not your usual barroom get-up. "You expect me to swim in *that?*" My question was less directed at Katie and Nigel than strategically stated for the record, in case something were to go terribly wrong.

"Yep, that's right," said Katie, taking a long, slow sip from the margarita that filled her oversized cocktail glass to the brim. "I do it four nights a week. Actually, it's a blast."

I was skeptical. Somehow, the idea of swimming in a 35-foot-wide indoor aquarium with real seawater, live tropical fish, a coral reef, and long tendrils of wavy sea plants hardly seemed like all that.

Katie, I had recently learned, in addition to being a part-time waitress and Go-Go dancer, was the *official* mermaid instructor at Sea Splash Bar and Grill on West 26th Street. According to Nigel, my TV producer, no one was permitted in its 35-foot-bar aquarium without a thorough tutorial from the one and only Katie Scholl.

This evening, I was to be the lucky mermaid-in-training, thanks to Nigel and colleagues, who thought this would be *the* perfect location to shoot a new segment of my show. I had already interviewed Catherine, an artist and one of its owners, about her inspiration for the bar's aquatic theme, and now I was ready for my mermaid lesson.

At first, I had a hard time focusing on Katie's long-winded instructions. Her wildly animated hand gestures, Ronald McDonald hair color, and oatmeal cookie complexion were major distractions. Apparently, I wasn't the only one with beauty challenges. As a grown woman, which was worse—having bad acne or going bald? I reasoned the acne was the lesser of the two evils, since at least it could be treated and people didn't automatically assume you were dying of cancer.

"Excuse me ladies…" said Nigel, checking his watch, as usual. "We have the restaurant 'til 7 and it is now exactly 5:48," he said. "We're ready to roll. Just

OPPOSITE Who doesn't love a frozen margarita with an orange plastic mermaid brim.
Personally, I prefer mine with Patrón tequila and rimmed with salt.

waiting for you two to finish up here."

"Okay, Nigel, we're almost done," I said, looking at Katie, who took another long pull of her margarita and addressed me with a steady gaze. The tequila seemed to be helping her focus.

"Seriously, Sheila, before you get in that water, you really need to know all the tank rules."

"Rules?" What rules? I figured you just wriggled into your mermaid suit, flopped into the aquarium and swam underwater for a few seconds until you couldn't hold your breath anymore.

"Yeah, like first of all, whatever you do, do not touch the front."

"Got it. And, just out of curiosity, what would happen if I did?"

"Probably nothing if you just brushed it. But, like, if you really put a lot of pressure on it, it could break."

I pictured a tsunami of shattered glass, frigid salt water and wriggling fish engulfing the restaurant and drowning us all, just like Shelley Winters in *The Poseidon Adventure*.

"Okay, what else?"

"No matter what, do not touch any of the coral at the bottom of the tank. It's not even real. It's actually more like cheap sculpture. Catherine makes it in her studio. It's clay but it's fragile and pretty sharp."

On top of the cascade of water, dying fish and glass shards, I saw myself slicing my arms and legs to ribbons on razor-sharp faux coral as I drowned.

Katie continued, mid-sip: "Be careful with your tail. Don't get too close to the bottom; you could stir up all the fish shit underneath the gravel. The water will cloud up and you won't be able to see."

"Makes sense," I replied, recalling the aquarium I had had in seventh grade and what happened whenever I accidentally dislodged my plastic scuba man from its pink-gravel bottom.

"All right, so let's go over this," I said, counting the rules off on my fingers.

"One, don't touch the glass. Two, stay away from the coral. Three, don't stir up the fish shit. Anything else?"

"No, that pretty much covers it," Katie said. "Now let's get you dressed and into that tank. You must be excited." She handed the bartender her empty glass and slowly lowered herself from her stool. Briefly losing her balance, she smoothed her acid-wash denim mini-skirt back down to where it belonged and gave me a double thumbs-up. "Where's your bathing suit?"

"Bathing suit? I only brought a top. They told me I'd be wearing a special mermaid costume."

"That's funny. I left a message at the production company to bring a one-piece or a two-piece," she continued, looking me up and down. "The costume's kind of thin but I guess it'll have to do—with nothing on underneath. Go ahead and use the ladies room to change. Then whenever you're ready, just go around the bar and through the door marked 'private.' Climb up the ladder and I'll meet you by the tank."

"Okay, give me a few minutes." So, that's how they were going to put me in—from up top.

As I spun off my stool, Katie said, "Oh yeah, one other thing: Make sure you wash off *all* your makeup. It could contaminate the tank and make the fish sick."

"Right."

Katie took several tentative steps, righted herself against the bar, and headed back around it. I was curious how she might perform in the tank later that evening in front of a rowdy crowd, with all those margaritas in her. This I needed to stay and see. As I headed toward the bathroom, I offered a short prayer to the Universe. *Please don't let me drown and please don't let any of the fish asphyxiate on my MAC Big Honey lip gloss.* Now that would be a tragedy.

Struggling to tie the straps of my black J. Crew bikini top behind my neck, I heard a faint knock on the door.

"Sheila....Principessa? Are you in there?"

"Audrey? Hurry up. Come on in." I gave the doorknob a quick twist and swung the narrow bathroom door in. What a relief to see Audrey's familiar face and comforting smile. I was really coming to depend on her kindness and compassion to help me get through what had quickly become one of the most difficult chapters of my life.

"Hi, my love. I haff brought you some stuff you're gonna need." It was a basic mermaid survival kit—a pair of goggles and two bathing caps. "One of the PAs picked them up for joo. I think you should wear both caps and put the silver one on top...It will look more glamorous that way."

Audrey moved in closer as I stepped forward and bowed my head. Then together, with all four hands, we carefully lifted my $1,750-custom-made-for-me-on-TV-human-hair-wig up and off my head like a crown full of precious jewels. By now, we had this routine down to a series of well-choreographed movements. The wig came off, I put on my double layer of bathing caps, and Audrey stepped forward again, this time helping me tuck the remaining wisps of hair on my head neatly underneath the caps.

I glanced at myself in the corner of the bathroom mirror. "This looks fuck-ing ridiculous," I said, pointing at my ears, which were squished flat and half sticking out of the caps at the bottom.

She shook her head gravely. "Sorry, but it's not like you really haff a choice. You can't swim in your wig, and if you take off those caps effrybody's gonna see you don't hardly haff any hair left."

"I know, I know. And thanks for the reminder."

"Sorry, love…"

"It's okay, Audrey," I mumbled. Her words were painfully true. I hated to admit defeat, hated to be reminded of the sorry state of my scalp. But, at the same time, I really appreciated all her support. When it came to my hair, she was a magician, making it as thick and shiny as a Pantene ad for the TV cameras, and then letting it quickly disappear, brittle and nearly non-existent, as soon as they stopped rolling. Hoisting the fragile wig-cargo off my head, carefully lifting it out of my hands and placing it gently on the white styrofoam form; washing, curling, and styling it for the following day's shoot—it had all become part of her daily routine.

Enough hair stuff; it was time to focus on my upcoming mermaid debut.

"You seem a little nervous," Audrey said.

"You would be, too, if you knew about all the tank rules."

Audrey gave me a reassuring pat on the arm. "Oh Sheila, you look great and you'll be a beautiful little mermaid. So jess relax, grow a tail, and go do your thing!" She gave me a kiss on each cheek, her positive attitude and good humor once again lifting my spirits, then turned and walked away the same way she had arrived—amidst her own personal cloud of heavy flower-scented perfume. I stood there, basking in it alone, wrapped in my yellow bath towel, wearing nothing more than my bikini top, a cotton thong, and a double layer of bathing caps. I felt like Charlie Brown, all by himself with that single curl at the front of his head, a puzzled look on his face, standing in the cloud of dust and dirt that Pigpen always left behind. At least I was in distinguished company—me and good old Charlie Brown, not sure exactly what to expect next.

But for all of Audrey's Jean Naté-scented compliments and well-meaning assurances, I *was* nervous. So much for fish tanks *lowering* your blood pressure. And besides, weren't mermaids supposed to be sexy sirens of the sea, with long, flowing hair? That sure wasn't me. Nowadays, it felt like I was in a continual state of hair humiliation. But this was neither the time nor the place to dwell on it. *Snap out of it, Sheila.* After the shoot was finished, I could spend the rest of the evening properly feeling sorry for myself.

Lately, I had discovered various truths about myself, some of them very encouraging. I had realized, for example, that I was capable of getting out of my own emotional way, that despite wrestling with unpredictable and often negative thoughts, I could regain enough composure to get on with the task at hand.

I started to wash my face with the slightly grimy hotel-sized bar of soap from the soiled white porcelain sink, scrubbing off all remnants of makeup, including the beautifully arched eyebrows that Audrey had so meticulously drawn on my face earlier in the evening to replace the ones I was losing.

I finally shoved my clothes and shoes in my gym bag and followed Katie's directions up the narrow wooden ladder. At the top, I stumbled into an elaborately constructed labyrinth of PVC pipes and valves, surrounded by a noisy array of whirring pumps, hissing motors, and buzzing fluorescent lights that cast their white-grey shadows on metal I-beams spanning the length of the room. I thought *Holy shit, this is exactly like Chitty Chitty Bang Bang*. But there was no Dick Van Dyke to greet me, only my abbreviated crew—Jake, the cameraman, and Tim, the sound guy—along with a somewhat sobered-up version of Katie.

"Okay, Sheila, are you ready!?" Katie asked as she skipped from beam to beam like a gymnast.

"I guess so," I mumbled as Katie handed me a damp, shiny pile of cloth. "So this is that what I'm going to be wearing?" I asked, holding up the skimpy pink and black polyester mermaid costume.

Examining Katie's homemade mermaid suit, I could see it had been quickly stitched together from two pieces of cheesy, zebra-print polyester-spandex blend. She had sewn some black patent leather fringes and cutouts to the bottom for a tail. I poked my hand through a hole in the crotch where the seams had come apart. Now I understood why a bikini bottom would have come in handy. *Jesus...I hope I can't catch crabs or an STD from wearing this thing.*

The costume was a huge disappointment. Call me naïve but I had fantasized myself decked out à la Daryl Hannah in *Splash*—and after all, weren't we in the theme bar of a similar name? I was counting on a garment redolent of maritime couture, something nobly consistent with mermaid myth and folklore. I imagined sparkly iridescence, shimmering fish scales, perhaps even a pair of sexy strapless clamshells to cover my boobs. Not some clumsy, home-ec project gone wrong. I could have done better in the Halloween aisle at Duane Reade.

Katie interrupted my undersea fashion reverie: "I'm going to go in, then I'll talk you through it." I was hopping up and down now, trying to keep my balance while shimmying and squeezing my ass into the mermaid suit, just like a pair of skinny stretch jeans. Katie jumped into the tank. "It's salt water, plus there's a pretty strong current from the pumps so the only way to sink is to exhale slowly," she said, blowing air out for effect. "Otherwise, you'll just float on top, which looks pretty dumb. It's not like swimming in a pool. And see these I-beams," she said, patting one of the grey metal structures that hovered six inches above the tank. "They're your *friends*. Put your hands up there *before* you come up for air. Otherwise, you can bang your head and they are *solid steel*. "So jump in whenever you're ready."

I looked over at my crew; they gave me the thumbs-up, and I kangaroo-hopped over to the edge. After double-checking to ensure my goggles and bathing caps were firmly secured, I carefully positioned myself under a friendly steel beam and plopped into the tank.

The water was cold and smelled exactly like you would expect a dirty fish tank to smell. I had another flashback to my seventh grade pet-store aquarium. It was the same smell, but stronger and ranker. My Dad was always after me about keeping it clean. I followed his instructions but it didn't matter; it still stank.

I kept one hand on the I-beam as I lowered myself into the cool, dark water. As soon as I let go, though, I popped back up to the surface. I lowered myself several times, bobbing back up in the current like a message in a bottle. I shot a semi-exasperated look over at Katie, who answered my question before I even asked it.

"You're doing everything fine except the exhaling part. That's why you keep popping back up. Take a big, slow, deep breath before you go under, then really exhale!"

On the fourth try, I exhaled hard and stayed down all right—too far down, because I kicked the bottom. I popped back up, gasping for breath and disoriented. I couldn't believe it: All I had done was exhale for six seconds, sink to the bottom, and then shoot right back up. The pressure and the current were no joke.

"Hey, that was pretty good. Way to go!" Katie clapped. "But don't forget about not touching the bottom."

"Yeah, right," I said, spitting out a mouthful of salt water.

"I know it's tough. Try it again and let's see if you can give the crowd a big wave on your way down."

"But there *is* no crowd," I said, knowing full well the only people at the bar were an intern, a couple of production assistants, Nigel, Audrey, the lighting guy, and another cameraman. Seven people hardly constituted a crowd, especially since all of them were on the payroll.

"Well, then, just *pretend* you're swimming in front of a crowded bar full of guys. How's *that* for motivation?"

I caught my breath, gathered myself and pushed off from the I-beam again, exhaling deeply and submerging, this time adding a little wave of my right hand to my mermaid repertoire on the way down. Just under ten seconds later, I popped back up. It was difficult to tread water, swim, or do much of anything with my legs bound together in the spandex fishtail.

"Not bad, not bad." Katie scooted around one of the main pumps to where I could hear her better. "You're starting to get the hang of it."

On the next pass, she wanted me to swim the length of the tank underwater. I took the plunge and exhaled *very slowly* on my way down but after a couple of strokes, I started going backwards. Dozens of rainbow-colored fish were passing me by on both sides, moving in the opposite direction to get out of my way. After a couple more futile strokes, I was completely out of breath. I bobbed to the top and, *oh shit*, as I made my up toward the light, I realized I had forgotten to wave.

"Damn, I couldn't do it," I said, spitting sour tank water out of my mouth and pulling off my goggles.

"Yeah, I know, you have to swim really, *really* hard. It's more like the ocean, like getting stuck in an undertow or a riptide."

"Well, I may not know anything about swimming in a fish tank, but I do know if you're caught in a riptide the last thing you're supposed to do is swim against it."

"Well, *whatever*." My lack of natural-born mermaid aptitude was clearly testing Katie's patience. "I think you know what I mean. Just swim real hard, is all."

I dumped the rest of the water out of my goggles, readjusted them tight on my face one last time, grabbed the I-beam, and pushed myself back underwater. *Focus, Sheila*. I started swimming like I was in the ocean *minus* a riptide and this time I remembered to wave. I managed four consecutive strokes before I was completely out of breath again. I popped back up to the top, reaching for my trusted friend, Mr. I-Beam, one more time.

"Awesome, Sheila. That was really amazing! That's exactly how it's done. Now this time why don't you try a somersault?"

"Forget it. I don't even know how to do a somersault on dry land…" I hated to put myself in the category of "uncooperative talent," but, sorry, an underwater somersault was way outside my mermaid comfort zone.

"Okay, okay. So here's what you can do: Take off the goggles, and when you get to the bottom, pull off your swim cap and let your hair flow like a real, sexy mermaid."

Uh-oh. Quick, I had to come up with an excuse—invent another creative hair-lie-on-the-fly to hide the shame of my rapidly balding scalp.

"Ahhh, well...actually I can't take off the cap. I mean I wish I could, but we have another shoot right after we wrap here. We won't have enough time to dry my hair and style it before the next call." I sheepishly avoided eye contact and felt that familiar, nerve-racking fluttering inside my stomach. I even had a name for it: The Hair Butterflies, with an emphasis on the "lies." I hated to lie, but had been told in no uncertain terms to keep my hair situation hush-hush. My television agent assured me my television contract would not be renewed if *anyone* from the network found out about it. And so it was that I found my stomach often crammed with the fallout from a flock of colorfully winged fibs—those little Hair Butterflies.

"Too bad, 'cause it really gets the guys at the bar going. The tight mermaid suit, the long hair flowing ...It looks *really* hot."

"I *bet* it does." I heard my voice booming enthusiastically over the sound of the whirring motors. Meanwhile, all I could think was, *Sure, that'll really get the guys at the bar going—a bald mermaid in Speedo goggles, flailing around furiously, blowing bubbles, flashing her best made-for-TV smile and Queen Mum wave. Yep, a real turn-on.*

In my peripheral vision, I caught sight of Nigel scrambling onto the platform. His presence on set usually meant one of two things: Either the shoot was going exceptionally well or there was a serious problem.

"Sheila, I think we've got it," he said, pumping a fist as he ducked under one of the I-beams. "It looks amazing from out front at the bar."

"Seriously?"

"*Yes*, seriously...wait till you see it, Sheila. You're absolutely gonna love it. I think we're good."

"R-r-really?" By now my teeth were chattering and I was starting to shiver. I looked at my hands; my fingertips were chalk-white and shriveled like raisins.

"Trust me—it looks great. You can jump out whenever you're ready. I'm going back downstairs to wrap up."

Katie and I watched as Nigel made his way back through the maze of beams, pumps, and motors toward the ladder. Katie swung from one of the upper I-beams like a chimp, spun around toward me and said, "See, Sheila. You were awesome. Do you wanna go back in one more time?"

With the pressure off and Katie egging me on, I decided to go for one final dive. Always the perfectionist, I was determined to put it all together for this one—the breathing, the breast stroke, the wave, and no tail flapping to stir up fish excrement or bust up the coral reef. And I was even willing to toss caution and my goggles to the wind, though there was nothing I could do about the bathing caps or the butter*flies*.

I inhaled deeply, slipped into the water, and exhaled slowly and surely. *Namaste. Think underwater yoga, Sheila.* I stretched my arms above my head on the way down, which helped me to sink faster. This time, I swam three full strokes, turned around and flashed my best Miss USA contestant wave. I hoped the cameras were getting all of this. Hey, as long as it made for riveting TV. As far as I could tell, nobody at the production company—with the exception of Nigel—gave a shit about what happened to me. Let her drown in an underwater toilet filled with fish. Who cares? Footage to capture ratings—getting the show picked up for another season—that was all that mattered.

I swam two more strokes, just about turning purple from lack of oxygen, and waved again, this time adding a big pageantry smile before finally breaking the surface for air. I flopped onto the platform like a big game fish being gaff-hooked onto the deck of a boat. My mouth tasted like salt and rusty metal; my nostrils were raw and burned. I was waterlogged, slightly nauseated, and strangely invigorated at the same time. I launched into a coughing fit from the water I had inhaled showing off with my last-minute underwater JonBenét Ramsey smile.

"Well, Katie," I said, finally catching my breath and spitting out the last of the tank water, "maybe I can come back some other time, take another lesson, pick up the somersault and a few burlesque moves." I had developed a new level of respect for Katie and her part-time gig as Mermaid-in-Chief.

"Sure, Sheila," she said, handing me my yellow bath towel. "Absolutely anytime. I'm here most nights after five. Just gimme a call. And, oh yeah, next time don't forget to bring your whole bathing suit."

CHAPTER 17

MISS UNIVERSE

When I first started crying it was definitely still July, because I had just celebrated my birthday. At some point, Tuesday became Wednesday—or was it Wednesday that became Thursday? What I do remember is I bought myself a red-velvet cupcake to eat and a blue Gillette razor to shave my head.

I had given up on all the doctors, the acupuncture and herbs, the prescribed lotions and over-the-counter potions that supposedly would bring about the rebirth of my hair. I didn't want to wear a toupee, a wig, or a weave. Marred by all-consuming hair thoughts, I was tired of explaining and sick of pretending. It had reached the point where the locks I was losing were calling all the shots. So, instead of trying to hide or deny my hair loss, I decided I would literally face it head on. *I couldn't stress about my hair falling out if I didn't have any—right?*

What I hadn't anticipated was the seemingly simple act of swiping a sharp little metal blade across my scalp to wipe it clean would land me in bed, depressed, confused, and swallowed up in a powerful range of emotions. Apparently, it was an aberrant choice and I had left myself woefully unprepared for the negative reactions it elicited in others, and for the profound impact it would have on my life.

While I know for sure it was still July when I bought that razor, it quickly blurred into August. I suspect it was still hot and sunny outside, but I couldn't be sure since I had drawn my Roman shades tight, turned off my phone, and set the thermostat at 65 degrees to drown out the world and freeze away the pain. The only thing I could be sure of was I didn't have anywhere to go because grief was my full-time job now.

Grief had replaced my lucrative career, the one in front of the TV cameras that kept me in the pages of all the glossy magazines. Deep down I had hated that job, but I wasn't sure how much I liked this new one, either. It certainly offered better hours and less of a commute. But it paid a whole lot less for a lot more work. Grief required that I lie in bed all day, every day, until further notice.

Like everything else in my life, I took my new job very seriously, which meant I would lie there until the Universe instructed me to do otherwise. I had

OPPOSITE Happy Birthday to me. I celebrated with a single candle and a red-velvet cupcake from the Make My Cake bakery in Harlem, New York.
OVERLEAF I moved to my Harlem apartment nearly two decades ago. In the master bedroom, I put together a series of images from a 1908 postcard of my grandmother's family.

no one to see, nothing to do. Just grieve.

At first I mourned the physical loss of my hair, the so-called crowning glory that made me a woman in the eyes of conventional society. Then I started to reflect on what this loss truly represented. The magnitude of it was almost impossible to comprehend. It was my hair that made me feminine and dignified, beautiful and whole. Picturing the Goliath-like enormity of what lay ahead, I became inconsolable. What was I going to do now? How could the Technicolor clarity with which I had always perceived and planned my life have so quickly turned into such a disorienting black-and-white blur?

I stayed barricaded in my bedroom, with my black wool, ribbed-knit ski hat pulled low to protect my new baldness from the nor'easter raging in my heart. Though I was determined to move beyond grief, somehow I became more panic-sticken with every step I took. If only I could pinpoint when I had lost my equilibrium, maybe I could go back, retrace my steps, and regain some balance.

Once in a while, I was allowed to take a break from grief to do something important like pray or take a pee or walk Dolby. But mostly I stayed huddled under my plaid wool blanket and goose-down duvet, hoping to make things right with the Universe. My impeccably laundered white sheets with the blue embroidery were normally crisp and clean, stretched across the bed with military precision. Now they were clammy and cold, soaked with tears and soiled with my own snot and shame. I had stopped reaching for the box of Kleenex on my nightstand and started wiping my wet eyes and blowing my runny nose on the 3,000-thread count Egyptian cotton instead.

I simply was not ready to face the world without hair. I was humiliated by my own appearance, paralyzed by self-consciousness, too embarrassed to walk outside without a scarf or hat. How was I—once *America's Best Interior Designer*, now totally bald—going to get along in a world that placed such tremendous value on a woman's appearance in general and her hair in particular?

It was there in my bed, lying uncomfortably in the arms of solitude, that I first became convinced the Universe was mad at me. I was being punished for something, and whatever it was, she was way beyond pissed off. But the more I tried to make sense of our misunderstanding, the more confused I became. My confusion turned to frustration and that's when I started to cry. I held onto my pillow, rocking back and forth, my upper body and morning breath heaving to the rhythm of staccato sobs.

The more I tried to stop crying, the faster the tears fell and the more furious the Universe became. If I was ever going to be okay, I knew I had to make peace with her. I kept asking what I had done wrong. Each time, there was no answer; she just hit back harder. Her first blow caught me by surprise, knocking the wind out of me and dislodging the chip from my shoulder. I staggered to my feet, tried to call a time-out and ask what I'd done, but she hit me again, this time crushing my pride, dislocating my ego, and shoving it to the back of my skull. I realized when I got back up that she had cracked my impenetrable veneer, exposing all my fears and flaws like the knotty grain in a piece of raw, unfinished wood. I had always kept my own vulnerability at arm's length; now it was a disturbingly intimate companion.

I threw my favorite Wedgwood basalt vase at her, but she ducked. Instead of hitting her, it crashed against my wall and shattered, leaving the kinds of shards you can't see until they find their way into the sole of your foot. She laughed.

Whatever I had done wrong, I wanted my hair back. Maybe Miss Universe was willing to barter: Could we make an exchange so she could return my femininity? I offered to return everything she had ever given me—the nice homes, the cars, the money, the lifestyle. She told me she didn't want any of it, that I should just fuck off. I had always been a good listener and besides, exactly who did I think I was, trying to take on the Universe in the first place? I was too small, too insignificant, and way too exhausted to fight anymore. So I did what she said and fucked off. I stopped asking questions and just lay there, day into night, night into day, wrapped in my sheets and blanket, my aching body twisted like a soft pretzel.

I continued to drift in and out of sleep, keeping one eye open just in case Miss Universe decided to come back for another round. Dolby stood by with his tail pointed, sturdy, vigilant, ever-protective, his scruff rising above the rest of his smooth white coat like a miniature mohawk. He lowered his head and growled, curling his upper lip to reveal the tips of his yellowing teeth. His normally sparkling eyes stared straight ahead with unaccustomed intensity.

I surmised that despite her disdain, the Universe was thoughtful enough to grant me a brief pardon, allowing me to temporarily disengage from life until I learned to trust my sadness. So from my eighth-floor bunker, holed up with grief, impregnated with my own tormented thoughts, guarded by my loyal companion Dolby, I lay in my bed and cried. And then I cried some more. And when I was finished crying, I rolled over onto my right side so I could weep. I wept and then wept some more. And while I wept, Miss Universe sat comfortably on the loveseat across from my bed with her legs propped up on my powder-blue ottoman, sipping a cup of chamomile tea, quietly watching with the hint of a smirk, as I suffered my emotional miscarriage.

CHAPTER 18

THE CANCER CARD

I hadn't intended to play the cancer card. It just sort of happened. Really, I swear. It was Monday and I was driving back to the city from a weekend upstate. I was speeding as usual, my lead foot (inherited from both my parents) firmly on the gas pedal. I didn't see the state trooper coming from the opposite direction until it was too late. I checked my speedometer then my rearview mirror and saw him swing a U-turn. *Shit. I just got clocked doing 75 mph in a 55 zone.* He came after me with lights flashing and siren blaring. *Pull over.* The last thing I needed was points on my license.

I was always in a hurry, even when I was on time. Today was different, though, because I had gotten a late start for a dental appointment in Manhattan. I never understood why everyone dreaded going to the dentist. My Father was the only person ever entrusted with the care of my teeth, so I simply couldn't relate to all this negative hoopla I constantly heard from friends about "hating" their dentists. It wasn't their fault you had trench mouth because you never bothered to floss.

But things had changed. It turned out that while I was busy losing my hair in New York, my Father had been far busier in Philadelphia, misplacing his wallet, losing his keys, and then his train of thought until ultimately he couldn't remember to forget that he had been diagnosed with an insidious degenerative brain disease called Alzheimer's. My Dad could no longer practice dentistry, so I scheduled a check-up with a Dr. Pavis. Even though he got a glowing recommendation from one of my college friends and was affiliated with Columbia University's College of Dental Medicine, I was feeling uncharacteristically apprehensive about a routine cleaning.

I rolled down my window to reveal a young, white-uniformed officer in a wide grey campaign hat who politely asked to see my driver's license and registration. His nameplate read "Gerald M. Varney."

There was no way around it: I was about to get a ticket. Not only was I "driving while black," but I was behind the wheel of a Range Rover. It didn't matter that mine wasn't shiny and black like the ones I saw barreling down Fifth Avenue in Manhattan or parked sideways in the crushed stone driveways

OPPOSITE I was photographed for *Domino* magazine in 2007, sitting on the back porch of my guest cottage in one of my favorite Catherine Malandrino summer halter dresses.

on Lily Pond Lane in East Hampton. Even though my green truck stayed filthy—the interior an enlarged leather-clad dog crate and the exterior forever disguised in mud and detritus that rarely saw the inside of a car wash—it was still a notorious cop magnet. Dolby made matters worse, going berserk with his growling and barking from the back seat, clearly mistaking this for a car-jacking. I fumbled nervously with my wallet, digging for my registration in a side compartment that never saw the light of day. I had registrations for three different vehicles tucked in there and almost handed the officer the wrong one. Apologizing for my overzealous miniature guard dog, I shuffled through the cards, found the one for the Land Rover and handed it to him, along with my driver's license.

I sat and waited for the predictable tongue-lashing about my excessive speed along with the usual question—"Whose car is this?"—to which I always took righteous offense. *No, I am not the housekeeper on the way to do the grocery shopping in my employer's country wagon. No, this is not my sugar daddy's ride and I am not on the way to pick him up from the train station.* Instead of returning to his cruiser to run my plates, the trooper looked back and forth between me and my driver's license several times. His face took on a startled expression. In my DMV photo, I was smiling and my thick hair was down to my shoulders. But in person, my head looked like a shelled Planter's peanut—bald and shiny. All I needed was some roasting and a sprinkling of table salt and I'd be the perfect bar snack for Officer Varney and his Troop K buddies.

The trooper looked down at my license one more time then back up at me.

"So, Ma'am, may I ask where you're going today in such a hurry?"

"Sorry officer, but I'm running late for an appointment at Columbia Presbyterian Medical Center in Manhattan."

"A doctor's appointment?" Close enough. I simply nodded yes. I could have corrected him, but what the heck: It was really just semantics. Dentists were doctors, too, right? He remained silent, staring down at my license for several more beats before handing it back to me along with my registration. *Now I was confused: Was I getting a speeding ticket or not?*

"All right, Miss, I have to ask you to slow down and please be more careful. And I hope things work out. My Mother went through chemotherapy and radiation recently. I know it's a tough battle."

I stumbled for a response. *Think cancer, Sheila.* I put on my best sick face and tried to find an appropriately deferential tone. "Oh gosh, I'm so sorry. I hope she's okay now. Thanks, officer. I really appreciate it. I promise I'll slow down."

"You have a nice day, Ma'am." He nodded and touched the brim of his hat.

"You, too," I mumbled as he turned and strode back to his vehicle.

For the next five minutes, I sat by the side of the road with my hazards blinking, trying to process what had just transpired. I had gotten out of a speeding ticket—a first in my lifetime—because the officer was convinced I was rushing to an appointment with my oncologist. (And now I was definitely going to be late to see my new dentist.) Did I really look that bad? I pulled down the visor, flipped open the lighted makeup mirror, then quickly slammed it shut.

Ever since I had shaved my head, this was all I got, day after day, week after week. It was exhausting. What was wearing me down was not so much the act of explaining once or twice that I *wasn't* sick with cancer, that I *wasn't* undergoing chemotherapy, that I *hadn't* lost my hair to a life-threatening illness. Rather, it was the accumulated weight of having to repeat it over and over to absolutely everyone I ran into—perfect strangers, friends, acquaintances, professional contacts, and clients. Sometimes I just went along with it. If you wanted to assume I had cancer then go ahead—assume away. Other times, I found it presumptuous and thoughtless, and it often left me feeling frustrated, annoyed, or angry, especially after I'd been forced to do it four or five times in one day.

I found myself having to constantly make preparations in advance of meeting people instead of getting together spontaneously the way I had always done. If I was meeting a friend and her children who I hadn't seen in a while for lunch on a Saturday, I would have to call in advance and let them know about my *Alopecia* to avoid scaring them or making them feel uncomfortable. Let them explain it to their kids however they saw fit: *Auntie Sheila looks very different now, but she's still the same Auntie Sheila.* If I didn't send out advance warning, a relaxing evening out just catching up with girlfriends would inevitably became an intense Q-and-A session about my health and my decision to shave my head. Everyone had an opinion. *If I were you, I would definitely wear a wig during the week for work, then take a break, take it off on weekends. If I were you, I wouldn't tell a guy I just met about the Alopecia; just wait till blah, blah, blah, blah, blah.* I'd always been a very independent and private person, confident in the choices I made. But I simply wasn't prepared for the multitude of reactions and opinions. It was something that had never crossed my mind when I made the decision to shave my head and it sent me reeling. I just couldn't understand why it would matter *so much* to so many people who *weren't* me and *didn't* walk in my shoes. It was becoming increasingly easier to simply make up excuses about why I couldn't get together with them. That way, I could just stay home and avoid the enormous hassle.

After my appointment with Dr. Pavis, I went back to my office with clean teeth, a new set of x-rays, and the news that I needed to have a tooth extracted.

While my new dentist seemed benignly pleasant and competent enough, he was still nothing like my Father. How could he be? I thought about my Dad. It seemed unfair that after all those years of playing by the rules and working tirelessly to build a successful practice, he hadn't even had a chance to contemplate retirement on his own terms. Life had its wonderful moments and divine gifts—and no question about it, my Father had been the recipient of many. But I was also learning that you might just as easily be dealt a bad hand, a devastating setback as unpredictable and random as a tidal wave; like a wall of water rolling in with the unrelenting speed and brutal force of a freight train, swallowing everything in its path. It didn't matter whether you knew how to swim. If you were lucky enough to survive, it forever obscured the way you saw the ocean. As I began to face my own predicament of being a middle-aged woman who suddenly did not fit into a world that placed enormous value on something I physically no longer had, there were some days I felt like an invisible hand was holding me just beneath life's surface, like a struggling swimmer under that merciless wave. While I never asked, I often wondered if there were moments when my Father—despite his stoic exterior—felt dispirited and breathless, as I often did nowadays.

Likewise, I had found a few blessings as a direct result of my hair loss. In addition to being faster when I swam laps now, thanks to the superior aerodynamics of my hairless head, another one of them was that I suddenly had more free time on my hands than I could ever recall. Shaving my head was like flicking on a light switch. Fair-weather friends and superficial acquaintances scattered like roaches across the kitchen floor. Once in a while, one or two would reappear, looking for crumbs of my former life, but eventually all of them vanished, crawling out of my world and into someone else's social life to find the sustenance I could no longer provide. Most important, though, now that my television series was canceled, I was finally able to refocus on my true passion—design.

It was unclear what exactly had happened with the show, but ultimately my contract was not renewed for a fifth season. From time to time, there were conversations about me doing holiday or other specials, but nothing ever materialized. And for some reason, I could never convince the folks at NBC's *Today Show* to invite me back, even though I had a contract as a contributor to do live on-air segments about design and decoration. It seemed odd, especially since

I felt honored to have my Harlem apartment on the cover of *Elle Decor* in May 2005.

they had been kind enough to let me "come out" on national television during a live segment about *Alopecia areata*. Five million people in the U.S. suffered from the disease. Al Roker interviewed me, along with a prominent dermatologist. I stressed that the condition was life-altering, *not* life-threatening; I talked about how *being* bald was far easier than *going* bald. They flashed to the current issue of *Elle Decor* that had just hit newsstands. It was May 2005; my living room was featured on the cover and the rest of my Harlem apartment in a 10-page spread, which included a photo of me standing with my hand on my hip, without a

ABOVE In the first photograph that was published of me without hair, I am standing in my Harlem
living room wearing an embroidered dress by Tracy Reese.
OPPOSITE My dining room is painted in a shade of Granny Smith apple green, one of my favorite colors.

single hair on my head—the first time I appeared this way in a magazine. While
the article never mentioned *Alopecia*, it did say I suffered from an "autoimmune
condition." And for as many truly thoughtful and lovely hand-written personal
notes I received from friends, fans, colleagues, and former employees who saw
the article, I still felt that I couldn't convince the world it was okay for a woman
to be bald. Probably because I hadn't convinced myself yet.

Usually when one of my projects was featured in a national magazine or

I made a special TV appearance, my office phone rang off the hook. But this time was different. No calls to be a guest on *Oprah*. No requests from newspapers to be interviewed about recent design projects. No emails from people wanting to talk to my agent about licensing deals. Not a single phone call regarding work. I take that back: There was one. It was from a woman in Des Moines who had seen the magazine spread. She wanted to know where I had bought the tan paper shade on the wire lamp that was sitting atop the side table in my living room.

The intercom on my desk buzzed. It was my Mother calling on line one.

"I just wanted to make sure you got my package. I sent it to your office like you told me."

"Yes, Mom, I got the package. And thanks for sending it so quickly." I had asked her if she had any old scarves she could spare, knowing full well she would easily be able to locate plenty amongst her large collection of fashion accessories.

Her box had arrived two days earlier. I didn't quite have the heart to tell her it had been tossed on the floor in the corner of my office and was lying on its side along with a bunch of other stuff I hadn't had time to focus on. I was too busy transitioning from being a woman instantly recognizable for her thick head of curly hair to the human embodiment of facial asymmetry. My left eye had lashes as long as a camel's, but no eyebrow. My right eyelashes were disappearing one by one, but the brow above them was still there, curling out of its own accord, stubbornly clinging to life. Then there was my head: Its hairlessness surely spoke for itself. Now I was seriously considering the option of a new scarf-accentuated look to cover it up.

"I went through all my dresser drawers and found some nice Hermès and Chanel ones. I even found a Pucci. I also stumbled across an old pamphlet on scarf-tying so I threw that in. Thought it might come in handy."

"Thanks, Mom."

"Anyway," my Mom continued, "I sent the best ones I could find. If you don't like them, don't worry—just give them away or throw them out. I don't need them back."

"I have to confess, Mom, I've been so swamped with work, I haven't had a chance to open the box yet. But I will soon."

That afternoon, I finally got to it. True to her word, there was an assortment of scarves, from bold, colorful striped ones to more subtle solids and paisleys.

My Mother and I had very different tastes in clothing and accessories, and

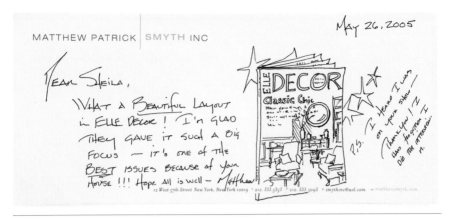

I received this handwritten note from Matthew Patrick Smyth, a friend and fellow interior designer, after he saw my apartment on the cover of the May 2005 *Elle Decor*.

these were not necessarily what I would have chosen for myself. But they would do, especially since I didn't own any.

I played around for a while, twisting, double-knotting, folding, tying, and refolding while watching myself in the bathroom mirror. I followed the directions in the pamphlet "How to Wear Your Hermès Scarf" that my Mom had enclosed. They were complete, step-by-step, and easy to follow, with diagrams and photographs. I felt a bit silly, like a little girl playing dress-up with her mother's makeup and shoes.

There were a number of looks to try: I could do a *cheval*, which was a nod to the equestrian world that had inspired designer Thierry Hermès when he first started his company. There was the belted scarf, knotted to the side where your belt buckle normally was. Another suggestion was "add dash to your raincoat with a bright splash of hand-screened color," accompanied by a photo of a woman walking down the street with an Hermès scarf tied to the back of her raincoat. Scarves on your head, cinched around your waist, around your neck or off your shoulders...scarves to make you look like an Argentine *gaucho*, a sophisticated WASP at the cricket club, or even, if tied correctly, Katherine Hepburn....

The problem was, I bore absolutely no resemblance to Kate Hepburn—with or without the scarf. I simply looked like myself, only a bit more ridiculous with a 24 by 24-inch piece of designer silk tied onto my otherwise hairless head. I quickly realized the reason Grace Kelly looked so stylish wearing a scarf was because she had a beautiful head of hair underneath.

I decided to try out my new look in public that same afternoon. Adjusting one of my new, colorful silk scarves in the mirror, I told myself if JLo could

rock this look, then so could I! I stopped by Yvonne's, a consignment shop on Madison Avenue, on my way home from work. While I donated a lot of my old casual stuff to a local church or the Salvation Army, I consigned most of my better designer clothes for sale. Today, I had a couple of dresses to drop off. I walked up to the counter, and a woman with brassy strawberry-blond hair appeared. She had one of those worn-leather complexions, a combination of freckles and a heavy tan.

She sized me up quickly and said, "Looks like you just finished a round of chemo."

Whatever happened to "Hello, how may I help you?"

"Excuse me?"

"I was wondering whether you just finished a round of chemotherapy."

"No," I said, but apparently she didn't hear me—or if she did, she decided to bulldoze ahead, anyway.

"My husband's been in chemo for three months. He has breast cancer. I bet you didn't know men can get breast cancer."

"No, I didn't." I didn't really care, either, but decided against sharing that sentiment, not wanting to appear rude, even if I was thinking that way. Hadn't she heard me say "No," as in "No, I am *not* undergoing chemotherapy"?

"Well, he's been going twice a week for the past few months and it sure takes its toll. He's been sick as hell the last couple weeks, had to take off work most of the time. I feel your pain, Honey. When did you get diagnosed? My Harvey, he found this lump on the left side of his chest last September, the week before Rosh Hashanah, had the operation in October, and as soon as he was over that, they started in with the chemo. You can imagine—"

Enough of her saga; I tried to be polite: "Listen, I'm really sorry about your husband, but I'm in a bit of a rush, I'm running late for an appointment, so if you don't mind just marking these items and writing up my receipt... I have an account under my name—Sheila Bridges." She finally stopped and focused on my clothes, holding each garment up to the light, checking for stains or holes.

"That Nanette Lepore dress," I volunteered, "I got it at Bergdorf's three months ago and have never worn it. The tags are still on."

All I got in return was a glare as if I'd broken some kind of unspoken agreement. Didn't I understand we were part of a special cancer club and that what we did was show mutual support? What did she expect? I was a novice—and an

OPPOSITE The colorful Emilio Pucci silk-patterned scarf was one of my favorites during the brief period when I wore scarves to hide my balding scalp.

unwitting one at that. I stood in front of the counter in silence, trying to adjust my Pucci scarf, tugging and pulling at it. I wasn't used to having anything touching my scalp and now my head was tingling. I wondered if Harriet Tubman's head had itched like this. Probably not. My problem was, I had been drafted into a club I didn't want to belong to. My membership was based solely on my appearance, and my main credential was entirely bogus. When I had a full head of light-colored, curly hair, most people assumed I was biracial. Now that I had shaved my head and wore a scarf, it obviously meant I had cancer and had lost my hair to chemo. Same damn problem. I just couldn't seem to win.

That evening, I met my friend Karen for a cocktail on the Upper West Side.

"Pretty scarf," she said as she climbed onto the wooden bar stool next to mine. I had just ordered my first cosmo with Grey Goose when a tall, attractive salt-and-pepper haired gentleman started toward us with a smile on his face. He looked older than my typical demographic.

Fans often approached me to tell me how much they enjoyed watching my television show. It happened everywhere—at the gym, the supermarket, the baggage claim in airports and, most frequently, in restaurants. *Here we go again,* I thought.

"Excuse me, ladies: I don't mean to interrupt, but I just wanted to tell you"—now it was clearly directed at me—"that I've been in remission for three years now. I saw you from across the way and wanted to come over and wish you the best of luck."

I looked at Karen, then back at our uninvited visitor. I could easily have let him off the hook, but decided I just didn't feel like it.

"Best of luck with what?" I asked, swiveling on my stool to look him dead in the eye.

"Ahh, you know…the cancer. It's a helluva fight. It sure was for me. Mine was prostate. What about yours?"

There was an awkward pause as I stared at him unblinkingly, thinking maybe I could bore a hole through his thick skull.

"You *do* have cancer don't you?" he asked.

"No, as a matter of fact, I *don't.*"

He looked surprised at first, then disappointed, then embarrassed. "Oh, my goodness, I'm so sorry, terribly sorry, to disturb you. My apologies and have a wonderful evening." He turned and shuffled back to his table with his tail between his legs.

"Geez, Sheila. That was intense. Poor guy. Why'd you have to give him such a hard time?"

"Give *him* a hard time? Spare me. So suddenly it's okay to walk up to a perfect stranger and start questioning them about the cancer you *assume* they have because they're wearing a scarf on their head? Give me a fucking break. Just because somebody had cancer doesn't automatically give him the right to get in my business. That man doesn't know me from a can of paint. I mean, honestly, do I look sick? Do I look like I have cancer?" I could feel my blood pressure preparing to launch. I waved for the bartender; I needed another cocktail.

"No, actually you don't look sick. You look great."

"Thanks."

"But seriously, Sheila, wouldn't it be a whole lot easier if you just slapped on a wig and called it a day? Then you wouldn't have to worry about random people approaching you like that guy just did. I mean, do you think it's really worth it? Wigs can be so stylish. I remember, growing up, my Mom wore all sorts of falls and hairpieces. Think about all the glamorous celebrities famous for wearing them—Dolly Parton, Cher...and what about Tina Turner?"

"I am not saying there's anything wrong with wearing a wig. What I *am* saying is I personally do not want to be famous for wearing or not wearing one. I guess if I had a choice I'd like to be recognized as a great designer, not as 'that bald woman who used to be on TV when she had hair.' The baldness? It should be a footnote, nothing but a footnote. Not the other way around. You're right, Karen," I continued. "It probably would be a lot easier to just slap on a wig. But trust me, there's nothing easy about *that* process. And for the record I *have* been wearing one, remember? How do you think I made it through the last season of my show? I didn't have a choice. I was forced to. We didn't shoot the episodes in sequence. I had to look the same even after I was losing my hair. In the business they call it continuity. Have you actually ever tried to wear a wig? And I'm not talking about just to a Halloween party but on a daily basis for eight or ten hours a day?"

"No I haven't."

"Well, I've got news for you: It sucks. It's hot and itchy, especially when you don't have any hair underneath. I got the best quality human hair, custom made, lace-front fancy-ass wigs, and it still felt like I was wearing a scratchy wool sweater on my head. I hated every minute of it. Did I ever tell you about that time we shot in L.A. with Mark Steines?"

Karen gave me a slightly puzzled look. "Maybe...I'm not sure. Tell me again."

"He's the *Entertainment Tonight* cohost?"

"Right."

"Anyway, it was this segment where Mark and I went furniture shopping on La Cienega for his *ET* office makeover. The production company booked this huge black stretch limo to drive us around all afternoon. So, the driver picks us up and he says, 'I'm real sorry, but my a.c. is broken down.' It must have been a hundred and freakin' twenty degrees back there. We're sweating our asses off on the black leather seats and all the windows are shut tight. Mark starts complaining and finally the guy rolls down the windows *and* the sunroof all at once. Then all of a sudden, we hit the freeway, he stomps on the gas, and there's this huge blast of hot air. I have to grab my wig with both hands to stop it from whipping every which way but out the window. We get to our first stop and my production team all look like they're in a panic. I'm not sure why. Then my makeup person shows me a hand-held mirror and I see for myself: Not only is my wig crooked and the hair all tangled up, but my eyebrows—they were drawn on in brown pencil—are melted and they're about an inch thick. I looked just like Groucho Marx!"

"Omigod." Karen put her hand to her wide-open mouth and laughed. "But I don't know, Sheila, it's just hard for me to believe there isn't a solution to your wig problem. There must be a way you can make it work. I mean, women have been doing it for thousands of years: Even Cleopatra wore a wig, for Christ's sake."

"Cleopatra, Chemo-patra...It's all the same to me. At this point, I really don't give a shit: I am *just not interested in wearing a wig*—if that's okay with you."

"Hey, no need to get defensive. I hear you: All I'm saying is it might be easier. Anything wrong with that?"

"No, nothing wrong with that. Listen, I chose to shave my head because I wanted to. Correction: needed to. It was my way of taking charge of a difficult situation I felt I had absolutely no control over. This may sound weird, but when your hair is falling out you get fixated on every single strand left. At least that's what happened to me. Every last hair suddenly became precious—which was strange since I never really cared a whole lot about my hair before. Suddenly they're coming out one by one and you're almost counting them. What a way to live, every day, counting your hairs, thinking, 'How many are going to fall out today? What am I going to look like tomorrow?' Can you imagine?"

"I can't say that I can."

I did my best to explain to Karen how shaving my head was my way of giving the Universe the finger. Resorting to the razor allowed me to fully acknowledge what was happening, to *really make it real*. With every stroke of that blade on my scalp, I felt like I was saying, "Okay, so you want to bring it, then bring it." No way was I going down quietly or passively.

"The bottom line was if I shaved off what was left of my hair before it fell out, there wouldn't be anything to obsess over anymore."

"Makes sense. But I still think you should stay open to wearing a wig every once in a while. Okay, maybe only when you need it for professional reasons."

"Well I think you really need to stop harping on this wig stuff. Of course, I get what you're saying. But you've known me long enough to know how I am. Once I make my mind up about something—that's it. This isn't about wearing some stupid wig or keeping up professional appearances or about how I relate to other people or them to me. It's about me and my own self-acceptance and trusting that I know what's right for me. You have to understand, this has been a humiliating ordeal. I realized a few months ago that if I was ever going to accept it and get on with my life, it had to happen from the inside out, not the other way around. I had my hair for almost 40 years; it was part of my body for my whole life. At the end of the day, the wig has to come off. I can't sleep in it. It's not a part of me. I have no real connection to it—physical or spiritual. I need to be able to wake up every morning, look myself in the eye and be okay with what I see—inside *and* out. And the funny thing is, I am good with what I see in the mirror, despite the fact that everyone seems to want me to feel otherwise. "

"Hey, I hear you loud and clear. And I really do believe you'll get wherever you want to go. You're obviously well on the way."

"Thanks. I sure hope so. Some days it doesn't feel like it. It feels like I'm treading water in a pair of steel-toed boots. Like today, for instance."

"I bet. Well, for what it's worth, I promise never to ask you about wearing a wig again."

"Seriously? How about we toast to that?" I raised my hand and shouted, "Bartender!"

CHAPTER 19

STAR TREK REVISITED

Our court time was scheduled for 1 p.m. in Central Park. Who cared if it was a Tuesday? Wasn't this supposed to be one of the perks of being an entrepreneur? The beauty of having your own business? Now that I was no longer in front of the TV cameras or bogged down with a zillion doctors' appointments, juggling the demands of my regular day job and personal life ought to have been a piece of cake. I had spent years steadily building my brand. I had established a successful firm, published my first design book, opened a retail store, and hosted an award-winning television show. I was the girl who created an amazing lifestyle but had no life. It finally dawned on me that it was no longer about working hard, but working smart. I was determined to regain my balance, resolved to get to know me better. After all I'd been through lately, I deserved to take the afternoon off.

I had a doctor's appointment later in the day—my annual OB/GYN exam— but figured there was plenty of time to hit some balls with Tony. He was one of my very A-Gay friends, who happened to be a professional photographer and also lived uptown, not far from me. Tony was handsome in a dark-chocolatey Richard Roundtree-John Shaft kind of way. We had met playing tennis in "The Jungle" as it was sometimes called—the courts at Frederick Johnson Playground in my Harlem neighborhood, where Althea Gibson had trained as a youth. The joke was, you could easily get a court but you might just as easily get hit by a stray bullet.

Other than wanting to get some exercise outdoors in the afternoon sunshine, one of the main reasons I wanted to play with Tony was I knew he'd let me work on my dreaded serve, by far the weakest link in my game. I couldn't pinpoint exactly what happened or when it started, but suddenly it was like I had a short-circuit in my brain and could no longer put the fuzzy yellow ball into the service box across the net, no matter how hard I tried. Tennis players had a name for it: The Service Yips. I could serve hopper after hopper of practice balls effortlessly and 90 percent of them would go in, placed almost exactly where I wanted. But as soon as three players strolled out onto the court to join me for a set of doubles, it all fell apart. I had *Star Trek* fantasies about the teleportation machine that Captain Kirk used to materialize, back aboard the

OPPOSITE It was great to rediscover tennis as an adult. While my serve still sucks, my forehand is as reliable as it was when I was a kid.

221

Starship Enterprise. Maybe I could borrow it to beam my opponents and partner off the court just long enough to hit a 125 mph ace.

I worked with instructor after instructor, trainer after trainer, trying to fix the mechanics of my serve. When all the coaching failed, I chalked it up to being a headcase, and decided to consult with a sports psychologist. She had worked with NBA players, Olympic downhill racers, and world-class golfers. But none of the deep-breathing or visualization techniques I tried at her suggestion worked either. I experimented with an underhand serve, a flat serve, a spin serve, a slice, and a reverse slice. Even the American Twist, or Kick as it was more commonly known, resulted in double fault after double fault.

My serve—sort of a soft, arching puffball—had always pretty much sucked, but I still managed to put it in. In high school, Lizzy Bernstein and I were the only freshmen to make varsity, playing second doubles, and kicking some major Quaker ass along the way. Backed up by strong groundstrokes, my puffball serve kept me winning enough matches to eventually play first singles and be named captain of the team. And how about all those Bridges family round-robin doubles tournaments my Father insisted on playing before we took him out to brunch on Father's Day? First it would be Sidney and my Mom versus me and my Dad. Then it was *"Rotate!"* and Sidney and I finally had parental permission to get up to our old antics—behaving like rowdy kids and cutting up while beating our parents in the set with no "Wait 'til your Father gets home!"

Now as an adult, any invitation to play, particularly with people I didn't know very well, was cause for some apprehension. The last time I played mixed doubles, I was partnered with an attractive, silver-haired gentleman named Jim, who had a hearing aid in his left ear and bore a striking resemblance to *The Price is Right* host Bob Barker. We lost the first set thanks to Jim's underwhelming backhand volley and my endless double faults. Now we were down 0-2 in the second, and it was my turn to serve again. My first attempt hit the net cord and sailed completely off the court—not even close. *Focus, Sheila. Positive thinking! You can do this.* I braced myself as I tossed the ball high at 1 o'clock.

"Go after it," I could hear Sidney's voice booming in my head. Sure enough, I felt my right wrist pronate just as my racquet struck the ball flush at the top of my toss. It felt good. I had done it! Then, as I looked up from my follow-through, I heard a *thwap,* followed by an "Owww!" and a chorus of "Are you okay?" from across the net. *Oh shit.* Not only had I just hit my own partner but leave it to me to nail him hard enough to knock out his hearing aid and send it clattering to the green asphalt, where it shattered into little pieces. I apologized

profusely as I scrambled to help pick up the flesh-colored plastic remnants, real-izing at that moment I should probably consider hanging up my tennis togs for good. No wonder I had performance anxiety for a friendly doubles match.

Today would be different, though. No games, no pressure. Just practice, all fun. We had checked in with our permits and been assigned Court 14. The bell rang. As we made our way down the steps through the crowd of players stream-ing off the dusty Har-Tru courts, an elfin woman decked out in a spandex Nike tennis dress the color of orange sorbet stopped me and said "Excuse me, Miss."

"Yes," I replied, thinking she probably needed directions to the ladies room, since there was no way she could see it from behind that oversized visor and those dark sunglasses covering almost her entire face.

She surprised me: "Don't you think you should be wearing a hat?"

I chose not to answer, instead giving her a look normally reserved for total morons. If I still had eyebrows, I would have raised one of them.

"I mean aren't you worried your head is going to burn?"

"No, I'm not." *What was it about my head that attracted so many nosey people? And why the hell did this one care whether I was wearing a hat?*

"Well, just so you know, you can get a bad sunburn—even when it's over-cast or cloudy like this."

I ignored her completely, and ran to catch up to Tony, who was already on his way to Court 14. The last thing I wanted was to waste precious court time discussing the weather and its relationship to my head with some nut. We started hitting and kept it up for nearly a half hour straight, working up a good sweat. My cross-court backhands, and even my forehand volleys, were sharp today. Instead of a match, we decided to play points. Tony agreed I should serve all of them so I could get in some good practice.

Wouldn't it be my luck that Orange Sorbet Lady was assigned to the court next to ours. Every time one of our balls strayed onto her side or vice versa, I caught her staring at my head.

"If it makes you feel any better, I'm wearing sunscreen." I finally volunteered. *Maybe that will shut her up*, I thought. But it didn't. She was relentlessly annoying, like a mosquito buzzing in your ear in the dark while you're trying to sleep. You keep swatting at it harder and harder, but it keeps coming back. The next time she saw an opening, she approached me by the chain-link fence behind our courts and

---

OVERLEAF A Father's Day card was sketched with colored markers by my Dad's friend, Bernie Mason, who worked in advertising. He even thought to include Kismet, my Himalayan cat, in his drawing. I was 14 years old at the time.

said, "You know, even if you're finished with your treatments, you really shouldn't have any sun exposure until several months or probably at least a year after."

That was the straw that broke this hairless camel's back. I felt like thwacking her with my freshly restrung Babolat racquet, but resorted to a verbal thrashing instead. I walked over and got in her face: "I don't know what you're talking about, but in case you didn't notice, I'm actually trying to play some tennis here. So, I would appreciate it if you would mind your own business and stick to *your* game so I can get on with *mine*. I really don't need any advice about sun exposure, thank you very much."

She blanched. "Well, excuse me. I was only trying to be helpful...."

"Helpful? How could you possibly think you're being helpful?!"

Tony came striding toward the net to see what all the commotion was about.

"Hey, what's going on?" he said. "Is everything okay?"

I turned and headed toward him. "Everything's fine. Don't worry about it. Let's just keep hitting." I walked back toward the baseline.

But everything wasn't fine. Now I was spraying balls everywhere. Half of them I sent into the net, the other half onto Court 13. I couldn't concentrate, couldn't relax. After about ten attempts at starting a decent rally, I finally gave up and shuffled back to the net and said. "Sorry, Tony, do you mind if we stop?"

"No—of course not." He approached me with a concerned look. "Is everything okay?"

"Not exactly. I just can't seem to focus. That woman next to us, getting all up in my grill ever since we got here, talking about my head...."

Tony put down his racquet, leaning it against the net post. "You're kidding. What did she say about your head?"

"It doesn't really matter. She just got under my skin. As you can see, now I'm all over the place. This is no fun. I'm really sorry. Besides, I have a doctor's appointment at four. I need to get home, shower, and walk Dolby. Can we play next week? Maybe we should switch it up, try the red clay over at 96th and Riverside. And I promise, no distractions next time...."

During my walk home through Central Park, I reflected on this latest confrontation over my head. Why did people have to be so intrusive? I didn't get it. I mean, even our national bird was bald. What was the big deal? It was as though a natural boundary had suddenly been erased between me and the rest of the world. When I had hair, people respected my personal space;

but now without it, it seemed like everyone could come right up to me and blurt out whatever popped into their head. I really didn't appreciate being approached by random strangers constantly making snap judgments and assumptions about my head and my health. Another thing I didn't get: Why was it that not a single black person had ever asked me about chemo treatments or cancer? Maybe my Harlem neighbors thought I was just making a fashion statement, taking a cue from my African sisters, who wore the look boldly and beautifully. Recently, I'd even been approached by a pretty black woman at the gym. She mistook my baldness for a sign I was gay and asked me out on a date. I told her I was flattered but that I was "strictly dickly." She seemed disappointed. I thought, *Maybe I should just design some T-shirts and get a preemptive message across.* I envisioned the shirts, with the word "NO!" printed in gigantic orange letters against a currant-colored background on the front and smaller words on the back.

I HAVEN'T JUST FINISHED A ROUND OF CHEMO
I'M NOT GAY
I'M NOT A HARI KRISHNA
I DON'T HAVE CANCER
I'M NOT MAKING A FASHION STATEMENT
I'M NOT AN ALIEN FROM ANOTHER PLANET

That should pretty much cover it for now. It was exhausting having to constantly explain my baldness to people I didn't know. Was the sight of my head so startling that it automatically warranted all this speculation and unsolicited commentary? It felt as if, at any moment of the day, I could be called on to justify my existence by anybody and everybody I met. And that was not a good feeling—not one that encouraged a sense of benevolence and trust toward my fellow human beings.

I made it to Dr. Klein's office on Park Avenue just in time. She had been my OB/GYN for what seemed like forever—entrusted with performing my only abortion when I became pregnant in my early twenties and a myomectomy (fibroid surgery) in my mid-thirties. She was pretty, with deep-set, dark eyes. Every year she looked basically the same with the exception of the style and coloring of her hair, which she kept changing. When I first started seeing her, it was long, straight, and chestnut brown. Now it was short, wavy, and more or less platinum blonde. Apparently she also loved to sunbathe, because she always appeared a bit too tan—not quite George Hamilton, but getting there.

I haven't just finished a round of chemo
I'm not gay
I'm not a Hari Krishna
I don't have cancer
I'm not making a fashion statement
I'm not an alien from another planet

NO!

I thought that maybe if I wore this T-shirt in public, strangers would stop harassing me about my bald head.

Once, I had commented, "Nice tan."

"I know, it's terrible for my skin," she said, "but we have the beach house and I really like to lie out on the weekends." I laughed. She reminded me of the girls I went to high school with who had houses down the Jersey Shore in places like Loveladies, Margate, and Barnegat. They would slather themselves in baby oil mixed with iodine, "lay out" in the blazing mid-day sun, and come back with these intense tans, often competing and comparing to see whose was darker.

Dr. Klein was always open to sharing personal anecdotes with her patients, and I found that endearing. She had a knack for putting you at ease, talking her way through the standard but sometimes uncomfortable gynecological proce-dures. She was smart, super chatty, and had a great bedside manner—the opposite of most of the overly clinical male doctors I'd been seeing, particularly during my *Alopecia* diagnosis and treatment.

I waited in Dr. Klein's busy reception area, surrounded by women in various stages of pregnancy, and was relieved to be called into the examining room by the nurse. I undressed, peed in the cup she gave me, put on the blue and white smock, had my blood pressure taken, got weighed, and answered some routine questions about contraceptives and menstrual cycles. The nurse left me sitting on the freshly papered metal table, my bare feet dangling between the socked stirrups, as I waited for Dr. Klein.

I heard a faint *knock, knock, knock* and the door swung open.

"Hey there, kiddo." She took one look at me and stopped dead in her tracks. "Oh my God, what did you do to your *hair?* Oh my goodness, oh my God, you look just like one of those aliens on *Star Trek!*"

"Hi, nice to see you, too, Dr. Klein," I said, as she approached me, clutch-ing her stethoscope in one hand. "So I look 'Just like one of those aliens on *Star Trek'?*"

"I mean no—well, you know what I mean—well, not exactly, but...do you ever watch *Star Trek?*" She motioned for me to sit up straight so she could start the breast exam, first the right one then the left.

"Not anymore, but as a kid—the original show—yes." I pictured Sidney and me glued to our parents' Zenith color TV, transfixed by Leonard Nimoy as Spock, with his pointed Vulcan ears, preternatural calm, and unassailable logic. Following Dr. Klein's cue, I lay back and lifted my arms above my head so she could finish up the breast exam.

"Well on *Star Trek: The Next Generation*—or at least I think it was *The Next Generation*—there's this whole alien race of bald women—not the Aaamazza-rites or whatever they're called; those are the little yellowish bald guys in togas ...I didn't mean them at all. I'm talking about the Centauri—is it the Centauri? Or maybe it's the Minbari, the Mubari?"

Where the hell's she going with this? I thought, as I put my feet in the stirrups and scooted down to the very end of the table.

"I have no idea," I mustered, feeling the speculum open inside me.

"Well, whatever, I'm pretty sure they were called Minbari. Close enough... Although, wait a second, maybe I'm getting the new *Star Trek* mixed up with that other new show, I think it's called *Babylon Six* or *Babylon Five*—something like that. Anyway, they had these bald alien women who were just gorgeous. Now what was the name of that species...? " By now, she was backpedalling so fast and furiously she had to hesitate and catch her breath.

"You know what? " she continued.

"What? "

"I'm so mixed up! Come to think of it, I'm almost positive it was *Star Trek: The Motion Picture*. There was this incredible bald woman who was one of the main characters at the beginning. What was her name? Lieutenant Ilia? "

"I don't know." I felt the final scrape of the Pap smear and then the speculum coming out of me.

"Well, I guess it doesn't really matter," she said, continuing about her business and finishing up my exam. "The point I'm trying to make is she was totally bald and she was also stunning. She had this absolutely perfect-shaped head. Just like yours."

"Just so you know, I'm actually not a species from another planet, but I was diagnosed with *Alopecia* last year, which is why I don't have hair anymore."

"Oh, goodness. I had no idea. I have a cousin who got it when we were teenagers. To this day, she never leaves the house without a wig. I can't even remember what her real hair looked like. Well anyway, you look great and you sure are lucky."

"Lucky how? "

"Well, because you have such a perfectly shaped head. Just like Lieutenant Ilia. I mean, if I had to shave my head, it's such a funny shape, it would look terrible, just awful."

"I was thinking maybe I could consider myself lucky if I *didn't* have *Alopecia*."

"Well, yes, of course, of course, but you know what I mean," she said, with a wave of her hand. "Anyway, everything looks really good here. You're familiar with the routine: We'll call you if there are any problems with the Pap smear. And here's your prescription so you can go ahead and get your mammogram when you have a chance." She handed me the little piece of paper.

"By the way, I forgot to ask, how are your parents and your brother doing? "

"They're fine." I said, not bothering to share that my Father had been diagnosed with Alzheimer's or that my Mother had recently undergone triple-bypass surgery.

"Well, great seeing you, kiddo. See you next year. Be well." She smiled, gave me a quick goodbye wave, and left the room.

So much for Dr. Klein's wonderful bedside manner. I was dumbfounded. I got dressed, paid my bill, and headed out to Park Avenue, thinking, *Did that really just happen? Did I really get compared to a freaking alien on* Star Trek *by my most-trusted doctor? And I was supposed to just sit there and let her turn it around so I took it as a compliment?*

I decided to walk back uptown instead of taking a cab. I needed to clear my head. Suddenly I wished I hadn't taken the afternoon off after all. Between that stupid woman at the tennis court and Dr. Klein's blurting out what she was really thinking…being at the office would have been far less stressful. Why couldn't people just keep their phony empathy and brilliantly insightful commentary to themselves?

I decided to stop at Dean & DeLuca on Madison and 85th to buy something to eat for dinner. Sushi maybe? Or perhaps a piece of grilled swordfish and maple-glazed carrots from the prepared-food section?

"What kind of soups do you have today?" I asked my fellow alien in a white apron behind the glass counter. (Yes, he was bald, too, but he was a guy.)

"We have black bean and andouille sausage, gazpacho, and uh…let me check." He lifted the round lid off the big pot.

"Looks like we also have a hearty chicken with vegetable."

As I stepped away from the counter trying to make up my mind, I heard loud giggling behind me. I turned around to see two cute little blond boys in matching blue T-shirts and white pants pointing directly at my head. They couldn't have been more than 4 or 5 years old, and looked virtually identical.

"Mommy, Mommy, look at the funny lady; she doesn't have any hair." They kept laughing and giggling: *Tee hee hee.* "She doesn't have any hair and she looks like a man." *Tee hee.*

I looked at the two boys, then up at their mother, a strikingly beautiful blonde with a long ponytail. I made momentary contact with her big blue eyes. She glanced away immediately, finished paying for her food, and hissed, "Come on boys, let's go," quickly hustling her two giggling Aryan Smurfs all the way out the door. *Another teachable moment squandered*, I thought, and bit into my dinner—a "hearty" oversized vanilla cupcake with thick chocolate frosting dusted with multi-colored sprinkles.

When I finally arrived back home, Dolby greeted me as enthusiastically as always. He grinned as his muscular little body twisted from side to side. Then he started jumping high in the air. I had to laugh. He didn't care if I had no hair. I was still the same Sheila, he was genuinely happy to see me, and couldn't help but show it. Why did everyone else seem to care so much? And why did random people—and more disturbingly, people I trusted—feel compelled to volunteer anything on their minds, right down to initiating irritating conversations about everything from cancer to sunscreen to space aliens?

Some days, I couldn't decide which was worse, the unsolicited comments or watching people's faces fall into expressions of pity when they looked at me. Now I was starting to receive phone calls from ex-friends I no longer spoke to. Apparently, they weren't satisfied with Googling catch-phrases like *sheila bridges cancer* or hearing rumors about me having some mysterious life-threatening affliction: They had to hear it from the source. The inbox of my office email account was flooded with messages asking for advice about buying wigs instead of what paint colors to choose. I was no longer fielding calls from magazine editors asking me to speak on national interior design panels; they had been replaced by requests to be the keynote speaker at "survivorship" conferences in places like Baltimore and Atlanta.

I was finally beginning to understand what my internist Dr. Lassiter tried to explain at my first annual check-up after the diagnosis. "*Alopecia* is an incredibly difficult disease, but not for the reasons most people think," he said. "It is in no way life-threatening, but it is completely life-transforming—especially for girls and women. A lot of people completely shut down and become severely depressed. They have such a tough time adjusting socially or just simply acclimating. Suddenly, they realize they're in this world that is so appearance- and hair-focused. It can be devastating for some patients."

As I was about to leave, he pressed a small piece of white paper into the palm of my hand. Scribbled in barely legible doctor's hieroglyphics, he had written a name—Dr. Evelyn Knapp—and a phone number. I looked up at him, slightly confused.

"Is that a 4 or a 7?" I asked.

"That's a 7," he said, double-checking. "Do me a favor. Give her a call. She's a psychotherapist. Very supportive, very discreet. Promise me you'll make an appointment to meet her. If you don't like her, you don't ever have to go back." While I didn't call Dr. Knapp, I also didn't throw the piece of paper away. I kept it on my desk, safe under an antique decoupage paperweight. *You never know*, I thought, *one day I might actually need it.*

"C'mon, Dolby, let's go out." I grabbed his leash and he beat me to the door. I needed to spend the evening catching up on work after playing hooky all afternoon, so I figured we'd just do a quick walk around the corner. We walked down 117th Street toward Lenox Avenue. The block, which was well lit and clean now, was lined with Bradford pear trees and red-brick row houses. When I had moved to Harlem back in 1993, pre-gentrification, the entire street was a series of burned-out lots, full of tall weeds and strewn with garbage, crack vials and rats—not exactly the safest place to park your car or walk your dog.

We circled back to St. Nicholas Avenue and came up the west side of Philip Randolph Square, where we saw two middle-aged black men sitting on a park bench. I nodded as we passed. They were regulars—hanging out, talking, smoking, and drinking from a bottle in a crumpled brown paper bag. I often saw them when I walked Dolby in the middle of the afternoon. Old enough to be working and too young to be retired, I figured they were unemployed.

We were almost out of earshot when I heard one of them casually say, "I ain't ever fucked no ugly bald bitch befo'."

"Yeah, me either, man."

On top of the afternoon I'd had, this was the last straw. Suddenly, the adrenaline was pumping through my veins. I came unglued. Jerking around, nearly giving Dolby whiplash and dragging his leash behind me, I marched back up to them, stood two feet in front of their bench and shouted, *"What did you say?"*

They both stared at me, speechless.

"I said what did you just say?!"

No answer. They looked confused. *Dumb and Dumber.* I thought. I had that unmistakably crazed look in my eyes—you know the one: Think Glenn Close in *Fatal Attraction*, except instead of wielding a 10-inch kitchen knife taken from Michael Douglas' Bedford kitchen, this script was written for an enraged bald black chick from Philly who might as well be carrying a loaded, unregistered semiautomatic Glock in her purse instead of lipstick. Just because I didn't grow up in the projects didn't meant that I couldn't get a little gangsta when I needed to. After all, this was Harlem.

"I didn't think so. I didn't think either of you stupid bitches had the balls to say anything now that I'm right here. No need to repeat what you said because I heard it loud and clear the first time. *'You ain't ever fucked no ugly bald bitch befo'?!* I don't know what makes you think it's all right to disrespect me with that kind of shit! What I do know is this ugly bald bitch wouldn't touch either of you ghetto-ass motherfuckers even if you were the last two hood rats on Earth!" By now I was shouting, pointing, and jabbing my right index finger at them as they squirmed on their bench.

I turned on my heels. "Come on," I said to Dolby, giving a tug on his leash and marching us straight home. By the time we were safely back inside the

I snapped this photograph of an alien-filled—I mean mannequin-filled— storefront
in SoHo, New York, with my BlackBerry.

apartment, I was trembling. Partly, I was disgusted with myself for having done something so stupid, so outrageously confrontational. What if they had had a knife or a gun and were drunk enough not to care? I could be lying on the cobblestones in the park, bleeding to death by now. Mostly, it was the out-of-control rage I felt pulsating through my body. Was I fast becoming one of those hard-core New Yorkers I absolutely loathed? Callous, rude, and Tarzan-tempered—hardwired for a fight every time someone bumped me on the subway platform or let the heavy glass door slam in my face on the way to the ATM. Or, God forbid, was I morphing into a quintessential American stereotype of *The Angry Black Woman*?

I recalled bits and pieces of Grand Master Flash and The Furious Five's "The Message," one of my favorite songs from high school:

A child is born with no state of mind
Blind to the ways of mankind
God is smiling on you but he's frowning too
Because only God knows what you'll go through
You'll grow in the ghetto, living second rate
And your eyes will sing a song of deep hate
The places you play and where you stay

Don't push me 'cause I'm close to the edge
I'm trying not to lose my head, ah huh-huh-huh

It's like a jungle sometimes it makes me wonder
How I keep from going under

That's right: I had been pushed *over* the edge and definitely lost my head. Instead of washing my foul mouth out with a bar of Irish Spring, though, I sat down on the hardwood floor in my living room, held my head in my hands and cried. *How am I supposed to get on with my life gracefully if people will not let me forget—not for one second—what I look like?* I'm a grown-ass woman—strong, smart, and successful, with my self-esteem fully evolved and firmly intact. *I like myself.* And yet...I sit here in tears, starting to hate what I might be becoming. The amount of hair on my head had no bearing on my meaningful relationships, my experiences, my travels, my accomplishments. But now, without any, I can't leave the house without getting into a fight.

I thought about all the little girls who looked like me, growing up in an ass-backwards world that cared infinitely more about what's on the outside than who lives on the inside. If this kind of stuff brought me to my knees, imagine how others must feel…Everything our mothers told us about beauty being only skin deep, while incredibly clichéd, was also absolutely true. But no one bought into it for a minute. Everybody—myself included—behaved as if it was only how you looked that really mattered.

Maybe some people really were convinced, deep down, that I was an alien from outer space. Maybe they really believed that having no hair also meant having no heart. Maybe they thought I was a mock-up instead of a real person. *Sure, you can say whatever you want to me but you can't hurt my feelings, because I'm a soulless mannequin with a rechargeable battery-pack instead of a heart, and antifreeze running through my veins. But beware of me and my species. We're everywhere, watching you humans, patiently waiting as we strategically plan to take over your planet when you least expect it. I'm just one of an entire nation of featureless, hairless, yet preposterously stylish beings frozen in intriguing and seductive poses in store windows throughout Manhattan. We take in your every word and gesture as you stare at us through the picture glass at J. Crew, Banana Republic, Barneys, and Bergdorf Goodman, coveting our fashionable outfits. Your naïve, benevolent nature is admirable, your words full of deep meaning and significance.*

"Oh my God, Helen, look—look at that dress! Isn't it gorgeous? It has to be Cavalli! I absolutely must have it!"

Yes, your enthusiasm and sincerity are touching, and we so wish we could be like you. But we're still biding our time, anticipating just the right moment because, you see, we are going to get you someday.

As I continued to sit on the floor, gradually working my way back to a better frame of mind, Dolby padded over to me, sensing something was wrong. He did his best Downward Dog before plopping down next to me. He touched my leg with his right paw, then nestled in close and rested his head in my lap. With that single, simple gesture, I instantly felt better, marveling once again how, more often than not, kindness and compassion arrived on four feet instead of two. And how words usually reflected nothing more than the fears of the person who spoke them.

Forget about praying to the Universe. Where was Captain Kirk when I really needed him? *Beam me up, Scotty. And hurry up. There's no intelligent life on this superficial planet they call Earth.*

OPPOSITE My beloved Dolby. Always by my side.

FRIENDS' CENTRAL SCHOOL
SIXTY-EIGHTH STREET AND CITY LINE
PHILADELPHIA, PENNSYLVANIA 19151
MERRILL E. BUSH, PH. D., HEADMASTER

CLAYTON L. FARRADAY,
    HEAD OF THE UPPER SCHOOL
CHARLOTTE B. DeCOSTA,
    HEAD OF THE LOWER SCHOOL

February, 1971

Dr. and Mrs. Sidney R. Bridges
Monument Road
Philadelphia 31, Pa.

Dear Dr. and Mrs. Bridges,

I am happy to report Sheila's progress to you. It has been delightful to watch Sheila. From a shy, hesitant person, she has turned into a happy, confident, productive student. Every day is happy for Sheila.

Mrs. Schwartz's report: " Sheila is a very conscientious student. She is mastering her reading skills with apparent ease. Her reading is fluent and enjoyable to listen to. Her progress is most satisfactory."

Sheila is not so enthusiastic about arithmetic, although her progress is good. She understands the work although she is not so much interested in it as in the language arts.

Sheila is interested in science and social studies. She listens well and contributes to discussions.

Sheila has a good sense of humor, which is enjoyed by our class. She has made a fine adjustment to school.

Sincerely,

Jane C. McGee

Jane C. McGee

JCMcG:ews

CHAPTER 20

HELL HATH NO FURY

The first time I went to see Dr. Knapp, I must have shed 10 pounds of pure water weight.

I spent 150 bucks to sit on a worn brown three-seat suede sofa with needle-point toss pillows for 40 minutes of talk therapy. The problem was, I could barely talk.

"What brings you here?" Dr. Knapp had ventured to ask.

"My internist, Dr. Lassiter, suggested I set up an appointment. I was diagnosed with *Alopecia areata* recently, lost most of my hair, then shaved the rest off."

I tried to form more words, but every time I opened my mouth, all I could do was gasp for air. The tears welled up, fell from my eyes, and rushed down my cheeks. I slouched over the box of Kleenex I had propped up in my lap, constantly blowing my runny nose and blotting my leaky eyes.

Encouraged by Dr. Knapp's calm demeanor and compassionate prodding, there seemed to be absolutely no reason to hold back. I didn't cry often so I de-cided if I was going to let it out, I might as well go for it. Whatever the activity, my parents had always taught me to give it my best shot. So that's what I was going to do—go for the blue ribbon as biggest crybaby ever.

For the first few weekly sessions with Dr. Knapp, it was more of the same. I struggled to find words to explain why I was so overcome with emotion. Then I was finally able to start talking. Once the words came, they flooded out. I told her I was seething with anger. I had a reservoir of it and I felt like I was starting to drown in it. I explained that I couldn't move through daily life anymore without being pelted with intrusive looks and derisive comments about my bald head—the endless Kojak references and cancer assumptions. I felt most of my friends simply didn't get it, so I had stopped sharing my thoughts or feelings with them. I was tired of being the poster child for "Chin Up." I felt jet-lagged, even though I hadn't been on an airplane in months. I explained how my entire life I had always felt "different," and that was difficult enough—without the added complication of this autoimmune condition, which physically amplified my feelings of alienation.

Dr. Knapp eventually got around to explaining the importance of grieving.

OPPOSITE My first-grade report card, written by one of my favorite teachers, Mrs. McGee, was sent to my parents in February 1971.

Sidney is wearing his favorite windbreaker and I am in my favorite blue and pink knit poncho.
My Dad took this photograph in 1972.

She spelled out how anyone who loses anything of significance to them needs to grieve the loss. Then, in time, let go of it in order to begin healing.

"Whatever you lose—a breast, an arm, a parent, your hair—it's crucial to acknowledge the loss and grieve. It's a process."

"How can you compare losing your hair to losing a parent? Seems kind of ridiculous. I mean, hair is hair...it's hardly the same as losing your mother or your father."

"It's not just hair—it's *your* hair. It was part of your body for almost 40 years. And if it was 'just hair,' everyone wouldn't be constantly hassling you about it, would they?"

"I guess that's true. But I mean it's not as if I have some terrible terminal disease like a lot of people."

"Just because you don't have cancer or some other life-threatening illness doesn't mean you haven't earned the right to be upset or to grieve."

What she said made sense. I found it ironic that I needed to pay a stranger for permission to feel the way I was feeling, to legitimize the emotional seesaw I had been stuck on and couldn't seem to hop off. I told Dr. Knapp I had hung on to Dr. Lassiter's little piece of paper with her name and phone number written on it for most of the previous year. I hadn't felt ready to call or make an appointment to see her until an incident took place that made me suddenly realize my life as I had known it would never be the same.

"One of my brother's best friends was getting married in New York, and we were all invited. My parents came up on the train to go to the wedding at a Quaker meeting house. Everything went fine at the ceremony, but when it was over and everybody started walking to the reception, my Mother started complaining: 'My feet hurt, my legs are bothering me. Why do we have to walk so far?' That sort of stuff."

"Mom, come on," I said. "It's only a couple of blocks. You can make it." My brother and I were forever on my Mother's case about her lack of exercise, stressing that, while shopping at Nan Duskin was competitive, it was not a recognized sport, and that open-toed purple suede Prada sneakers with a wedge heel did not legitimately qualify as athletic shoes.

We stepped out of the way as the rest of the wedding guests gradually passed us on the sidewalk. Our progress slowed with my Mom shuffling behind me and my Dad. I kept creeping ahead of both of them, then stopping to turn around. "Mom," I eventually blurted, "What is going on? Maybe you should have worn some more comfortable boots."

My Mother was a woman of a certain generation—meaning she did not leave the house without her makeup, perfume, and lipstick perfectly applied and every hair in place. Any given day of the week, she looked her best; there was never a question about sacrificing fashion for comfort. So why should today be any different?

"I need to sit down," she said.

I looked at my Dad, who simply shrugged and said nothing. This man of few words was even quieter than usual. He seemed uncharacteristically spacey, I thought, even strangely vacant.

They paused in front of a brownstone. "Okay, just stay here, both of you," I said. "I'll be right back." I hustled into the street to try to hail a cab. We were going west, against the traffic. I stuck out my arm and an off-duty taxi pulled over.

The cabbie rolled down his window. "Where you going?"

"That way." I pointed in the opposite direction from where he was headed. He waved his hand no and started to roll up his window.

"Wait a second. I've got my parents over there and my Mother isn't feeling well. Please, we're only going around the corner to 17th Street." He looked over at Mom and Dad, who were now both resting on the stoop, and motioned for us to get in.

"Mom, Dad, come on, let's go." I barked. "Get in the cab."

I ushered my parents into the back and I jumped in front. Less than a minute later, we were at our destination; I handed the cabbie a five and told him to keep the change. My parents sat down at a table at the reception, obviously relieved to be sitting comfortably. I knocked back a couple glasses of Champagne, which helped me relax a little, but I still felt like I was a teenager, babysitting, although now it was for my parents instead of the neighbors' kids.

For the first time I could remember, I felt fully conscious and aware of their ages. Suddenly, they seemed old. Really old. Even though they were in their seventies, I had never thought of them that way before. They just never seemed to look or act their age. But tonight was different. I couldn't pinpoint exactly what it was, but something had changed since I had last seen them—like they had grown old overnight.

My initial reaction was to fuss over my Mother.

"How are your feet? How are you feeling? What do you want to eat? Do you want a glass of wine? Here's a napkin. Do you need anything else? Another helping of pasta? More shrimp maybe? You need to go to the bathroom? Let me find out where the ladies room is."

Sidney was busy with his groomsman duties—speeches, toasts, and so forth. He stopped by periodically to check in on us. I didn't want to ruin his evening, so I hadn't told him what happened on the way over. Maybe part of me thought not mentioning it would make it go away. It kept gnawing at me, though.

After the reception, my Mom and Dad took an Amtrak train back to Philadelphia and I went back to my Harlem apartment. When I spoke to them on the phone, late that night, everything sounded fine.

But then it all started to unravel. Over the next couple of days, I tried to get hold of my Mother but couldn't. I found out later that she had driven herself to church that Sunday. She was supposed to serve juice and work with the preschoolers, but when she got to the parking lot she didn't feel right so instead of getting out of the car she just turned around and drove directly to the hospital. They checked her in through the emergency room and it turned out she had suffered a heart attack. The following day, she had triple-bypass surgery. When I called home and spoke to my Dad that evening, he didn't even mention it.

"What's going on Dad? Can I speak with Mom?"

"She's not here."

"What do you mean she's not there? Where is she?"

"She's at the hospital."

"What's going on? Is she okay?"

"Well, ah…she went to the hospital."

My Father, who was normally on top of everything, couldn't even seem to tell me what was wrong with my Mother. All he could say was she was at the hospital. It was bizarre. I ended up paging her doctor, who explained what happened and said "you and Sidney need to come home right away." So that's what we did. The three of us spent Christmas Day by my Mother's bedside in the intensive care unit. As difficult as it was to see her withstand another tremendous health blow, I was equally worried about my Father's peculiar behavior. Even though he wasn't the one who was officially in a serious condition, I suddenly felt panicked about the inevitability of both of them passing away.

Over the course of the next 48 hours, I started to feel increasingly helpless and ultimately overwhelmed. It felt as if my whole world were collapsing and that no matter how hard I tried to shore myself up mentally, eventually my shoddy intellectual scaffolding would come crashing down on top of me. It was just too much to handle. First my *Alopecia*, then my Mother's heart attack, and now something wasn't right with my Dad.

My Father clearly needed to see a neurologist. Naturally there was some resistance, but I eventually finagled him into seeing one. I drove down from New York for the day to accompany him on his initial visit. The nurse showed us in to Dr. Kaplan's office and, after introductions, he said to my Father, "Dr. Bridges, I'd like you to remember three things—a pencil, a rose, and a book. I'm going to ask you about them a little later, okay?"

"All right."

"A pencil, a rose, and a book," the doctor repeated.

"Okay." A couple of minutes later, after some routine health-related questions, he asked my Father, "Now what was it I asked you to remember?"

I watched my Dad's face strain as he tried to recall those three simple words. He squirmed in his chair, grinning and chuckling, trying to play it off. The same man who had finished college in two years and was the smartest man I'd ever known could not retrieve, from the recesses of his mind, three nouns he'd been given just minutes earlier. Furthermore, it turned out he could no longer remember his own telephone or social security numbers or the county where he lived. As we suspected, he was in the early stages of Alzheimer's, our modern-day version of what used to be called senility.

It was painful to see my Father's intellect and dignity stolen by a thief I knew little about up until that time. Whenever I witnessed him get into an in-depth conversation, it was with trepidation, as he often got lost and retreated. He stopped playing tennis and confided it was because he couldn't remember the rules or how to keep score. A few of my friends' parents had suffered from dementia so I was vaguely familiar with its effects and symptoms. But there's nothing like watching from close range as someone you love grapples with the disease. Only then do you truly comprehend the magnitude of this corrosive intruder that barges into your mind, roils your thoughts, and snuffs out your memories, one by one.

I suddenly felt as if my whole life had been turned inside out. Everything I had ever known—all my accumulated thoughts, routines, and memories—seemed to rush toward me in a flash. I caught a glimpse of them before they receded, just as quickly, into an unrecognizable blur. Gone was my hair, but more important, so were the two fiercely independent if sometimes frustratingly stubborn parents I had grown up with. There would be no more Friday night pinochle games, Saturday evening jam sessions, or Fourth of July barbecues with Aunt Carol's deviled eggs. No more games of badminton, croquet, or horseshoes. No more cocktail parties with glasses clinking, familiar voices, and laughter rising and falling with the crescendo of conversation. No more deep-sea fishing charters or trips to Egypt. No more jetting off to Rio, Bahia, or Curaçao for carnival.

I felt lucky that both my parents were still alive. But now, instead of looming larger than life as they had when I was a child, they appeared so much smaller. Vulnerable instead of invincible.

I tried my best to put these feelings into words for Dr. Knapp.

"It's weird. I don't know how to explain it exactly, but I can feel my Father's absence even though he's still here."

"And how does that make you feel?"

"Terrible. Absolutely terrible. Incredibly helpless. Angry."

Like most psychotherapists, she wanted to plunge deep into my relationships with my family. I wasn't thrilled at the idea of shining a spotlight on the ambiguities of my childhood or my parents' idiosyncratic ways. I was extremely guarded at first, fiercely protective of my family's private dysfunction. Gradually developing confidence and trust over a period of months, I eventually began to reveal more of the events I thought were instrumental in shaping my personality.

We talked a lot about my childhood shyness and sensitivity, about how there seemed to be no room for either of these traits at home or at school. In a world where effective communication was considered the key to success, it was made very clear to me that being quiet or reluctant to speak was unacceptable. As I grew up, I learned to compensate for my own reticence.

"I've always felt like my shyness is mistaken for aloofness. When I first meet people, sometimes I don't say much. Then I almost always hear back that they thought I was unfriendly or stuck-up or something." It had been an impediment and I still felt plagued by it, despite the fact that most of my adult acquaintances would hardly describe me as "shy." I explained how my Mother would get stopped from time to time by people who had known me as a child. They would tell her how they'd seen me in a magazine or on TV and almost invariably remark how surprised they were I had become "so successful" given how shy I was as a kid.

"I mean, do people really buy into that kind of stuff? That kids who're shy are somehow stunted? Just because you don't say much, it doesn't mean you aren't thoughtful, observant, contemplative, or intelligent. In fact, I'm probably more wary of people who talk all the time. It seems like they don't really listen or pay attention all that well because they're so busy talking."

"And as far as the whole sensitivity issue was concerned, I felt like the message was always, 'Suck it up and get tough.' There was always this underlying suggestion that it's a bad thing to actually feel stuff, that you're better off blocking out or anesthetizing anything that's painful or uncomfortable. Hell, I would much rather bear the burden of feeling everything than trying to pretend that nothing bothers me at all."

Dr. Knapp encouraged me to reflect more on my childhood. Could I remember the sorts of things I felt sensitive about when I was little? I recounted how when I was four or five years old, Sidney constantly told me I was adopted. I'm not sure I fully understood what he meant by that, but I did have an intuitive sense he was saying I didn't really belong in our family. While it was typical older-brother teasing, I took it to heart, crying inconsolably until my Mother intervened. But instead of growing "thick skin," as she suggested, I developed a razor tongue instead, which I used at will whenever my brother hurt my feelings. As I got older I found it quite effective to ward off his bullying. I remember him calling me "pee pee pants" for days after I had wet my bed. But then, thanks to a stroke of good luck, I found his stash of soiled Fruit of the Loom briefs hidden in a plastic Jack-O-Lantern at the back of his closet. I coined the phrase "BM Boy" and he never said another word about my having wet the bed again.

I went on to explain to Dr. Knapp how I felt my heightened sensitivity as a child had evolved into a surprisingly useful tool as an adult, that it somehow translated into an aesthetic sensibility that was a strong asset in my career as a designer.

"If you want to be really good as a designer, you need to be completely in touch with your senses in order to see things in a way people don't normally see them. You've got to be able to discover nuances in ordinary things and find beauty or create it where sometimes it doesn't exist. You have to access the sensitive, feeling part of your personality just as easily as you can command its pragmatic, logical aspects. That's what allows you to manipulate space, color, light, and composition, and to translate them both artistically and practically into tangible, livable environments."

Most of our sessions were spent discussing all the feelings, emotions, and impressions I had kept bottled up for most of my life. I loved my parents, but I also felt deeply resentful about their double standards. Between my brother and me, I always felt like I got the short end of the stick. This was a significant splotch on my upbringing. As an adolescent, I was fraught with frustration about it, but there was nothing I could do. So I simply learned to stuff it, say nothing, and retreat to my third-floor bedroom.

If I complained about something I thought was unfair, my Mother's stock response was simply "too bad"—always uttered with an air of nonchalance. She was casually dismissive of my arguments, but my Father didn't even bother to respond. His stern silences spoke volumes. Once they were fixed on a decision, I could never persuade, cajole, or sway them otherwise. It started in my early childhood, which was understandable, but continued unrelenting, well into my adulthood, which I found very difficult to bear. The message was clear: Their house, their rules, their money. They held all the power; I had none. As a teenager, I set my sights on getting out from under their strict regime as soon as possible. I was champing at the bit to break free.

In high school, people would ask me, "Have you ever thought about going to Penn or Temple?" I would answer, "No, not really," as politely as I could. But what I was really thinking was, *Not in a million years*. I felt like a caged animal. I wanted to get out of Philadelphia and as far away as possible from my parents' iron grip.

Their habit of giving then taking away also started when I was young. By age 11, one of my two front teeth was beginning to cross in front of the other, so my Father, being the ultimate stickler about all things dental, made sure I wore braces to correct the overall alignment of my teeth, but in particular to make sure I didn't get too comfortable looking like Bugs Bunny. He sent me off to an orthodontist named Dr. Wittaker, who filled my entire mouth with metal braces and tiny rubber bands. Once they came off, two and a half years later, my Mother told me she and my Father would no longer be paying for my horseback riding lessons. When I objected, her response was a matter-of-fact "too bad." They had spent too much money on the braces, and anyway, riding was dangerous: I could very easily fall off and smash up my expensive new orthodontia.

Sidney got braces, too, and had to wear a retainer. Nobody ever took away his tennis or basketball, though. I guess his favorite sports weren't deemed all that dangerous. Meanwhile, I desperately wished I could come up with my own means of paying for horseback-riding lessons, but I was only 13 and what could I do? So I just quietly shed my rabbity little-girl look and hid my hurt behind two rows of perfectly aligned white teeth, which I flashed in an obligatory smile for strangers but rarely for my parents.

I couldn't wait to drive. As soon as I turned 15 and a half, I got my learner's permit. My father patiently taught me how to drive in Fairmont Park and I took an AAA driver's-ed course for the insurance discount. I passed the DMV exam and got my license at 16. My parents let me drive their extra car, my Mom's old Camaro. Senior year of high school I drove myself to school every day. And finally, my girlfriends and I could go to all those dance parties on weekends without worrying about how we were going to get home at the end of the evening. I was thrilled—and my parents were encouraging. They trusted me and said I could have the car as long as I was a careful, responsible driver. Sidney showed no interest in driving in high school, but when he finally decided to get his license right before his senior year of college, my parents promptly took the Camaro from me and gave it to him. When I reminded them of their promise, they made it clear there was to be no discussion or explanation—just "too bad," followed by silence.

Dr. Knapp asked me whether I really ever put up a fight. "It wasn't worth it," I told her. "How do you rise up against 'too bad' and stone silences when you're an adolescent?"

In my early twenties, I quit my retail job at Bloomingdale's and decided to go to design school. I got into Parsons, one of the most prestigious (and expensive) of its kind in the country. But when I asked my parents to help with the tuition, they were not on board. It was another case of "too bad." So I worked full time and took out student loans, vowing I would do it all on my own without their

---

OVERLEAF I love playing with textures—in this case, a lavender grass cloth, which I put on the walls of a guest bedroom in a client's home in lower Manhattan.

PREVIOUS PAGES Bedrooms are one of my favorite spaces to design and decorate. Here, at a client's home, I used light-colored nightstands to offset the dark, wenge wood walls.
ABOVE AND OPPOSITE I lived with a small, cramped kitchen until I opened up the space. Tired of all-white kitchens, I chose blue, custom-made cabinets instead.

OPPOSITE AND ABOVE As a designer, I have always enjoyed experimenting with color
and texture in fabrics, furniture, and wallcoverings.

Spaces are always more visually interesting when different furniture styles and periods are mixed together.

I used both antiques and contemporary pieces to decorate this client's living room.

help and never ask them for anything again. At the time, I felt I could not trust them to give me a leg up when I needed it.

Around the same time, my brother decided he wanted to get a Master's degree in English—which would allow him to study Post-Colonial, Shakespearean, and Gothic literature at Oxford University. So my parents wrote a check for his tuition. Then he decided he needed to get another graduate degree at Columbia University Teachers College in New York, this time concentrating on educational administration and leadership. My Mom and Dad wrote another check. An immersion program in Guanajuato, Mexico, to learn Spanish. Another check—and I wrote the one for the airfare. While my brother had always been a recipient of many prestigious academic fellowships—a testimony to his sincere commitment to and passion for teaching—they did not always provide him with a free ride. Maybe my parents wrote checks because my Mother had also been a teacher and held a Master's in Early Childhood Education. Perhaps she and my Father fully understood and acknowledged the value of my brother's desire to further his education, whereas my goal represented a fleeting interest in getting an impractical degree from some art school they hadn't really ever heard of.

Sometimes the checks had nothing to do with academia but my brother's interests or indulgences—like a pair of expensive new orthotics for his tennis shoes or an overdue credit card bill. Those were the ones that bothered me the most, particularly because I listened to my Mother constantly complain about them. Maybe if I had acted more like my brother—dutiful rather than dissentious—I, too, could have had some help to lighten my financial burdens.

Strangely, I never begrudged Sidney over the double standards; however, he did occasionally fan the flames, which only added to the burn I already felt, saying stuff like, "Horesback riding isn't a real sport anyway. All you do is sit there while the horse does all the work."

The precedents were set when we were young. I became accustomed to the routine. Besides, Sidney was my older brother and only sibling, so naturally I idolized him from the get-go, hanging on his every word. At five, it made sense to me that Mr. Goody Two Shoes always got to be Batman—the mysterious Caped Crusader—while I was stuck playing his corny sidekick, Robin. While my brother could sock it to our imaginary villains, using words like POW, BAM, BIFF, BOOM, and KAPOW, the only thing I got to say was "Holy cow, Batman!" I was way too shy and compliant to speak up and say I was sick of being The Boy Wonder, and wanted to be Catwoman, instead.

As I got older, I rationalized that maybe my Mom and Dad were simply trying to toughen me up to make sure I could hack it when I grew up. The way my parents saw it, it wasn't easy out there. Better to be able to take care of yourself than rely on other people. Eventually those feelings began to shift, though, as I began to recognize that Sidney was far from perfect and often acted more like he was the younger sibling even though he was three years older. I realized that sometimes we cripple the people we love by handing them crutches they don't really need. I intuited that every time my Mother wrote Sidney a check, she might as well have handed him a shopping bag along with it. Kind of like those big black-and-white John Wanamaker bags he always had to lug when we were little. I had a hunch that someday he might trip and stumble over them.

Despite whatever feelings I had about what went down when we were kids, the feelings I had then are not the ones I have now. As Sidney grew older, his brotherly bullying was replaced with outward kindness and empathy—two of the qualities he possesses that I admire most.

I will never forget the first Christmas holiday when I came home to Philly without a single hair on my head. For the first time I could remember, I was fully absolved of all Christmas duties—decorating the tree, setting the table, walking Dolby, etc. Instead, I hid in my bedroom like a teenager with terrible acne, too ashamed and self-conscious about my appearance to come downstairs and face company. Each time I heard the doorbell ring, my heart sank further as I wondered how I could possibly greet aunts, uncles, and family friends looking the way I did. Sidney sensed what was going on, came up to my room, and refused to leave. Amidst my tears, he reassured me that everyone downstairs loved me and that nobody cared one iota about my hair: The people sitting in my parents' living room cared only about seeing *me*. He waited patiently until I pulled myself together. I found out I could rely on his strength as mine floundered, and I finally emerged only because of his support and compassionate understanding.

I spent weeks telling Dr. Knapp more of the same—my pent-up stories of what I considered the immensely meaningful, as well as the flawed, aspects of my upbringing. The sessions helped me articulate most of it and put it in perspective. It was all those years of constant reinforcement of the double standard that fueled my need for financial independence. I became convinced that if I could figure out how to be totally self-sufficient I could never be hurt. If I paved my own way, made my own money, and was in charge of my own decisions, nobody could say "too bad" or take away anything of significance to me.

Perhaps my parents were subconsciously preparing me for the innumerable challenges I'd face in the world beyond their grasp. It turned out that I would eventually face the same types of double standards as an entrepreneur. It was an occupational hazard being a black woman with her own business, working in an elitist profession dominated by gay white men and rich married socialites. If I went after anything I wanted or called out my male contractors on their mistakes, I was considered "aggressive" rather than "assertive." They could be so condescending. Sometimes what I really wanted to do was just punch them in the face and say, "See, now *that's* aggressive," as they wiped their bloody noses.

If I didn't mince words and told a difficult or incompetent employee with a lackadaisical attitude what I thought, I was considered "harsh" rather than "direct." If I did anything without a big Cheshire Cat smile on my face, without giving my assistants or colleagues a big gold star and a pat on the back, I was labeled "*The Devil Wears Prada* with a tan." Men could say and do as they pleased without having to constantly edit their behavior or be worried about being labeled a bitch. There was no escaping it. I loved what I did for a living, but there were days when my professional frustration bled into personal irritability.

Instead of keeping everything bottled up as I had learned to do as a kid, I was encouraged by Dr. Knapp to let it out in writing. "It doesn't have to be anything formal or that makes perfect sense," she said. "I don't care if you doodle while you do it. The goal is simply for you to get it out. When you feel angry or pissed off, you need to find an outlet other than the gym. Just write. You don't even need to go back and read what you wrote."

At first it was hard to do. Even though I had kept journals in my twenties I felt self-conscious about my writing. Of course, I went back and read it. I wanted the words to flow, to sound more poetic. Regardless, the more I wrote the less burdened I felt. As a kid, if I had the courage to speak up and express my hurt or frustration, it was called "talking back" and I got in trouble. I carried this habit of suppression firmly into adulthood. Like an old, comfortably fitting knapsack, it had become such a part of me I didn't even realize it was there anymore. Even if I couldn't say the words out loud, now at least I could get the feelings out. It was better than having them locked inside, festering.

I shared my thoughts with Dr. Knapp. She had comments; I had counter-comments. Together we dissected my past, taking it apart, sifting through bit by bit. I told her I thought maybe I needed a time-out from New York City. I explained one of the reasons I had moved to The Big Apple was New Yorkers' reputation for tolerance and respect for other people's differences. Despite its promise, though, as soon as I had taken a razor to my head, the city hadn't delivered. I felt like I was living in Cancerville and that it was time for a sab-batical. I began the process of rearranging my life so I could work from the country instead of the city, which wasn't all that difficult, thanks to some basic reorganization on my part and a global phenomenon called the internet.

We spoke a lot about how I was always willing to take risks in my profes-sional life, but how I had become highly risk-averse in my personal one. That after losing my hair I had begun second-guessing myself instead of trusting my instincts and judgments as I always had. I went on and on about how often I felt my trust had been violated throughout my life—not just by my parents, but by close friends and boyfriends.

I told the story of my good friend and roommate who had stiffed me for almost a year's rent when she moved out to follow some guy to Los Angeles. Even though the company she worked for had bought out her share of our two-year lease, she never sent me the money. She was in love and she married the guy. Then she had the audacity to complain to mutual friends that I constantly left mes-sages on their answering machine asking for her to send a check—as if her annoy-ance at my calls justified her behavior, breaking the agreement we had made.

I shared several similar stories with Dr. Knapp. I told her that one of the big-gest betrayals of trust I ever experienced had to do with Stephen. Our relation-ship didn't work out and we broke up. But he still called often. I likened him to herpes: A virus that just won't go away, it lays dormant and harmless most of the time but it's always there, patiently waiting to wreak havoc. Sometimes he called several times a day, confiding in me at length. I was so rattled by my recent hair loss and with trying to find my way in a world that didn't exactly embrace the new me that I enjoyed the distraction.

Stephen was dating a young beak-nosed blonde named Maggie. I had never met her, but had seen her from afar at a cocktail party hosted by a fellow member of our country club. She blended in seamlessly amongst the haughty, preppily clad, lock-jawed WASPs she had grown up with, whereas I was the club's first, and only, black member. Stephen didn't hesitate to share stories about her insecurity and temper tantrums over silly things. When he was really on a roll, he used words like "inspid" and "vacuous" to describe her.

"I don't get it, Stephen. Why would you date a girl who throws crockery at you and whom you don't even really respect? She sounds ridiculously childish and immature. But what did you expect? She's what—at least 20 years younger than you?" It did occur to me he could be leaving out all the parts about their torrid romance and hot sex. Then again, it was doubtful—and who wanted to go there, anyway?

Other than Stephen's new "relationship challenge," we also chatted about the more mundane details of our lives, such as our latest projects. I was renovating a tiny guest cottage on my property and he was fixing up a big new house. We figured out we each had something to offer the other. I needed my renovation finished in time for the arrival of my summer tenants at the beginning of July. I had a storage unit near Albany full of beautiful furniture, and he was living in a partially furnished house. We decided to barter his construction services for my furniture and decorating expertise. We were two grown, consenting adults, and even though we weren't dating, we still cared for one another and had tremendous mutual respect for our professional abilities. So why not?

At first, it all went off without a hitch. Within a couple weeks, my bathroom was plumbed and two of the walls were framed up. My diamond-shaped, thick-set terracotta bathroom tiles were installed, as were a pair of new windows. I chose paint colors for his home. I gave him a beautiful espresso-colored leather club chair from Coach, along with another from Paris; a Christian Liaigre syca-more and iron bookcase/console from Holly Hunt; some handmade rugs and light fixtures; and a Bograd Kids six-drawer dresser and my old brass bed frame, both for his younger daughter, Lindsay.

Stephen invited me to a dinner party at his house, where I hadn't been since our breakup. "You should come. It'll be fun, casual—no big deal. Maybe 10 people, and I'm going to cook."

"Carpentry cuisine?" I asked.

"Not this time," he said with a crooked smile.

It would require meeting the "vapid" girlfriend; she would be the hostess. I wasn't sure I wanted to go, but I figured what the heck. I didn't have plans for Saturday night and I would probably know some of the people there anyway. So I accepted his invitation.

But then something went awry. Stephen showed up at my house early Friday morning and quickly started loading his DeWalt circular saw, compressor, Shop-Vac, and buckets of tools into the back of his red Toyota Tacoma pickup. From my bedroom window, I saw him get in his truck and start to back away from the cottage. I flew down the stairs and out the back door.

"Hey! What's going on? Where are you going with all your stuff?"

"I can't finish the job. I'm pulling out."

"What are you talking about? I've got tenants coming in a few weeks."

"I've got too much other stuff to focus on, more important stuff. This is a tiny job, it's just not worth my time."

"You can't do this. You can't just pull out now. We had a deal. The walls aren't even done yet!"

"Sorry, I can't finish it."

"This is bullshit. What the hell am I supposed to do? I can't finish it myself."

Our conversation erupted into an argument, then exploded into an epic shouting match that moved from the driveway to the side of my house to the front porch, then back to the driveway.

"Maggie said she doesn't want me working on your house," he finally admitted. "She doesn't want me hanging around you. I'm spending way too much time over here."

"Since when have you ever listened to that idiot?! Besides, we had a deal and I already gave you almost $15,000 worth of furniture. That Holly Hunt bookcase alone is worth $5,000 and the club chair from Paris cost me four grand. That's way more than the work you did."

He laughed and shrugged his shoulders. This was the other side of him, the one I didn't like, the one that made me break up with him in the first place, the cold and twisted Stephen that usually only showed up when he drank too much.

And then he got in his truck and said the two magic words, without even knowing the power they held, yelling them back over his shoulder in his most cavalier tone, just before he sped out of my driveway: "Too bad."

Too bad, I thought. *Did he just say what I think he said? Too bad?!*

I was fuming. After I calmed down, I needed to figure out how to get to the bottom of this. So I called Dave, Stephen's best friend since the fifth grade.

Dave confessed the dinner was actually an engagement party, that Stephen had given Maggie a ring, and they were going to announce it Saturday evening.

"Why the hell would he get married to a woman he doesn't even like? And invite me to the surprise engagement dinner? What an asshole. He calls me every day, we talk, he bitches about her, he's even told me how much he still loves me, and now he's friggin' engaged to her? He comes to my house, takes all his tools and doesn't even have the balls to tell me what the hell is going on? What a fucking coward. Is this some kind of sick joke? If I didn't know him any better, I'd say he had a master plan to humiliate me."

Shockingly, instead of coming to Stephen's defense, Dave agreed with me wholeheartedly.

I hung up the phone and started pacing back and forth. Talk about getting blindsided. There is no way I'm going to let him get away with this. I picked up the phone and called Antique Delivery Express. They were a local trucking company I used regularly for furniture pickups and deliveries for clients. I had done business with them steadily for at least ten years. I reached one of the guys on his cell phone.

"Hey, Conrad, this is Sheila Bridges. Where are you right now? I have a problem and I need a huge favor."

"We're in Hudson. We just finished packing up a bunch of furniture and we were about to take a lunch break. But if it's urgent..."

"Yeah, well it is. If you don't mind, could you meet me at 247 Hillside Road in Tivoli? It's right off Route 9G."

"Sure. No problem."

Twenty minutes later, I pulled into Stephen's dirt driveway. A big Penske box truck drove in right behind me.

"What happened to your regular truck?" I asked, concerned the bright yellow rental might draw too much attention.

"It's in the shop. Broken axle. We're supposed to get it back next week."

It was too late to worry about it. I knew Stephen would be at a job site at least until late afternoon and that he never locked his doors. He was a trusting country boy and I, a wary city girl. When we were dating, sometimes he would

ABOVE Dolby oversaw my cottage renovation and the barter agreement that had gone terribly wrong. OPPOSITE In the early 1900s, the building that is now my cottage in upstate New York was used for violet propagation. Here, it was photographed post-renovation.

OPPOSITE AND ABOVE On the walls of the dining room and bedroom in the guesthouse, I used my Harlem Toile De Jouy wallpaper. The Piero Fornasetti dining chairs are from Italy.

drive down to Harlem and leave his Porsche parked on the street with the doors unlocked and the key in the ignition. It was some crazy entitled shit I couldn't relate to, but what could I say? Nobody had ever broken into his house or stolen his car so he wasn't going to change his ways.

I was antsy and moved quickly through the house. Reminders of the life Stephen had built with his new woman were everywhere. On top of the urgency of my errand, they added to my discomfort. There were snapshots of the happy couple posing for the camera—positioned meticulously on mantels and tables, next to small ceramic bowls filled with citrus and pine-scented potpourri. The evidence was in the sterling silver framed photo of Maggie wearing sunglasses with her head thrown back, laughing. Even if she was a true numbskull, it painted a far different portrait of their relationship than the one he'd given me on the phone. Why had he gone so far out of his way to mislead me into believing it wasn't all that serious?

As I pointed out individual pieces of furniture, tersely announcing "that one" and "now that piece over there," Conrad and his assistants quickly recognized their status as repo-men and picked up the pace, working efficiently yet carefully, blanket-wrapping each piece before hustling it out the door and into their truck. "That brown leather club chair, and that one, too."

In the master bedroom, I was shocked to discover that not only had Stephen and his new girlfriend been sleeping in the same bed where he and I had slept at my house—the one I gave him for his daughter—but also on exactly the same white cotton sheets. I bet Maggie had no idea. What a douchebag. Gross.

"The bed goes, too. The frame but not the mattress. Just pile everything else on the floor." I didn't want those sheets back.

I guesstimated how much of the furniture I'd given him would cover the work he'd done to date and settle our barter, taking no more, no less. As Conrad's truck backed out of the driveway, I shut off the lights, closed the door tightly behind me, and drove home on pure adrenaline. I decided to busy myself with gardening and invited a friend over to help me weed one of my flower beds.

When Stephen's first call came in, I knew it was him, thanks to Caller ID. I let it go to voicemail then played back the message. It was obvious he hadn't been home yet. Ever the narcissist and master of manipulation, he was playing his usual sheepish game with the same old honey-coated forked tongue.

"Hi, Sheila. Listen, I'm really sorry about what happened earlier and I'd really like to see you so we can just talk. Maybe we could get together for a drink. I have to pick Maggie up at the train station in Rhinecliff later, so let's try to get together before that, okay? Call me back as soon as you get this. Bye."

My girlfriend and I looked at each other, sitting in the mulch under the oak tree. He called again an hour later and I listened to the message. "Where are you? Call me back. Let's talk. I want to get together."

A few minutes later, the call I'd been waiting for came in. He hissed and spat into the phone, ranting and raving at his highest pitch about what he was going to do to me if I didn't return his furniture. He threatened to call the police and have me arrested. I imagined him arriving home, gradually noticing all the stuff that was missing, quietly percolating a boiling rage, racing from room to room, his Sperry Top-Siders squeaking, his eyes squinting with his normal Silly-Putty complexion deepening to ruby red.

By the time the Dutchess County police reached me by telephone, I had attained the studied calm of a practicing Buddist monk. With a little help from my furniture vigilantism, our Karmas had been reversed and the script had been flipped: Now it was Stephen's turn to be out-of-control pissed off. Meanwhile, I leveled with the officer, explaining that I had taken back some furniture, which was mine. No, I hadn't broken into Stephen's house; no, I hadn't stolen anything. I had receipts for all the pieces, and they were now back in my possession. He was welcome to stop by and see the unfinished mess of a cottage my ex had left me with, if he'd like. No doubt, the police wanted nothing to with a messy domestic situation involving some angry guy, his PMS-y ex-girlfriend, and their fight over a bunch of fancy furniture and unfinished construction.

The morning after the dinner party, I heard from Claire, Dave's wife. "What a bizarre evening," she said, laughing. "The baked chicken with rosemary-roasted potatoes was delicious, but there weren't any chairs to sit on!"

When I spoke to my Mother later that weekend, I told her what had happened. I was a little worried what she might say about what I had done. She knew about Stephen, but had never met him. Neither had my Father or brother, which was a good indication that as far as I was concerned the relationship hadn't been going anywhere. My Mom's reaction to the furniture episode caught me by surprise. She giggled. Then she laughed loudly. And finally she said, "Sure sounds like he's never dated a black woman before."

"Yeah, I would say that much is true." I chuckled.

But then she became serious and said, "More important, it's pretty obvious he didn't know you; he didn't know you well at all."

"That's probably true, too."

My Mom was right: Stephen never really knew me at all.

ABOVE Every summer when I was a child, we went to visit my Mother's relatives in Virginia. In this photograph with my brother, Sidney, I am comfortably seated on my Uncle Dick's tractor, in my cousin Bernard's lap.

CHAPTER 21

OLD MacBRIDGES

I was in love with my cousin Bernard—pronounced "Ber Nard," like it was two separate words. He was a young man, 18 years old, and I was a little girl of five. Of course, I had no idea how scandalous it was to marry your own adult relative, unless you lived in sixteenth century England. Even if I had known, I wouldn't have cared because Bernard had a huge, unkempt Afro, skin the color of Swiss Miss Instant Cocoa, and eyes the color of rain. He was John-Boy from the Waltons, but black, and minus the hairy, prune-sized mole on his lower left cheek. He was the grandson of my Aunt Net—my grandmother Azalia's sister Annette—and therefore my second cousin.

Bernard lived on my Aunt Net and her husband Uncle Dick's 60-acre farm in Amelia, Virginia, along with his three older brothers—Wilbert, who was known as Dickie; Randolph, called Bubba; and James. They were raised by their grandparents because their parents had tragically died young. What I loved most about Bernard, aside from his good looks, country drawl, and slow southern cadence, was that he smelled of shucked corn, sweat, horsehair, and the diesel fuel from the Ford pickup he drove. I saw him only once a year but that didn't matter. Neither did the fact that our union would be taboo and considered statutory rape. We could work around that: It was nothing but logistics—pure logistics. What I felt for Bernard was so genuine and immeasurable that I convinced myself he would wait for me.

I was still in diapers when we began our tradition of visiting the Virginia farm every summer. My Mom, Sidney, and I would make the trek via Greyhound bus or be driven by my Aunt Baby's husband, Richard. My Father would stay behind in Philadelphia. He wanted as little as possible to do with those uncouth roughneck farmers—my Mother's people. To him, they were the Beverly Hillbillies—only East Coast, with no oil or cash. Besides, my Dad was busy, he needed to keep working and couldn't afford to take time off to spend in Virginia—a hugely convenient excuse to avoid a do-nothing stay in a ramshackle farmhouse with no air conditioning or working toilet.

Most evenings, when Bernard would go out with his brothers, I tried to wait up for him. Bernard had an extra cot in his room, which is where I usually slept. I would doze off, then awaken, startled but giddy, to the squeak of the screen door before it slammed shut, announcing their return. I hoped Bernard hadn't been out messing around with any of those hillbilly "fast girls" I sometimes heard my grandmother and aunt fretting about. When Bernard slipped into the room, I always pretended to be asleep. I lay there hoping tonight would be the night when he finally drummed up the courage to tell me he loved me before proposing and whisking me across the tobacco fields on the back of Uncle Dick's tractor, deep into the nicotine night, to tie the knot. Never mind that all of our three-handed children would have had seven toes and IQs equivalent to a bale of hay. Love was love, and I was smitten.

The only serious impediment to our eternal bliss was the plumbing situation. While I was okay with hand-pumping well water for drinking, and bathing in a big tub filled from buckets heated over the wood-burning stove in the kitchen, I was deathly afraid of using the old wooden outhouse in the middle of the night. Sidney convinced me he had seen a big corn snake slithering through the grass out back early one evening and that it was just waiting for me to pull down my pants so it could jump up and bite me in my private parts. The fact was I would have rather wet the bed and slept in my own puddle all night than gone outside in the dark. But I didn't want to appear childish. I also could not bring myself to use the lidded "slop bucket" kept in the bedroom just in case I couldn't hold it. So I stayed awake half the night, legs tightly crossed, anxiously awaiting the rooster's crowing at sunrise. Only then was it safe for me to head outdoors, at which point I sprinted out the porch door.

Maybe I could get a job baking bread or shelling snap peas to pay for some indoor plumbing. I didn't like asking my parents for money, but I was even willing to consider approaching my Dad about an increase in my weekly 50-cent allowance. A new bathroom couldn't possibly set us back all that much. *Don't worry Bernard, I have us covered. That will be my contribution to our never-ending happiness—a bathroom with a flushing toilet.* I also figured I needed to make up for my other contribution, from the previous year's visit, which was a case of the chicken pox that Bubba, Dickie, James, and my beloved Bernard all promptly came down with in all its contagious and itchy spendor. For sure, I was their favorite cute little cousin from Philadelphia, with my long plaits and quiet yet tomboyish ways, but I owed them one for the chicken pox.

Other than the lack of indoor plumbing, there was nothing I could recall not loving about those times in Virginia. My days were spent barefoot—something I was never allowed at home in Philly, even though we had plush carpeting everywhere. No frilly lace or French eyelet dresses. It was Danskin knit shorts and Crayola-colored striped tops all the way. I could wear my favorite clothes day in and day out, 'til they got really dirty, and no one seemed to mind.

My Aunt Net was an amazing cook, using all her homegrown fruits and vegetables, making everything from scratch instead of in the microwave. I remember her home-baked breads, handmade sausages, and freshly churned ice milk. I can still smell the homemade buttermilk biscuits baking, the fresh eggs being fried, and the thick slabs of bacon sizzling in their own grease in the big black cast-iron skillet.

I got up at the crack of dawn each day so I could ride between Uncle Dick and Cousin Bernard in the front seat of their rickety old pickup, heading out to the barn to milk the Holsteins, feed "pig slop" to the hogs, and then go out to tend the cornfields. At some point, Uncle Dick would drive me back to the house on the tractor to get me out of the way of the many daily chores these men needed to perform in order to make a living. It was a working spread that required back-breaking labor—not some gentleman's hobby farm. They grew and sold tobacco, corn, wheat, and lumber harvested from their own land. They hunted with their hounds, slaughtered animals they raised, and even sometimes shot small vermin like squirrel, possum, and wild rabbits, which my Aunt Net prepared in the smokehouse or salted, boiled, pickled, and baked into delicious dishes. I was willing to try almost anything, including my Mom's favorite—pickled pig's feet. There was something about being close to nature and having my hands and feet in the Virginia dirt that made me truly happy. But what is pleasure without a little pain?

There was a one-eyed orange tabby cat who lived in the barn. I can't quite recall his name, but I'm pretty sure it was something stunningly original and inventive like "Cat." Uncle Dick had shot Cat in the left eye when he caught him in the henhouse making a meal out of some baby chicks. The poor cat scrammed and managed to survive, looking like a furry miniature cyclops with an indented skull and half an ear. I was so completely taken with animals, it didn't matter to me that Cat was an ornery one-eyed outcast. Part of what I liked so much about four-legged creatures was that my shyness was a non-factor. Words, which never came easy, didn't rate with them. I was more inclined to communicate in the realm of gesture—a language they spoke and seemed to understand. Like most felines, Cat was independent in nature, full of cat-itude and indifference. One day, I saw Cat heading toward the barn and I became particularly determined to befriend him.

"Here, kitty-kitty…here, kitty-kitty," I said, approaching cautiously. Cat ignored me. Okay, so if you won't come to me, no problem, I'll come to you.

This old black-and-white photograph was taken while I was still in diapers. I am barefoot, sitting
in the grass on the farm in Virginia, alongside Sidney and Cat, the one-eyed tabby who lived in the barn.
OVERLEAF When I was four years old, I was photographed by my Dad at a petting zoo in the Pocono
Mountains. I was always happiest when surrounded by four-legged creatures.

Cat continued on his journey, paying me absolutely no mind, as I crawled behind him on my hands and knees, doing my best feline imitation. I was unwilling to give up: If Cat wouldn't make friends on my terms, then I would do it on his.

Apparently I followed Cat for at least several miles, under barbed wire, through picket fences, across neighboring farms and cornfields, over berms, and eventually scaling one small Appalachian mountain, completely losing track of time, until Cat either got hungry or tired of his one-eyed expedition and wandered back to the farm at nightfall. When I appeared in the darkness on the dirt road, still making tracks behind Cat, everyone seemed frantically out of character—particularly my Mother, who cried hysterically. Why all the fuss? I wasn't bothering or hurting anyone. All I had done was go on a wonderful long walk with my new furry friend.

"Oooh, somebody's in trouble! Somebody's gonna get it!" My brother taunted. He couldn't wait for me to get the countrified beat-down. This was one time he hadn't instigated anything; I had created this mess, this glorious misadventure, all by myself. And sure enough, that's exactly what I got, a beat-down—*POP, POP, POP, POP, POP*—with my Mother's bare left hand on my backside.

She grabbed both of my shoulders, lifted me off the ground, and shook hard: "You could have been hurt by someone or eaten by a pack of wolves! You scared us half to death," she sobbed. "Don't you ever, ever run away like that again. Do you understand me?!"

I was completely unaware that everyone on the farm had been in an all-out search for me ever since I disappeared. These were pre-Amber Alert times. It was the South in the late sixies, after the Civil Rights Act had passed but well before white celebrities caught the bug of adopting cute black babies. My Mom and all the rest of them simply didn't get it. I hadn't run away. I was just following Cat. Amidst the tears and sobbing—by now I, too, was crying from the harsh scolding and spanking—all I could think to say, in a meek little voice, was, "I'm sorry, Mommy. I'm sorry."

I'd like to believe those idyllic early times down in Virginia sowed the seeds of my desire to one day own a farm. Unlike most young girls who had fairy-tale princess fantasies about designer wedding gowns, Skittles-colored brides-maid dresses, and handsome, princely husbands, my daydreams rarely if ever involved any beings who walked on two feet—the one exception being Cousin Bernard. My dreams were all about nature, land, water, horses, dogs, and cats. Well into my thirties, my Mother used to joke about how when I was little I used to say, "I don't want to get married. I don't want a husband. Eeeuuuuwww. Yucky. I just want to have animals. One day I'm going to live on a farm."

Mom found my childhood proclamations endearing, having shared her father's love of animals and grown up with a pet pig herself. But on the flipside, I could never convince either of my parents to let me have the menagerie of creatures I wanted so badly, no matter how clean I promised to keep my room. Instead, my shelves ended up packed with plastic-and-resin Breyer Model Horses, and porcelain and glass animal figurines I bought with my allowance. My stuffed animal collection was just as vast—each of them with a name and its own important role within the hierarchy of my extensive animal kingdom.

And so it came to pass, many decades later, that I found myself creating my own real-life animal refuge at my property upstate. While I did not own cattle or grow tobacco or corn, I rototilled and sowed seeds in big wildflower fields, filling them full of red poppies, blue cornflowers, larkspurs, orange cosmos, Black-eyed-Susans, and forget-me-nots. I eventually put in several gardens, including one dedicated to vegetables and herbs for cooking, where I grew an assortment of lettuce greens, kales, swiss chard, and lots of tomatoes of every imaginable variety.

My four-footed menagerie started with my quarter horse Red. From my perspective as a rider, he had given me the very best years of his life. Now, at 26, he was retired, suffering from navicular syndrome (the degeneration of the navicular bone and tissues in his front legs) and bad arthritis. He had survived a

Do not let animals
through this gate

NO
SMOKING

bout with cancer. I spent so much money over the years on his care—the endless equine vet bills, monthly farrier costs, and the fees for boarding him at fancy farms so pristine you could lick the barn floor. Most months, Red's expenses were more than you could expect to pay for a one-bedroom rental in a decent neighborhood like the West Village. It was time to cut back and move him home.

Horses are herd animals, though, which means they crave relationships with others of their kind. So I added a youngster to the mix—Harley, a 4-year-old Tobiano Paint, who had a completely black coat with the exception of a white marking on his withers, and three white socks (the area above his fetlocks). I bought him after seeing a picture on a flyer at the local tack shop. He was a 1,000-pound puppy, bratty and constantly up to teenager-like antics. He always made a mess out of his stall—treating feed and water buckets and anything else he could get his mouth on like it was toy to be played with and tossed around. Now I had my eye on a retired, 7-year-old polo pony that I had been introduced to by a friend in Connecticut. His name was High Jinx On The Money, which I hated, so I had decided I would rename him Ponzi Scheme if the purchase went through.

For me, horses are living, breathing art—exceptional sensitivity, grace, and agility poised on four legs. The relationship between a horse and its rider is based on mutual respect, patience, and trust. At best, it's an honest, communicative collaboration between a 120-pound person and a 1,200-pound athlete. At worst, it's a frighteningly dangerous ride atop an unpredictable wild animal completely at the mercy of its fight-or-flight instincts. The horse-rider partnership is one I understand well, a bond I feel lucky to have shared.

As a child, riding helped me build self-confidence. I knew that if I treated an animal with kindness, I could reap seemingly infinite rewards. Whether we were walking through the woods, jumping a crossrail, or galloping down a polo field, when my body and my horse's were fully in sync, it was an indescribable high. I had been passionate about them as long as I could remember, and despite the hard work their care entailed, it was worth it to be able to look out my bedroom window and watch them quietly rolling in the green pasture or grazing contentedly with their long tails swishing from side to side. It warmed my heart and fed my soul.

I found my sheep on craigslist.org, acquiring a small starter flock of four— three Jacobs and a Shetland. I named them Eeny, Meeny, Miney, and Moe. Once a year, in late spring, I sheared their thick, oily, nappy wool, then washed and spun it into usable yarn I hoped to incorporate into a line of home furnishings. I designed and built a chicken coop for my hens, who were pasture-raised, antibiotic-, hormone- and cage-free. Every week, I brought cartons of eggs to the city and gave them to my Harlem neighbors, who were impressed by their pastel hues and farm-fresh taste.

Adding to my ever-expanding animal family were my two new Australian Shepherds, Jax and Wheeler. They came from a farm in Virginia, where they were bred to work with horses, cattle, and sheep. Wheeler, smart and always ready to work, was a big goofball, sloppy and sweet. He was forever looking for something to herd—particularly my snow shovel and vacuum cleaner, and sometimes even the sheep. Jax, his half sister, was stubborn but also sweet. I thought of her as my "special-needs Aussie." Thanks to the dumb blonde down the road, Jax had brain damage and would never be a "normal dog." When she was a six-pound, 10-week-old puppy, my neighbor's 100-plus pound Rhodesian mix did a quick "grab 'n' shake" on her, putting her into a coma. After 10 days, she woke up, but had very little vision, no depth perception, and a host of serious neurological issues that would plague her for the rest of her life. Like anyone who has been in a coma, Jax had to relearn the basics: how to stand, eat, and walk. Sadly, the only thing she would ever be able to herd was her own tail.

One of the truths I learned from years of owning animals is how their behavior more often than not reflects how they are raised, trained, and treated. It's pretty much the same as with children. You see so many parents living in total denial about their maniacal, ill-behaved offspring, and there are just as many pet owners who do the same thing. All I'm saying is if your son acts like Damien from *The Omen*, it doesn't help to continue pretending he's a little angel and wouldn't hurt a fly. Similarly, if you've been tipped off that your St. Bernard is a latent Cujo because of his history of killing small animals and pets in the neighborhood—stop trying to convince everybody he's Lassie.

My puppy mishap aside, living upstate had many perks. One of the biggest was the Red Curry House & Garden Center. Located in a big red-and-white barn next to the Sunoco station, it was the only place I knew in the tristate area where you could get delicious, authentic Indian food and at the same time fulfill all your basic landscaping needs. The conversation would invariably go something like this:

"Hi Bernadette, how're you doing? I'd like to place an order to go."

"Good, Sheila. What'll it be?"

"Two vegetable samosas, please, one meat samosa, one order of Chana Bhaji, two pooris, one Tandoori shrimp, one chicken Korma, one garlic Naan.... On second thought, make it two garlic Naan.

OPPOSITE The portrait of me and my horse Red, in upstate New York, taken by my friend and fellow horse lover Nick Xatzis, is one of my favorite photographs.

ABOVE According to the French novelist Colette, "Our perfect companions never have fewer than four feet." Sadly, Sadie, Simone, Dolby, and Trouble have all passed on since this photograph was taken.

OVERLEAF LEFT Peanut, Milo, and Spike are three of my baby Nigerian Pygmy goats.

OVERLEAF RIGHT The brown-and-white fuzzy stuffed animal in my hand is actually a purse in the shape of a horse that one of my friends gave me as a birthday gift.

"Got it," she would say, scribbling fast on her pad. "Anything else?"

"Yes, uhm...I'll take two Colorado Spruces—the six-footers—three sugar maples, and one white pine—a five-footer. Also, I'd love that Crimson King that's to the left of the parking lot, if it's for sale."

"You got it, Sheila!"

"When do you think Raoul can deliver them?"

"I'll have him give you a call and set it up for later this week."

"Great," I would say, taking my place at one of the tables by the row of stainless steel chafing dishes warming over cans of Sterno.

Ever since I had decided to spend more time in the country than in the city, it seemed as if my appetite had grown ten-fold. My daily caloric intake was now equal to that of Michael Phelps, but minus the swimming. Maybe it had to do with all the fresh air or the fact that I was constantly working outdoors, shoveling manure, hauling buckets of water and bags of chicken scratch, and lugging bales of straw. My day started at 5 a.m.—feeding horses, sheep, dogs, and mucking out stalls before I sat down at my desk to work. I took multitasking to a new level, weeding my garden beds while checking emails at the same time.

Despite the fact that I was doing a lot of physical labor, I was packing on the pounds and it wasn't exactly pretty. I dreaded going to Manhattan because it meant I had to fit my new muffin-top into something other than my favorite Carhartt coveralls or oversized camouflage cargo pants. My regular city clothes were bursting at the seams. What do you mean I can't wear my Wrangler denim overalls or my army fatigues to the opening at the Whitney? Given a choice between buying a pair of red-soled Louboutins or a new pair of insulated muck boots and leather barn clogs, it was a no brainer. Sorry, Christian, but I've got to have proper footwear for the farm.

Since moving upstate, I had developed a new philosophy of consumption. Why eat just one peanut butter cookie when you could enjoy the entire box? Why only a single glass of Pinot Grigio when you could drink the whole bottle? Weekends at my house had become a series of alcohol- and food-filled free-for-alls with friends. I enjoyed cooking and baking—something I rarely did in the city because I hated my cramped kitchen. I also liked the idea that I knew where most of my food was coming from. It was hard sometimes to cook for one, so why not cook for a 'family' of four? You never know who might drop by. And if they didn't, I was plenty hungry.

More important than my insatiable appetite, however, was my hunger for a connection to the Universe. I felt inspired by the natural beauty surrounding

My brother, Sidney, was experimenting with depth of field and focus when he took this photograph of an African Daisy in Upstate New York.

me—whether it was a Cooper's Hawk soaring overhead or a pair of bushy-tailed red fox kits playing hide-and-seek in a hollowed-out log. Every day, nature taught me spiritual lessons about living in the moment—about appreciating what stood in front of me. I learned to stop, discover, and admire. Otherwise, I might miss the flock of wild turkeys out for a Sunday afternoon stroll across my front lawn. I now realized the importance of stopping to notice the new spider web that had been elaborately spun into the corner of my front porch, between the wooden railings. Today, fresh with drops of dew, its fragile asymmetry glistened in the muted morning light; tomorrow it would likely be gone. My trust in nature was devout: I trudged with confidence through ten inches of mud in order to feed my sheep in mid-March, knowing that by the end of May, I would be walking the same path on lush green meadow, instead. Trusting in nature helped mend the broken fence between Miss Universe and me. And with each new day, I gradually began to see trivial events and personal challenges differently. Here, without all the noise and even without the hair, I saw these routine occurrences as prudent, yet humbling gestures. She was finally helping me understand that it was okay to trust her—and myself—again.

The bullseye of a paper target used for shooting practice was taken out by my friend's 12-gauge Mossberg shotgun. The small holes are from the shots I fired with my air rifle.

CHAPTER 22

GIRLS, GUYS, GUNS

The first time I ever fired a friend's 12-gauge shotgun I blew a hole through the middle of the bull's-eye but nearly took out my right shoulder with the recoil. When I felt ready to make my own personal gun purchase, I bought an inexpensive and lightweight Gamo air rifle. After I got the hang of it, I moved up to a 10/22 Ruger carbine rifle and then on from there. Initially I did target practice with an antique side chair that had pristinely turned ebonized wood legs and was upholstered in green and white gingham fabric from Cowtan & Tout. I had used it in a segment about shopping for antiques with Matt Lauer on NBC's *Today Show*. Now it was tattered and the upholstery was all shot up full of bullet holes.

If I was going to be a gun owner, I wanted to be as good a markswoman as possible. My new boyfriend, Jonathan, wasn't particularly into guns, but his son Nick was a U.S. Navy Seal on special assignment in the Middle East. I figured I might as well get some tips from a real pro, so I asked Jonathan: "When you speak to Nick, can you ask him if he'd mind giving me some pointers?"

Until I moved north, I would not have called myself a gun enthusiast by any means. I still don't. While I do firmly believe in Americans' right to bear arms, I also think we need much stricter gun-control laws. Owning a rifle to me has always been more like owning a vacuum cleaner: Most of the time, it sits in my closet collecting dust; once in a while, I feel compelled to use it. I quickly discovered that hunting was to upstate New York what golf is to Florida. Most of the local guys I knew shot wild turkey and deer during the winter hunting season, and it seemed as if just about everybody owned at least one firearm.

It wasn't until I took my first NRA basic safety class that I discovered my own naïveté about America's gun culture. The course was taught at a local Huntsman's Lodge in a nondescript Quonset hut outfitted with wood paneling, framed Molsen Golden posters, stuffed deer heads, and an assortment of other taxidermy mounted on stained wooden plaques. A certified instructor named Chris—a man of Shrek stature with small yellowish teeth that reminded me of kernels of corn—slowly talked us through the 145-page manual that detailed every bit of minutiae you could ever want to know about each individual component of a handgun with diagrams. He explained the difference between revolvers and semi-automatic weapons. He familiarized us with all the terminology, from misfires and hang-fires to standing- versus bench-rest positions.

I found the mechanical design of firearms fascinating in its pure functional simplicity. Growing up, I was well aware of the small Italian handgun my Father kept in his bedside table drawer. He had been given the gun by his godfather, Mr. Brown. It stayed in a box in the very back, on the right, behind cigarette lighters, shoe horns, and black nylon socks. My Mother made it explicitly clear that guns were not toys and were strictly off-limits to children. Naturally, I became curious, my fascination fueled. So one day when I was probably nine or ten years old, I snuck into my parents' room while they were out, opened the drawer, carefully took the gun out of its box, held it in my hand, hefting its cool weight for just a few seconds, then quickly slipped it back into its hiding place.

I knew from my Mother that my Dad also kept a registered revolver at his office, which was in one of the roughest sections of West Philly. When she was growing up, they called it "The Bottom." My Dad's office had been robbed. The thieves broke in by taking out a window air conditioner on the second floor. They took everything that wasn't nailed down, including dental instruments, office equipment, money, my Dad's collection of artwork and his own photos—the ones he had shot, developed, and framed himself. "They even stole the toilet paper out of the bathroom," my Mom told me. The only thing they left hanging on the wall was a framed charcoal drawing of me and Sidney, sketched by an artist on the boardwalk in Atlantic City during one of our family

OPPOSITE My Dad's vintage Italian Rigarmi .25 caliber semi-automatic handgun was a gift
from his godfather, Mr. Robert L. Brown. It's mine now.
ABOVE The charcoal drawing of Sidney and me was sketched in 1972 by a boardwalk
artist in Atlantic City, New Jersey. I was eight years old.

weekends down the shore. They probably figured they couldn't sell it—it was too identifiable. Or perhaps, the benevolent side of me wanted to believe, they decided to keep these two innocent little kids out of it.

About a year after the burglary, my Dad was held up leaving his office one night. The perp held a gun to my Father's head, but a drug dealer on the block saw what was going down and yelled, "Yo, leave Doc alone!" So the guy put the gun back in his pocket and walked away. Everyone on the street knew and respected my Father. No matter how successful he became, he refused to move his office to a safer area. He insisted that all black people should have access to outstanding dental care, even if they didn't have insurance or a lot of money. His steadfast philosophy was that everybody—including hustlers, pimps, and dealers—deserved a chance to have their teeth cleaned and their cavities filled.

T he NRA instructor's other responsibility was to make sure our gun license applications were filled out correctly. Of course, I was obsessively compelled to complete mine perfectly; so, as usual, I was the one who got stumped and came up with the asinine questions.

"On page one, where it says race, what is the correct abbreviation for black? There're only three spaces. Is it BLK or BLA, or what?"

"Uhm. Not sure. Probably either one works, but you should check with the Sheriff's office when you turn the application in to be sure."

A brief pause and I raised my hand again. "Sorry, ah, where it says hair color, I'm not sure what to put. Is there an abbreviation for bald?

"Not sure about that one either, ma'am. You could try BLD, but I would definitely suggest checking with the Sheriff's office."

The dark haired woman two seats away leaned forward with an annoyed look and said, "You could just fill in your hair color. I mean, like, whatever it is when you let it grow back." *I should be so lucky*, I thought.

The top of the first page of the application read: I HEREBY APPLY FOR A PISTOL/REVOLVER LICENSE TO: (Check one only)

- CARRY CONCEALED
- POSSESS ON PREMISES
- CARRY DURING EMPLOYMENT

I had checked off the box for "Possess on premises" since the gun permit was for recreational sport and target practice. Leaning over my shoulder to double-check, our instructor saw that and, pointing at the form, blurted, "No, no, no—wrong! You always want to check 'carry concealed.'"

"Sorry. Anybody have any Wite-Out?" Everyone shook their heads "no" in unison. "But wait a second, I don't need to carry a concealed weapon and I don't need it for work." I envisioned myself packing a 9 mm Smith & Wesson in my Louis Vuitton purse while shopping for brass drawer-pulls at Restoration Hardware, or tucking it into my L.L. Bean canvas tote as I popped into Maison Gerard on East 10th Street to look at Art Deco side tables. "It's just to protect the livestock on my property from coyotes, or for target practice or shooting clays. You know, recreational stuff. I mean, who needs to carry a concealed weapon around here? There's practically no crime."

Suddenly, everybody leaned forward or yanked their heads around; all eyes were on me like I was a complete imbecile. They weighed in, one by one.

"I'm gonna carry a revolver in my handbag," the blonde nurse sitting next to me volunteered.

"Same here," said the dark-haired lady who had spoken up about my hair color.

"Why? Not that it's any of my business, but I'm just curious. I mean, home invasion is one thing, but do you really think it's that unsafe around here during the day?"

"Well, I work the late shift at the hospital. By the time I get home, it's real dark, the middle of the night, and I have to walk from my garage to my house." The guy sitting next to me, who was wearing baggy jeans, military style combat boots, and a camouflage jacket, had been ominously silent throughout the morning. He finally spoke up: "Why? Because you never know," he said in a raspy Clint Eastwood whisper.

"Never know what, exactly?" I turned to ask.

Our instructor piped up enthusiastically: "I keep a loaded gun on a rack above my bed. I made sure my fiancée, mother, and grandmother all have weapons easily accessible. Hell, we have so many guns in the family if you added up what they all cost it'd probably be more'n what we paid for the house!" Maybe this guy was onto something. How about designing a collection of upholstered headboards with hidden gun compartments for Gander Mountain, the outdoor-equipment chain? I could call it "Bangin' in the Bedroom."

The woman next to him interrupted. "Fear. Most people carry guns out of fear."

"Fear of what?"

"The unknown," the quiet guy sitting next to me answered without skipping a beat. Most of my fellow students nodded knowingly. That said it all—summed up, for me, the most disturbing part of gun culture in America. Fear of the unknown. Like popping off six rounds with your new Colt .357 Magnum Revolver was going to blow a deadly hole in your paranoia.

Once we finished reviewing the manual, we were informed we would have to pass a written exam. "There's a test?" I asked, feeling the sweat start to break out on my forehead. "Nobody ever said anything about a test." I felt my heart rate going up. First that damn application form, and now a written exam...I hated standardized tests; the last one I could recall taking was the SATs, and I was still getting over that. Hey, wait a second, this wasn't fair: Weren't all these things biased and wasn't I, as a black person, automatically disadvantaged and predicted to score significantly lower than my peers... Then I took another look around the room at those "peers" and, as our instructor quickly reassured me, started to feel a little better about my chances:

"Don't worry, Miss Bridges. It's all True or False and multiple choice. You can take as long as you need. Feel free to ask me questions. And by the way, there's no essay." No essay? Thank God. I had already imagined possible topics—How could Dick Cheney's hunting accident have been avoided with proper safety precautions?—and begun to fret about what I could possibly come up with to write.

I scored a 94—tricked only by two questions whose answers were not A, B, C, or D but "all of the above."

A favorite weekend expedition upstate was shopping at Walmart. They sold absolutely everything you could possibly want for your home— some brand names I recognized and others I hadn't ever heard of. Sure, I would have liked to buy a Sony portable CD player, but I settled for a Coby instead. I also acquired a pair of slouchy brown boots called Dawgs that looked like an uglier version of UGGs—if that's possible. Sometimes I was seduced into buying things I didn't really need. One time, it was a pack of tube socks. They were on sale: Buy eight, get two free. What was I gonna do with all these tube socks? Wear them under my riding boots, I guess, and send the extras to Wilt Chamberlain.

I zig zagged through the aisles, tossing a 10-piece towel set, Dirt Devil cordless hand vac, a new tea kettle to replace my old rusted one, a jumbo 24-pack of Scott bathroom tissue, and a large box of Saltine crackers into my shopping cart. My cell phone vibrated, then rang inside my jacket pocket. I checked the incoming call. It was Cynthia, one of my childhood friends from Philadelphia.

"Hey there!"

"Hey—what's up, chicka? How are you?"

"Good. How are you?"

"Fine. What're you up to on this lovely Saturday morning?"

"Running errands. Right now I'm in Walmart."

"Walmart? What the heck are you getting there?"

"Let's see...a hand vac, a couple dozen rolls of toilet paper—I was almost out. What else? Oh yeah, a new tea kettle, some towels, and a gun."

"Did you just say a gun?"

"Yep."

I heard laughter followed by rustling, a pause, and then Cynthia came back on the line: "Hey—are you still there? Oh, my God. I almost dropped the phone. I can't believe you're at Walmart buying a gun..."

"Sure, why not?"

"You are too friggin' hilarious."

"What did you think—I'd be shopping for Mary-Kate and Ashley fashion accessories?"

"Okay, but a gun. What—did you all of a sudden go redneck on me?"

"Hardly; I'll explain later but I gotta go. Can I call you back? I need to hurry up and pick up this rifle. I have a bunch of questions about the scope and stuff, and I've got to get out of here in time for my manicure–pedicure appointment."

"Sheila, you crack me up. Who else has to hurry up and buy a gun so they're not late for their mani-pedi?"

I chuckled along with her. "So I'll talk to you later, okay?"

"Okay, bye."

What Cynthia didn't seem to understand about my life upstate was that every day was *Groundhog Day*, with me in the Bill Murray role of Pittsburgh weatherman Phil Connors, determined to catch these varmints because they were wreaking havoc all over my property. Groundhogs—or woodchucks, as they were more commonly known—are cute little brown creatures but they were also destructive bastards, devouring everything in my gardens, munching on my clapboard house, and using their long black nails to dig an elaborate network of burrows and tunnels that was compromising the foundation of my out-buildings. Their handiwork was also dangerous for my horses, who could easily break a leg if they stepped into one of the holes.

Dolby, who had diligently kept the woodchuck population in check, was sadly no longer with us. He ended up with the cancer everyone thought I had.

First the diagnosis was lymphoma, then melanoma. He was put on steroids and went through rounds and rounds of chemo over several months, which made him sick and cranky and the brown fur on his face turn ashen. I had hoped we could extend his life by a year or two. But despite multiple surgeries and visits to the veterinary oncologist, for which I wrote numerous large checks, the cancer metastasized. It took over his muscular little body and weakened him to the point where he needed to be put down. Dolby held out until I left for a trip to Beijing, at which point he made it very clear that it was time for him to go by growling and snapping at anyone who came within a foot of him. He must have sensed I didn't have the courage to do it myself. I delegated his care to my friend and neighbor, Jared, the only person I trusted enough to make the right decision if things took a turn for the worse.

When I got back from China, I buried Dolby high on the hill, near a stone wall, overlooking the Hudson River. I had his headstone engraved with his name, his dates (1994-2008), and the inscription, "Loyal Friend and Companion." It was by far one of the most devastating losses I had ever experienced. Dolby was not just a dog, he was family. We were a pack of two, the bond between us immutable. His passing left a cavernous hole in my heart, but in it was the beauty to have surrendered to a special type of unaccustomed and unconditional love. It arrived in my life unexpectedly—on four perfect little white paws—and I was able to hold onto it for fourteen years.

Without Dolby to hold off the marauding woodchuck population, I needed to break out the big guns from Walmart. I had tried every humane solution I could find, starting with all sorts of store-bought repellents, including fox urine and coyote dung. I applied homemade concoctions—mothballs, dog piss, ammonia, and epsom salts. I tossed gas cartridges down their burrows. I tried motion and noise devices. I even resorted to blasting music from my Walmart-bought CD player—Salt-n-Pepa, De La Soul, and Run-DMC, to be exact. But my woodchucks were way too wily and persistent for any of that. It appeared that they liked my taste in garden vegetables as much as my preferences in 80's hip-hop.

In the process of trying to evict them from under my hay shed, I set at least one Havahart trap, baited with apple slices and veggies, almost every night. Whenever I checked the traps at dawn, though, if I ever saw any furry movement inside, it was usually black and white instead of brown. *Oh no, not again*, I would sigh with frustration as I threw an old beach towel over the trap and loaded it into the back of my truck. Then I would speed toward the Livingston Bridge with all the windows down, hoping to get across the river before the skunk funk took over the truck, settling into the upholstery for good. On the other side of the river, I'd find a place to pull over and set the cage down on the ground asap. I remember one time in particular when I opened the trap door, but the cute little skunk just sat there, immobilized.

"Go on, go on, now. Git. Go on. Skedaddle!" At least I let you live, Mr. Skunk. Better to be estranged over here than dead; there must be plenty of nice skunk families on this side of the river. Maybe one of your French cousins like Pepé Le Pew lives around here? I poked at him with a stick through the back end of the trap, tipped it up, and he finally scampered out. It didn't matter what kind of varmint I caught—possums, feral cats, rats, rabbits, squirrels, even the occasional baby woodchuck: The second they realized the trap was open, they'd make a run for it. Every once in a while, though, there was one like Mr. Skunk who would pause, stop, and turn back to look at me in astonishment that I'd actually set him free. He stood tall on his hind feet, and I could have sworn I saw him wave graciously with one of his front paws before he bolted like Speedy Gonzales into the woods.

One of the best (and most surprising) perks of living upstate was that not one person said anything about my head. Ever. Not once. I take that back: Once in a while, someone might make a discreet indirect reference. But I never felt verbally or emotionally assaulted as I had in Manhattan, where it happened so often I'd come to expect it. One time the chubby check-out woman at the Home Depot in Catskill volunteered "Did you know we offer a 10 percent discount to military servicemen and women?" as she scanned the little plastic pots of rosemary, lavender, and oregano plants I was buying for my herb garden.

"No, I didn't know that," I answered with a polite smile. And she left it at that. I realized I was wearing my favorite camouflage cargo pants and a matching army green T-shirt, so her assumption made sense. I thought about the thousands of young men and women shipped off to Iraq and Afghanistan with blind faith and trust they'd eventually make it back home safely. While they were in the line of fire, manning tanks and heavy artillary, searching house to house for terrorists and weapons of mass destruction, I had the luxury of loading an assortment of pink tea roses, Velvet boxwoods, and 40-pound bags of pine bark mulch into my orange Home Depot shopping cart.

The reason the cashier's question didn't bother me was it didn't put me on the defensive about my health. I wasn't backed into that familiar cancer corner, forced to engage in a conversation I didn't want to have about an illness I had been lucky enough *not* to have been diagnosed with. She hadn't insinuated anything negative about my head. Her question allowed me a quick, easy answer without the burden of revealing any intimate personal details to a perfect stranger.

When I had bought my property several years earlier, I remember a few Manhattanites telling me that upstate New York was the place where people moved because they "couldn't cut it" in the city. On the one hand, they may have been right. Let's just say there was a significant percentage of the local population that didn't exactly look like Kate Moss. Nor could they be considered "highly gifted" in the cultural IQ department. People had heard of the Mets, but never the Met. The beautiful, svelte, stylish intelligentsia I spied plying the cobblestoned streets of the Meatpacking District were definitely nowhere to be found up here. Or the few times they were, I knew to immediately duck and steer clear.

On the other hand, perhaps some of my congenial Republican neighbors simply didn't want to live in the city. Maybe they didn't appreciate being awoken at 2 a.m. by blaring car alarms, ambulance sirens, random gunshots, honking truck horns, or music pumping from a mufflerless Honda Civic racing up Amsterdam Avenue. Maybe it didn't bother them that they had never stood behind a velvet rope in front of Nell's or seen Prince having cocktails at Moomba, that they'd never been to a private party for Russell Simmons at the Bowery Bar or eaten a steak frites dinner at 3 a.m. on a formica tabletop at Florent. Perhaps, at the end of the day, they just wanted to be able to make a legal right turn on red. Could it have been that the idea of living in a place with more highrises than apple trees made them shudder? Very possibly.

There was little or no chance top model scouts would be combing the Crossgates Mall off I-87 for the next Gisele anytime soon—unless of course they wanted one with a double chin and major adipose. There were a lot of seriously fat people in my new neck of the woods, and I don't mean just your run-of-the-mill overweight folk. I'm talking Fat Albert size: One—maybe even two—tons of morbidly obese fun.

Tattoos were also extremely popular in these parts; many folks were tatted up to their ears with the American Flag, "Donnie's Girl," butterflies, daggers, Guns N' Roses, and dragons all over every visible part—and probably some invisible ones, too. Josie, the check-out lady at Tractor Supply, was a good example. She was vampire-pale, skinny, green-eyed, had six kids, no college degree, and more than a dozen tattoos all over her—exactly like Angelina Jolie, the only difference being that she wasn't shacking up with Brad Pitt, and didn't

My Father photographed, developed, and printed this image of my property in upstate New York.

have to worry about being stalked by paparazzi.

If upstate New York was the rural outpost of figurative and metaphorical leprosy, I quickly became an accepted exile in the colony. No one stopped to shriek or stare when I pumped gas at the Mobil Xtra-Mart or ate my Adirondack Bear Paw double-scoop ice cream cone sitting at a picnic table outside the local Stewart's. Maybe they were just enlightened enough to mind their own business. I passed by toddlers and their country bumpkin parents in the aisle of the local Agway and people smiled at me—some of whom had toothless, gummy smiles. Children riding squeaky-wheeled grocery carts at ShopRite didn't point or giggle. Small daily occurrences like these amounted to unexpected blessings, allowing me the emotional breathing space I so desperately needed to begin the healing process. When I had hair, I had always taken simple graces such as respect for my privacy for granted. Never again. It was incredibly ironic to me that, for all of New York City's supposed sophistication, open-mindedness, tolerance, and intellectual firepower, for all its purported embrace of diversity and eclecticism, in the end, I needed to escape its presumptuous air and protracted grasp, moving upstate to this redneck paradise in order to finally catch my breath.

CHAPTER 23

HAVING IT ALL

My close friends came to visit me upstate while my frenemies checked in on the phone periodically, expressing their sincere concern about my decision to do the reverse commute and spend way more time in the boondocks than in Manhattan. They were all worried, though about exactly what I was never sure. Maybe they thought I'd been raped by a scarecrow or stabbed by a lumberjack. Or, if I was indeed still breathing, either sucked into some kind of *Blair Witch Project*, or dangerously content to swing in my hammock by a swamp deep in the woods, playing my harmonica while being eaten alive by swarms of West Nile-virus–carrying mosquitoes.

When they did call, the questions were all pretty predictable: "How are you? What do you do up there? Aren't you afraid, being all by yourself? Don't you get bored?"

I wasn't afraid and I most certainly wasn't bored. Okay, so maybe I found the *Farmer's Almanac* far more interesting reading than the May issues of *The New Yorker*, but so what? I wasn't bothering anyone. I had fashioned a perfectly happy, interesting, fulfilling, and—by city standards—highly unconventional life for myself. And in the process, I felt like I had finally regained some balance.

"Who are you dating up there? You must be seeing someone."

"No, I'm not really dating anyone," I would say, even though I was. He was a lovely man who had been married for 27 years and recently gotten divorced. We met playing tennis. He didn't Google me, nor I him. There were no emails or texts involved; no downloads, uploads, kilobytes, or megabytes. I let my guard down and we got to know each other. I was able to share what I wanted to share when I was ready to share it, just like back in the old days—when the pterodactyls and brontosauri freely roamed the Earth. He gave me keys to his house, baked me delicious cheese tarts filled with plump golden raisins, and shoveled my walkway during snowstorms. He said "God bless you" when I sneezed and picked up all the used tissues strewn over the bed sheets when I had a bad cold and couldn't reach the wastebasket. He was handsome, kind, and passionate. There were no games.

OPPOSITE In 1961, my Mother bought her first silver charm, a baby cup, to celebrate the birth of my brother, Sidney, her first child. She continued to collect the charms until she gave me this necklace for my 40th birthday. I continue the tradition by adding to it every year.

For me, the challenge in my twenties was how to not lose myself when I was in a serious relationship. Now, twenty years later, I was trying to learn how to let a man do things for me instead of being an island unto myself. I had grown accustomed to doing it all—jump-starting my car, fertilizing my lawn, and paying my bills—sometimes all at the same time. And while I didn't know what the future held for us, I felt I had finally attracted the type of man who was worthy of my trust.

As for my friends, it wasn't that I was trying to hide anything from them. I just didn't necessarily feel like giving them another opportunity to scrutinize the men I was dating or pass judgment on how I spent my time. I had finally decided to live my life by my own rules instead of following the old store-bought, paint-by-numbers kit.

"So, you must have a ton of free time now that you're up there so much," said my friend Sarah. "What do you find to do all day?" Maybe she thought I had quit working and was sitting in a rocking chair on my front porch all afternoon, darning old socks or knitting a wool scarf and matching mittens. Knit one, purl two. Or perhaps she was concerned I spent my evenings stargazing and chasing fireflies, collecting them in a Ball mason jar after carefully poking holes in its lid. It was like another version of the same question I used to hear all the time after my television show ended.

"Now what are you going to do since you aren't on TV anymore?"

"I'm going to do what I did before I had a show." It was almost as if they forgot I had had a lucrative career as an interior designer and that was what got me on television in the first place.

"Well, actually," I told Sarah, "I'm busy with my regular design work for clients. I also spend a lot of time with my friends and working outside, I guess." She sounded skeptical. "Friends? Like who? Do I know any of these people?" As if to imply that friendships in the Hudson River Valley had far less clout than those born in the 'burbs.

"I doubt it. Anyway, guess what—I just put in 15 new pear trees last week!" Maybe she could share a modicum of my enthusiasm for my attempt to live a greener, more sustainable lifestyle.

"That's great. Hey, I have someone I want to introduce you to. I think you might really like him. His name's John, and he's a friend of Brian's from Citigroup."

His last name had better be Deere, was my first thought. But, sure, what the heck, I wasn't married, I was always open to meeting new people, and a friend of Brian's might very well turn out to be a friend of mine....

"He went to Stanford undergrad and Harvard Business School and he just got divorced."

"Why'd he get divorced?"

"I don't really know. I think they just grew apart."

"How long were they married?"

"I'm not sure exactly—maybe 20 years. I'll have to ask Brian. There is one thing you should probably know."

"What's that?"

"I think he was having an affair with a young analyst from work."

"Oh, really?"

"Yeah and, uh, I think the analyst was actually a guy."

Oh please, Sarah. Did she think I was desperate? "Ah, I see. Well, I'm sure John's a great guy, but I think I'm better off on my own right now. So, thanks, but no thanks!"

Even though my parents had met on a blind date, when anyone suggested setting me up, I usually declined, especially since I no longer had hair. These days it seemed my friends only wanted to fix me up with two types: Either older versions of the assholes I had already dated in my twenties or physically challenged social misfits, which is apparently how they thought of me. I simply had to meet the gremlin from the gym with the harelip, the pointed shoes, the permanent limp, and the bum arm; the dwarf with the lazy eye and the gigantic Frida Kahlo–style unibrow; the nerd from down the hall who was "so much fun" but happened to have a lisp, an eye-patch, and a peg leg with a kickstand. Exaggerations aside, I was unclear about exactly what interests I shared with these guys. While I certainly didn't want to date a male version of myself, I wasn't sure that I had enough in common with these men to make a go of it. I was beginning to wonder whether our mutual friends thought the fact we both had good credit was enough to assure a match made in heaven.

What happened to all those handsome, rich, athletic, buff Ivy League assholes I had attracted all through my twenties and thirties? The ballers and shot callers? They were gone. Long gone. As my Mother often reminded me, one of the unexpected blessings of losing my hair was it "weeded out all the riffraff." I had to admit she was right. The kinds of men I used to date no longer approached me. Many of them were still single, but now they were dating women half my age. As these guys got older, they managed to stay in the George Clooney mold—forever desirable and elusive, with a bevy of age-inappropriate, Bambi-eyed beauties on their arms. Meanwhile, we—their female counterparts—were relegated to the Miss Marple spinster roles, old grey mares put out to pasture. Even Bridget Jones and Carrie Bradshaw had finally hooked up for good. I had about as much chance of reversing this trend—and the ageism it represented—as I did of altering the world's perception of female beauty and its relationship to hair. I hated the double standard, but what could I do?

These days, I just didn't care anymore whether you graduated from Princeton or were a partner at Debevoise & Plimpton. I wasn't interested in dating a man who needed to download an app on his iPhone to figure out how to roast a marshmallow on a stick. I didn't need a man who could write all the big checks he wanted to, but was emotionally bankrupt. What I really wanted was someone who owned a Kubota backhoe, who could install a sump pump, who knew how to use a Troy-Bilt log splitter to chop a cord of perfectly seasoned wood, without taking off his left arm, before neatly stacking it on my back porch.

Most of the men I had dated in the city fit the former description; it was a safe bet they knew how to call AAA for road assistance but had never actually changed a flat tire. Right now I was in a new phase where I wanted smart, dexterous men who smelled like turpentine, freshly cut grass, or rift-sawn oak. My taste in men was like my taste in furniture. It was fickle, which made it tough to find a satisfactory date. Some days I swooned over a mahogany neoclassical pedestal table with mother of pearl inlay I had seen in the window of a Madison Avenue antiques shop. Other days, I drooled over a distressed side chair with chipping yellow paint—the perfect patina—I found at the flea market. Meanwhile, most of my single women friends were still searching for Blair Underwood's stunt double—a 6-foot-something, handsome, unattached but emotionally available guy with a highly successful career who drove a late-model sports car. *Good luck*, I thought.

What my Mother had said about the "riffraff" wasn't gender specific. My new life helped weed out some of my female friends as well. For the first time in a long time, I slowed down enough to take inventory. I serendipitously let some of my more "high maintenance" friendships slip by the wayside. I sorted out the perpetual takers from the sometime-givers, the ones who would offer support and compassion when it was called for from the ones who couldn't or wouldn't. It was always easy to find a crowd of adoring female fans (and haters) when things were going exceptionally well, but when they weren't you found out who your true friends were. If my Mother was having open-heart surgery and all you could think to do was harass me about choosing the perfect paint color for your mudroom, then chances were I'd be showing you the door a long time before you got a glimpse of my Benjamin Moore paint chips.

"Sheila, hey, I'm in a bit of a hurry, but would you mind giving me your housekeeper's name and phone number? Do you know of a good accountant? How about a real-estate broker? Can I get your painter's phone number? What was the name of that hotel in Hong Kong? Who's your caterer? Can you recommend a good upholsterer? A wallpaper hanger? A reliable electrician?"

Obviously I was happy to give referrals to friends—and I would ask them for the same—but if the only time I ever heard from you was when you demanded a resource, then all friendship bets were off.

I grew apart from some of my platonic male friends as well, particularly those who had recently gotten married. Their wives didn't seem to want me around, especially if the road to getting their player–boyfriends to the altar had been long and bumpy. As with most marriages, the wives were in charge of the social calendar and it made a lot more sense to them to fill it with other married couples. If they were going to have single women hanging around, those singletons were going to be her friends, not his. Having grown up with plenty of unmarried and divorced aunts, this seemed odd to me. Some of them were my Father's friends from long before my parents' marriage. My Mother never seemed to be threatened by any of them, and there were probably some she didn't even like. But she tolerated their presence simply because she knew my Dad valued their friendships. So what was the big deal with my friends' wives? Were they that insecure?

Ironically, when it came to dating, being single turned out to be a liability. Most of the people I knew who were having full-blown affairs were married— both men and women cheating on their spouses with other married men and women. It made total sense. If you were going to risk stepping outside your marriage, it was better to be doing it with someone who had as much to lose as you did.

For some reason, I convinced myself that relationships in general would get easier as I got older. It turned out the opposite was true. I also hadn't expected them to be quite so transitory or disposable. I struggled with some of my alpha female friends, too—particularly those who had given up their careers to live in the suburbs and raise families. I'm guessing some of them thought my life was shallow, frivolous, and devoid of meaningful responsibility. It didn't help my case if I shared stories about going snowboarding in Dubai, flying to the Winter Games in Torino, a birthday dinner in Vicenza, or two weeks at polo school in Argentina. I totally understood why they were compelled to hang

OPPOSITE I took the VW photograph in Vicenza, Italy, while I was attending a birthday celebration. The ticket stubs are from events at the 2006 Torino Winter Olympics games.

ABOVE LEFT I was on a polo pony at a friend's ranch in Argentina.

ABOVE RIGHT The detail of the ceiling of a galleria in Turin, Italy, inspired the design of my Torino Damask wallpaper.

out almost exclusively with other moms who had kids the same ages as theirs. Likewise, I had a lot more in common with other single, financially independent women who were focused on their careers and/or entrepreneurs who ran their own businesses.

I was able to make peace with the notion that as we get older, our lives stretch in unpredictable ways, and we need to shift in new directions to meet those changes, even though, sadly, it also meant sometimes relationships that used to work no longer do. What I didn't necessarily get—what made me uncomfortable—was seeing several of my old friends channel their inner CEOs to the point where they would still call me fairly often but almost never had time for a conversation. They approached their household tasks, wifely duties, recreational tennis games, and Zumba classes with the same level of intensity and competitiveness they had when they were working their way up the corporate ladder. I would get these 12-second drive-by calls that would go something like this:

"Hi, Sheila, How're you? What's going on?""

"I'm fine. Just busy, I guess. Right now, I'm really excited because I just found out that one of my new wallpaper designs is going to be featured in the Cooper Hew—"

"You know what? I'm in the car pool line, I just got to the front and the girls are about to jump in. Can I give you a call back later?"

"Oh, okay. Bye," I would say, dumbfounded, thinking, *Hey, wait a second. I didn't call you, you called me.* I might not hear back for another three weeks. Either they were way too busy or they just couldn't relate to my life anymore, just as I couldn't relate to theirs.

When we finally did catch up, they often seemed completely frazzled and utterly burdened by the stresses of motherhood, even though they had enlisted small armies of professional helpers in their quest to achieve the perfect cul-de-sac lifestyle. Apparently, the way you raised children nowadays was to ensure them a full competitive edge: You gave them absolutely everything money could buy; you over-scheduled their days with a thousand important activities essential to their development. As mother and social secretary, it was your responsibility to shuttle them to and from playdates and all their other scheduled appointments on time. Your husband's job was to fill up the bank account, write the checks, and make guest appearances on weekends.

"Sorry Sheila, but this weekend is a little tough. Peter has soccer practice at ten on Saturday, Mandarin lessons at one, millinery class at two thirty, and then it's off to the allergist at three thirty. India has ballet at nine, tennis intensive at eleven, theater workshop at one, Regent rock climbing at two thirty, and papier-mâché at three thirty. Aiden has jazz piano at eight thirty, Metropolitan metal-smithing at noon, Fairfield fencing lessons before Tae Kwon Do, and conversational Russian at three thirty. I need to get to the dry cleaners to pick up Carl's suits by two and be back to meet the caterer at three, the florist at four and then the kids have to all be home and dressed by five because we've got Susan Greene coming to shoot the children for the Christmas card. She's the professional photographer from Glamour Shots in the Paramus Park Mall. Maybe we can get together next Saturday."

Good grief! It was exhausting just listening to this. Forget about the 4 year old; I was the one who needed a nap. Didn't kids ever get any down time anymore? Weren't they ever allowed to "just play," to use their imaginations and make up games? Weren't my friends at all concerned that they were grooming the next generation of entitled assholes? But what could you say? Were you going to be the first one to convince your Suburban Supermom friends that it was all just a little bit too much?

I was never surprised when their kids acted out or their relationships with their husbands fell apart. Most of their men had been cheating on them for years and they chose to turn a blind eye, far more concerned about maintaining appearances and holding onto their toney lifestyles than being positive role models for their children. I felt like some of them had become professional nags—overbearing, bossy, and controlling—hassling their husbands and riding their kids' backs about everything from keeping up their extracurricular schedules to what topping they should order on their Domino's thin-crust pizza. God forbid I should have the rare pleasure of riding in the front passenger seat of their Volvo SUV on our way out to dinner.

"Thomas, make a right at the light. I said right, not left. Okay, now go straight for half a mile, then left at the Citgo station." Who needs GPS when you're married to a world-class back-seat driver?

"Thomas, what are you doing? Are you not listening to me? I just said left at the Citgo. All right, we're due at the restaurant now, so when we get there you can just drop us at the door, we'll go in and get the table and you go find a parking place."

"Thomas, did you confirm the dinner reservation? What?! I thought your secretary was going to do that."

Totally exasperated—lips trembling, jaw clenched, brow furrowed—she

OPPOSITE My Harlem Toile De Jouy wallpaper is in my upstate New York kitchen.
ABOVE Later, my porcelain dinner plates would have the same designs as those on the original wallpaper.

would jump out of the car before it stopped moving. Contrary to what most people believe, you don't have to be the CFO of a Fortune 500 in order to properly emasculate your husband and the father of your children.

I would glance over at Thomas with a look of compassion that said, "So very sorry, pal." Then I would jump out, following Boss Lady into the restaurant.

In situations like these—and they happened more than you might imagine—I often found myself thinking, *How do these guys stand it?* If this is who I have to become in order to fulfill the married-with-kids dream, then I think I'll pass.

Once in a while I mustered enough courage to offer an unsolicited opinion. It was usually something along the lines of, "Hey, our parents worked full time while they raised us and I think we managed to turn out pretty okay without all the extra professional help and wall-to-wall extracurricular activities. Sometimes, it gets to be too much, don't you think?"

So shoot me for having a momentary lapse, for forgetting the Number One Rule of Maintaining Friendships with Married Woman Who No Longer Have a Career: Don't ever, under any circumstances, question or offer advice about their parenting or marital skills. Ever. Not even when they ask for it. You don't have a husband or children, so what the hell do you know about dealing with men or raising kids?

Maybe we could make a deal. Perhaps in exchange, they could adhere to the Number One Rule of Maintaining Friendships with Single Women Who Held Onto Their Careers: Don't ever, under any circumstances, question our choice to have a meaningful occupation, our decision not to get hitched, or our biological urge not to have children.

But, seriously, rules like that would never work, even for me. Just because you're not an entrepreneur doesn't mean you can't come up with a brilliant business idea; just because you don't have a husband doesn't mean you know nothing of the minds of men. I knew it would go a long way toward keeping the peace if we could just agree to respect one another's personal choices. Many times, the grass appears greener in someone else's life, especially when you're in the middle of having a very bad day.

All of these "confrontations" with my friends who had become fully committed suburban wives and mothers led me to reflect on the myth of Having It All. Most of them had bought into it wholeheartedly. But what if it was just that—a charade drummed up by a dim-witted man and his allies to keep us women forever running uphill on life's treadmill, wearing six-inch stiletto heels, competing with—instead of appreciating—one another, always striving to do more, have more, be better, even though we were doing a bang-up job already? Weren't we strong and motivated enough of our own accord? Who really needed the added social and media pressure to be Super Woman, to become the perfect daughter, sister, girlfriend, wife, mother, friend, sister-in-law, godmother, aunt?

What if Having It All was overrated? Or if it turned out to be one gigantic elaborately constructed sexist Ponzi scheme we were sold on since we were little girls, one that robbed us of any significant returns on our emotional investment? How come I never saw my male friends clamoring like crabs in a bucket to Have It All? How come you never saw men on *Oprah*, all choked up as they talked about desperately vying for it? I came to believe you could manifest your own version of Having It All and that maybe it wasn't about having everything as soon as possible but instead being satisfied with having some of it, some of the time—and forget about having all of it, all of the time.

It started one sunny autumn afternoon. I was out in the country driving with the top down, still barreling down the winding road to Having It All. I saw a deer crossing up ahead and braked quickly to a crawl. Where there's one there are always more to follow. Sure enough, two more does came over the embankment, bounding out from behind a row of trees whose clotted colors had changed with the season. They were followed by a little spotted fawn on stilt-like legs trotting unsteadily across the asphalt. I waited until they had all passed in front of my car and across the road before accelerating again. But after about 100 yards, I suddenly thought, Having It All sure sounds like a lot of responsibility; like a helluva heavy mother lode to carry around all by yourself, unless of course you want to throw your back out. So what's wrong with trusting in the belief that it's perfectly okay not to "have it all?"

I checked my rearview mirror to make sure no one was on my tail, slowed down, made a U-turn, and gradually sped up, heading for home with a smile on my face, feeling the warmth of the sun on my bare head and the crisp, dry wind chasing my back, thinking about the stretch of road in front of me and the beautiful Indian summer days ahead.

CHAPTER 24

BLUE RONDO À LA TURK

I found out from my friend Diane about the *Godiva Getaway Weekend Experience Special* offered by the Providence Downtown Marriott for Memorial Day weekend. She had reserved two rooms—one for herself and her husband, the other for their three boys. Their middle son Alex was my godson.

The Marriott extravaganza was $199 per night and it included a buffet breakfast for two, complimentary parking, and assorted Godiva chocolates. Just what I needed—a romantic getaway to Rhode Island, where I could start my day standing in line at the omelet station before piling as many overcooked, translucent grey sausages as I could fit on my white breakfast plate. And much later, at the end of the evening, after gently pulling the polyester-blend, flame-retardant, patterned drapes shut to block my glorious panorama of the parking lot, after brushing my teeth and easing back the beige synthetic-fabric bedspread, I could finish it by savoring the delicious chocolate amenity that had been strategically positioned on my crisp white pillowcase by housekeeping.

Okay, in all seriousness, the real reason I was even considering signing on for the Godiva deal was it conveniently coincided with my 25th college reunion. In addition to Diane, a few of my other good friends from Brown had called to say they were going. I was on the fence about it and they were trying to coax me. Twenty-five years sounded like a long time. It was hard to believe that a quarter of a century had blown by so quickly. I had attended my fifth and 10th reunions and had had a great time, so why was I feeling so conflicted about my 25th?

I heard from Donna, who lived in Maryland and worked as a perinatologist in high-risk OB at Johns Hopkins. She was leaving her husband and two young children at home. "Come on," she said. "You really should go! It'll be fun."

Celeste, my roomate senior year, texted me several times, then called. She sounded almost as excited as the day she got accepted by Weill Cornell Medical College: "Sheila, you've gotta go. It'll be a blast to see everyone. I'm driving up from North Carolina and I'm rooming with Petra!"

But for all of my friends' enthusiasm, I wasn't totally convinced it was worth getting stuck in bumper-to-bumper holiday weekend traffic or a 30-car pile-up on I-95 to head back to Providence, and mingle with a bunch of folks I reasoned

---

OPPOSITE In a portrait of the four of us, taken by a family friend in 1969, I was five years old and my brother was eight.

were liable to be no more intriguing than they were the first time around. How much better could they be? No doubt we had all succumbed to the inevitable physical changes that accompany middle age, which meant that all those big, handsome, sexy football players I had crushes on freshman year would have gone from brawny to beefy—or worse. A tire around your middle equals pudgy not pretty. I imagined all my male classmates who wore thick, fluffed-up mullets and drippy Jheri curls in the 80s now resorting to comb-overs to hide bald spots roughly the shape and size of Texas. Most men just don't age as gracefully as Paul Newman or Sidney Poitier; they sport realistic reminders of their advancing years. One could only hope they had enough restraint to let it happen naturally and not resort to plastic surgery. I pictured the likes of Bruce Jenner or Billy Crystal, who could have easily presented themselves as distinguished older gentlemen but instead opted to have their faces stretched so they looked more like the Japanese hostess who worked at Benihana.

I suspected my female classmates may have fared better than our male counterparts, since most of us could now finally afford the time and money to take a lot better care of ourselves than when we were in college. Back then, our friends and roommates gave us bad touchups, colored cellophanes, peroxide jobs, or asymmetric shag haircuts. We bought slightly rank, dingy used clothes from the Army Navy store on Thayer Street. Our eagerness to have our long, tapered fingernails painted *Fuschia Fiasco* or *Tangerine Dream* by the girl in our Comp Lit class instead of a professional manicurist at a salon bespoke of our youth. Either that or we desparately yearned for our hands to look just like Alexis Carrington's on *Dynasty*—even though we were broke. Okay, so maybe there would be more crow's feet perched on our faces than in Hitchcock's *The Birds*. And, at our age, what could be wrong with a couple of extra pounds jiggling here or there or a few stray grey hairs on top, especially if they had been carefully coiffed and tended to like a well-trimmed Bonsai? Better that than the big, crimped hair full of mousse tucked under a Buten painter's cap; the tacky dresses with gigantic shoulder pads; and the high-waisted, ripped Lee jeans disguised by black-knit leg warmers—the perfect Jennifer Beals *Flashdance* ensemble. We were "together" women in our late-forties now, confident in our mature good looks and tastefully age-appropriate fashion statements.

As usual I worried about my own appearance, mostly wondering if going back to campus meant I'd be thrust into irritating Q-and-A sessions about my head. I assumed the vast majority of my classmates knew nothing of my hair loss. I'd finally become more adept at handling the annoying question, at letting it hang in the air momentarily, ducking to get out of the way before it boomer-anged back to its sender. But it was always lingering in the back of my mind. Seeing a shrink had helped me learn *not* to take it so personally, not to let it seep under my skin. "Like water off a duck's back," my friends upstate constantly reminded me. I understood better now that often, what people said out loud was merely what was on their minds—unripened or misplaced projections of their own fears and insecurities, prematurely verbalized.

What if the reunion turned out to be an opportunity for people to brag about all their accomplishments since graduation? *Hey everybody, I was an unpopular computer geek in 1982, but look at me now: I'm a billionaire with a private jet, a trophy wife, adorable dimpled, freckle-faced kids, and a postcard-perfect lifestyle.* I already stayed in touch with the classmates I cared about, so did I really need to go to a reunion to see them? My freshman roommate, Laurie, who had the distinction of being the only practicing female thoracic surgeon in the state of Rhode Island, also reached out, kindly offering me one of her guest bedrooms if I decided to come; our friend Lisa was coming from Dallas and staying with her.

"I'm not sure," I said, especially because in the back of my mind I knew what I really should be doing was heading to Philly, instead. We had put my parents' house on the market and I needed to continue packing. My Father's condition was steadily deteriorating and it was becoming harder for my Mother to manage caring for him—along with our big, old house and property—by herself.

I told my Mom that I couldn't make up my mind about my reunion. "Just go," she concluded. "You really should go. You loved college. It was such a special time in your life and you just don't know—you may never see some of those people again. You can come home next weekend and pack. There's no rush. It can wait." She was right. It was highly unlikely I'd be at my 50th. Twenty-five years could be the right amount of elapsed time to have gained some real-life perspective, some "grown" knowledge and experience. And I had to admit, the more I thought about it, the more curious I became about how things had panned out for my classmates. With everything going on in Philadelphia, I hardly felt gung-ho about the reunion weekend. But I decided to buy myself a new dress for the class dinner, just in case. Like most women I know, I had a closet full of beautiful clothes but nothing to wear. Maybe a shopping trip would be the pick-me-up I needed to get in a celebratory mood. I went to one of my favorite boutiques, Catherine Malandrino, on Broome Street, downtown in SoHo.

As soon as I walked into the store, I spotted a lovely little black cotton dress hanging on the rack and took it off to have a closer look. *Perfect.*

"Would you like me to start a fitting room for you?" said a strangely familiar voice from behind me. When I turned to face the salesman, I had an immediate flash of recognition. It wasn't just the whiny voice but his face. *Shit. What's his name? C'mon, Sheila. Think! You know this guy—what the heck is his name?* I racked my brain. Then it hit me: It was Kimon from Bloomingdale's. The nitwit salesperson who had the gall to ask if my Father had fucked a Swede. I would never forget that offensive comment or that face—even though now, 25 years later, it was no longer youthfully chiseled but bloated and slightly doughy. As I followed him to the fitting room, I noticed he had a round bald spot the size of a hamburger bun on the back of his head. *Well, I'll be damned,* I thought as I swung the shirred fabric curtain closed.

I handed him the dress and my American Express card at the cash register, hesitated for a moment, then decided to say something. "You used to work at Bloomingdale's."

"Oh, my God. Yes I did, but that was, like, 20 years ago. How did you *know?*" he asked as he rang me up and wrapped my dress in yellow tissue paper.

"Actually, we both worked in Men's Designers—on the first floor."

"Holy shit. You're kidding! No way! I can't believe it. Wow, you've got a great memory. What's your name?"

"Sheila... Sheila Bridges."

"Doesn't ring a bell. Do you still work at Bloomie's?"

"No." I chuckled. "I wasn't even there for a whole year."

"So, what do you do now?"

"You mean for a living? I'm a designer."

"A fashion designer?"

"No, an interior designer, actually."

"Wow. It's so funny that you remember *me* because I can't exactly place you..."

Of course, you can't, I thought as he handed my card back. "Well," I said, "I looked much younger and had a lot more hair then."

He still couldn't seem to recall.

"By the way, my name is Kimon."

"Yes, I know that. Have a nice day, Kimon," I said as I smiled, took my shopping bag, turned, and walked out of the store.

I was oddly reassured by my interaction with Kimon. It bolstered my belief that most people *don't* really change all that much. Some folks pay close attention; others don't. And there are still others who remain astonishingly clueless—even after 25 years. In this case, it felt good to be the one who was clued in.

I hadn't expected to feel so emotional when I first returned to the Brown campus on Friday afternoon. It had been fifteen years since my last visit. It caught me by surprise. Being back there was like unexpectedly bumping into a good friend whose smile is eclipsed by your own when you see them from across the street. Someone who knows you well enough to recognize your walk—a crony you had been in cahoots with long ago but with whom you'd lost touch, even though you once felt deeply connected. The feeling was familiar. It was the same one I felt back in 1981 when I was still in high school and visited the campus for the very first time, with my Father.

The much-anticipated annual campus dance, held that Friday night of our reunion, was a bit anti-climactic for me, probably because my expectations were way too high. It was like having your friends go on and on about how amazing a movie is—"a must-see!" Then when you finally go, it's a let-down because you already read the book. Part of my disappointment had to do with the overwhelming crowd—current students, their friends and families, faculty and alumni of all ages—with everybody stumbling around their old stomping grounds in the dark, like a horde of zombies. But instead of having their arms out in front of them like in the movies, these zombies were clutching—and chugging from—red plastic tumblers full of cranberry juice and cheap house vodka on ice, paid for by movie-theater–style paper tickets that most of us had ordered online in advance.

The get-ups ran the gamut. For the women, they ranged from low-rider skinny jeans to skimpy one-shouldered and spaghetti-strapped numbers, from vintage shifts or colorful cocktail dresses to frumpy, festooned silk-taffetta gowns. The men were clad in everything from pin-striped business suits to jeans with hoodies, from tuxedos to trousers with sport coats, Nehru collars, and striped rep ties—even the occasional leisure suit. Everybody was shod in every type of footwear from stilettos, wing-tips, sandals, sneakers, flip flops, and Hush Puppies, to clogs and cowboy boots. A few people even dared to walk the campus green in bare feet, a choice I deemed more unsightly than unsanitary. (Although it didn't help that the walkways were sticky underfoot and reeked of spilled keg beer.) The crowd was certainly representative of the confluence of styles that was uniquely Brown. In the words of Whodini, "The freaks come out at night." The problem was, I didn't recognize hardly any of them. Why didn't I see more folks I knew? And why did so many faces look so goddamned young—like they could have been my own kids?

One of the things I loved most about my alma mater was that as an institution,

TOP I was photographed alongside Donna Neale, *left*, and Joyce Bishop, two of my
college buddies from Brown University.
ABOVE I am tearing up the dance floor at "Funk Nite" with friend and classmate Rich Taylor.
Petra Thomas is in the foreground.

it never aspired to be greater than the sum of its parts. You could graduate from Brown and go out into the world, encouraged to do great things. It seemed to me that a place like Harvard, for instance, would always be greater in name and reputation than the students themselves, or the contributions they made. Even if you won the Nobel Prize in physics or discovered a cure for AIDS, Harvard would still always be bigger and more important than you.

Within the next 24 hours, the reunion venues got smaller, and I finally saw everyone I really cared about seeing. My core crew was there at our class picnic, the same girls I had been friends with since freshman year, when we were only eighteen: Donna, Diane, and Celeste, my roommate Laurie, and her friend Lisa. Even Arnold, my head counselor, who lived down the hall when I was a freshman, was there with his ten-year-old son, Cameron.

Arnold was three years older than me and had been my college boyfriend's best friend. When Kevin and I broke up, Arnold and I grew closer as he shared many secrets of our ill-fated romance, such as the fact that Kevin's mother never liked me because I hadn't worn a proper slip or stockings under my dress the first time I had gone with his family to church. Arnold had been more of a class mascot than a classmate. The reunion would have felt decidedly empty without him.

I had even managed to convince my friend Joyce to crawl out of her hermitic shell, set aside some of her more misanthropic tendencies, and come down from Cambridge to hang out for a few hours at my hotel. We had been roommates in Brooklyn when we first graduated from Brown, living together in a boxy two-bedroom apartment whose only distinguishing feature was the tiny stackable washer-dryer hidden in a closet behind white hollow-core, bifold doors. Twenty-five years later, she still had the kind of big, contagious laugh that seduced you into laughing with her until you keeled over because your stomach hurt. It was the kind of infectious laughter that I was convinced could lure strangers, sway dignitaries, persuade world leaders to break treaties and topple Fascist regimes.

And among the hundreds of other Brown denizens, there was also a slew of folks I always thought seemed nice but whom I never really took the time to get to know: The heavy-set girl with the short, wispy bangs from my Italian class; the clean-cut, soft-spoken boy in the zippered cardigans I used to sit next to in Engineering 9 who reminded me of Mr. Rogers. It felt good to have an opportunity to reconnect with these people and find out we had more in common than I would have ever suspected back in the day.

Much to my surprise, I even saw my very first freelance design clients at the

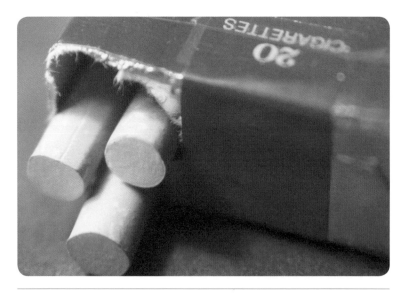

Lark filtered cigarettes were my Father's favorites. He took this shot of the pack. As a child,
I made him lots of clay ashtrays in art class because he refused to quit smoking.

reunion picnic—the couple that felt compelled to target me with their personal
diatribe that fateful Monday more than two decades before, attempting to put
me, with my unruly appearance and ratty hair, in my place. He hadn't aged
much at all, but still had the same elephant breath, and she had the same big,
warm smile and picky hair. They had their two kids with them—a boy and girl,
both of them playing the roles of real, life-sized teenagers in their casual yet
chaotic demeanor and awkward confidence. I wondered if one day my
ex-clients might have a problem with their own daughter's appearance. How
would they inaugurate her to the socially acceptable beauty standards she would
need to follow as she grew up? Would they teach her that it was okay in our
culture to be objectified as a woman, constantly striving for physical perfection
that was unattainable? Would they prepare her for our societal preoccupation
with youth and beauty, explain to her that she would be constantly judged by
both men and women based on her looks? As loving parents would they sit her
down at their breakfast room table and tell her she wasn't good enough for some
random guy because of the way she dressed or styled her hair?

Even funnier still, far from telling me I wasn't "trophyesque" enough, now
suddenly the husband kept pawing at me, telling me how great I looked and
even calling me a "rock star." I thought of Bono and Bruce Springsteen, with
crowds of adoring fans frantically screaming their names. I laughed to myself,

Plato wrote: "Music and rhythm find their way into the secret places of the soul."
My Father took a photograph of his own hand on his Baldwin baby grand.

wondering exactly what he really meant, then eventually decided not to over-analyze for a change, but to take it as a compliment and simply leave it at that.

When I arrive home and ring the doorbell, my Father answers the door. He carries my bags into the house as he's always done, just like when I was in college and home for the holidays. The only difference is he no longer knows my name. He still sometimes speaks, though rarely. When he does, the words don't always form real sentences. Everything seems to come out jumbled and repetitive, as if improvised yet *ostinato*. My Mother often speaks for him now, which I find ironic, since he was always so reserved and quiet by nature, as opposed to my Mom, who is relentlessly chatty and blessed with the gift of gab. Either way, her voice has become his.

My Father is in perfect physical health. No heart trouble, diabetes, or hyper-tension—like my Mother. No emphysema or lung cancer after smoking nearly a pack a day for most of his life—since he was only 15. The only positive contribution Alzheimer's made to his life was that one day he simply forgot to pick up his pack of cigarettes and light up.

His mental capacity continues to diminish daily. He has become a shadow of the man he was. He spends most of his time in our sun porch, sitting on the red leather loveseat, slumped over but not asleep. He has developed a strange new habit—a nervous tic of sorts—constantly rubbing his right thumb and index finger together, as if he is perpetually adding a dash of salt to his favorite coconut cream pie recipe. His baby grand piano remains in the sunporch, too. On it sits a stack of wrinkled sheet music by Chopin and Brahms, hidden behind books containing Rachmaninoff's *Piano Concerto No. 2*, Mozart's *Piano Concerto No. 23*, and Erik Satie's *Gymnopédie No. 1*. The ecru pages filled with black musical notes and bars are exactly where he placed them a couple of years ago. They still read like braille to me since I quit taking piano lessons all those years ago. His metronome sits in its wooden case, undisturbed too, without a pulse, shut tight.

Behind the Baldwin are the floor-to-ceiling bookcases he built to house his large collection of novels, and art and photography books. Books on gardening, Merck manuals, *Encyclopedia Britannica* sets, well-worn hardcovers, and tattered paperbacks—one of which, unbeknownst to both of my parents, was responsible for most of my sex education as a teenager. When they were out to dinner, I would scale the shelves for my Dad's copy of *The Happy Hooker*, authored by a Dutch former-secretary turned prostitute named Xaviera Hollander, and published in 1972. I would sneak the book down from the very top shelf and into my bedroom, poring over pages of highly explicit accounts of her life as a New York City madam. I remember reading passages aloud to my friend Nancy, pausing every once in a while, at the juiciest parts, to watch her jaw drop.

All of my Dad's books still line the sagging shelves, framed by marble and metal bookends, along with the thick black vinyl portfolio binders of his photographs, each one labeled meticulously in black Sharpie marker: Art Museum, Nassau, Mummer's Day Parade, Costa Rica, Colorado, Niagara Falls, Fireworks! Montreal, Memorial Day, The Philadelpha Zoo, Hershey Park, and Great Adventure.

Today my Father is wearing a starched white button-down cotton shirt, a beige Ralph Lauren cashmere vest, wool gabardine slacks, his favorite brown leather belt, and shoes. He still knows how to tie his own necktie into a perfectly arranged knot. He is dressed for work but no longer has a job or anywhere to go except for the occasional doctor's appointment. This afternoon he is sitting in the blue upholstered chair in our living room with his head tilted way back, asleep, with his mouth wide open. A CD is playing on his stereo as always and I recognize the track immediately. It is one of his favorites: Dave Brubeck's "Blue Rondo à la Turk." There is a rarely a day when we don't have the stereo blaring, since the music seems to soothe him—reaching him in ways we no longer can.

It looks like my Mother may have gained a couple of pounds since the last time I saw her and the skin on her face has brown splotches from too much time spent in the sun when she was young. Her diabetes and hypertension cause complications from time to time, and I worry she may be at risk for another heart attack from too much stress. She just had a procedure done last week at Wills Eye Hospital to get rid of the floaters in her left eye. She's also suddenly anemic, and I'm not sure why. Her doctor recently diagnosed her with osteoporosis, which she seemed to take, like everything else, in stride. Her body is broken down but her mind and spirit are lucid and fully intact. Mentally, she's still got it going on. Sharp as a tack. She drives herself to the beauty salon to get her hair done and a manicure every other Friday, and to church service and Bible study on Sundays.

She continues to dress in stylishly color-coordinated outfits, like the dandelion-yellow Valentino sweater and canary-colored paisley pants with the matching Ferragamo patent leather shoes on her narrow size seven-and-a-half feet. At wedding receptions, she's still the first person to enthusiastically jump out of her seat and onto the dance floor in anticipation of The Electric Slide.

It's a good thing my Mother taught kindergarten for 35 years. She possesses the type of interminable and superhuman patience required to properly care for my Father. She is kind to him most days, but sometimes she loses her temper. I suspect it's mostly out of frustration. He is not the man she married 52 years ago. This is not what she bargained for or how it was *supposed* to be. Their relationship gives new meaning to the vows they took on July 16, 1960: *In sickness and in health. For better and for worse.* Surely nothing can be worse for her than this.

She calls me five times a day and drives me absolutely crazy the same way she did twenty years ago. A decade past. Five years gone by. Yesterday.

"Do you know your Father had the nerve to put his keys in the dishwasher!"

She speaks to him like he's five years old: "Come on, Sid, it's time to eat dinner. Now let's wash your hands and sit down at the breakfast table. Would you like some Coca-Cola? Or maybe a glass of chardonnay?" Tonight they're having one of her culinary specialties: a Celeste mushroom–cheese pizza zapped for three minutes in the microwave. It's a good thing, since lately it appears my Father has forgotten how to hold a fork in his hand.

Gone are the two young, feisty parents I grew up with. They were generous as often as they were tough. Selfish on Thursday, selfless by Saturday. Imperfect, but always intent on doing "the right thing." They embarrassed me like all our parents do, by talking too much or saying too little, showing up in my room uninvited or picking me up from the party at the wrong time. They seemed fiercely independent and unstoppable then. I feared them almost as much as I loved them, seeking their approval and wanting to make them proud. Now, they cling to each other as if aware of the fragility of their future, completely co-dependent and increasingly reliant on their two adult children. Maybe I could ask the Universe to attach my Mother's mind to my Father's body. Then I would have one whole, complete parent—one whom I wish might live forever.

T he time had come to pack it all up. What do you do with all the stuff you've collected and inherited over the course of a lifetime? The proof of a well-lived life with all its spectacular moments, bittersweet memories, and unpredictable mishaps. Do I simply throw out the old wood and graphite tennis racquets and trophies; my parents' bowling balls; my Mother's handmade, hooked-wool bathroom rugs; my Father's old Lionel trains; my grandmother's cut-glass punch bowl; and all the hideous, misshapen clay ashtrays I made for my Dad in art class? What do I do about these closets full of stuff my family had acquired, and more important, what about all the intangibles we've accumulated over the years and are now quietly hoarding in our hearts?

The basic stuff was a piece of cake—getting rid of pairs of old wide-wale corduroys, worn shag rugs, vacuum cleaner bags, and used mop heads. Even some of the bigger pieces were easy—like the prosaic Scandinavian furniture and the gargantuan Mitsubishi TV in the basement, the one my Father and brother were glued to all those nights, watching the Eagles and Sixers games. But then there are things that really don't hold any inherent value but are suddenly viewed through softer, more nostalgic eyes. Some of them become powder-coated with sentimentality; they take on new depths of meaning. The more I packed, the more reflective I became. *Hmmm. Should I keep the rusty old ironing board?* Probably not. The white pedestal dining table in our breakfast room was not just the place we ate every day as a family, but where my Father helped me cram at 5 a.m. for those dreaded chemistry tests when I was in tenth grade.

My bottom dresser drawer was still full of the artifacts from a former life. It spoke of a little girl who had a thick head of untamable hair: Rainbow-colored scrunchies, Goody hair ties, Conair blow dryers, diffusers, bobby pins, hot rollers, elastics, hair clips, headbands, and curling irons of every barrel size

My Dad shot and developed this photograph of me in the rose garden of our backyard.
Gardening and photography were two of his great passions.

imaginable. I dumped all of it into a large black contractor bag, without any sadness or self-pity—but with compassion and empathy for a young, naïve girl with
the two thick plaits who knew nothing of the twists and turns in the road ahead.

What do you do about the personal things, the stuff that really *does* matter?
What about the tangible evidence of my parents' various hobbies and interests
beyond their work and careers, like all of my Father's photographs and 35mm
Ektachrome slides? I was the subject of so many of those images, as were my
brother and Mother. There were thousands of them. I left the difficult task of
dismantling my Dad's darkroom to Sidney. It was a place where I had spent an
inordinate amout of time when I was young, particularly during the awkward,
metal-mouthed, ugly-duckling years around the sixth and seventh grades. My

My Father photographed this hybrid tea rose in our backyard. We developed this image together in the basement darkroom of our family home.

Father's parents had given him a chemistry kit as a gift in 1944, and after that he always wanted to be a chemist. When one of his experiments, involving a Reynolds ballpoint pen and some potassium nitrate, blew a hole through their basement wall, they firmly suggested he convert his chemistry lab to a darkroom. Photography was the perfect hobby for my Father. It was an artistic yet socially acceptable medium that allowed him to indulge his fascination with toxic chemicals—mixing all those darkroom solutions—without blowing anything to smithereens.

For two years, I spent my Saturday nights alongside my Father in the dark as he projected his negatives onto a piece of crisp white Kodak paper. Much to my Mother's dismay, we would use the washbasins in our basement laundry room to hold trays of chemical developer and fixer. I would use a pair of rubber-coated tongs to move the paper gently around in the trays, waiting for the egg timer to ring and foggy resemblances to gradually appear before they suddenly accelerated into clear focus—the silhouette of a familiar face or a colorful back-yard flower blooming off the page. We would rinse the prints and hang them up to dry using clothespins on a line, like freshly laundered socks.

"Too much cyan and not enough magenta," my Father would pronounce grave-ly as he examined a photo, jotting down notes and numbers. We'd go back at it again and again until each image was entirely to his satisfaction. It was tedious and exacting work, honest in its simplicity, that taught me the importance of attention to detail and patience. I learned that there were no shortcuts, that the creative pro-cess was often slow and arduous, but its results could be highly satisfying. Those hours in my Dad's darkroom also taught me what it meant to be passionate about a particular craft, to relish a valid and satisfying pastime of your own choosing.

My parents had saved all the mementos they thought held any significance, which turned out to be almost everything pertaining to Sidney and me. My pink baby bunting, knitted by my Aunt Dodie; my first pair of shoes; every school report card and class photo; and every postcard I had ever sent them—all the way from horseback-riding camp to my first trip to Greece to see the Acropolis in Athens.

If the walls of our house could talk, I thought it would be fascinating to hear what they had to say. That we were all crazy? Maybe, but I sort of doubted it. Like all empty houses, no doubt the rooms had echoed on the day my parents moved in. They filled it with their stuff and transformed it into a home that was rich with conversation, music, laughter, and life. There could be no denying there was love and light in that household, streaming in through its lead-paned windows, trapped within its old stone walls. Sometimes that love was doled out in rations or expressed in peculiar ways that only the four of us fully under-stood. But love was there—under the wall-to-wall carpet, in the Lalique vase on the glass coffee table, and sitting atop the butter-yellow Formica countertop in our kitchen.

For whatever mistakes my parents made and whatever valuable yet ambigu-ous lessons my brother and I learned, the love in our home was real. It was the only house I had ever lived in, the only place I have ever called home. As two young black professionals in the early 1960s, my parents could not get a mort-gage from a commercial bank. My Father cashed in his G.I. Bill benefits from the Air Force and my Mom borrowed the rest of the money from her mother. My Mother went back to work when I was three so she could pay my grand-mother back. My Father promised my Mother, who was pregnant with me when they moved in, that one day he would make this slightly dilapidated house and overgrown property into a beautiful home where they could raise their two children. And he made good on that promise.

Though I often took it for granted, our home was a place I felt I could always go—with the exception of that one disastrous Christmas. The following year, for the first and only time, I didn't go home for the holidays. I did it mostly to make a point; it was my own stubborness that kept me away more than my Dad saying I was no longer welcome. But the next year, there I was, with Dolby loyally in tow, showing up at the last minute on the morning of December 25th, as usual, wryly complaining about having to trim the stupid Douglas Fir all by myself. It wasn't until many years later that my Mother shared with me my Father's regret about what he had said. She told me he sat on the side of the bed one night not long after Christmas, his back turned to her, and cried. She had only seen him that emotional once before during their marriage—when his mother (my Nanna) died. "He thought maybe he had been too tough on you," she said. He had expressed to her that maybe—just maybe, given my sensitive nature, I had taken what he had said to heart. He asked her "What if she never comes home again?"

My Father, being of a generation where stoicism and strength were trade-marked and admired, was not particularly demonstrative with his feelings. He was not the kind of Dad to give you a piggyback ride or swing you in the air until you were dizzy and breathless. But I'm convinced, now more than ever, that his love was deeply imbedded in the aperture of every camera he ever owned—from his first Argus C3 to every Leica and Olympus, to his last Pentax. I felt it, for sure, expressed quietly with the click of the shutter—every single time he snapped a shot.

My Mother had a different way of expressing it. Sometimes instead of gush-ing and wearing it on the sleeve of her gun-metal grey Perry Ellis blouse, she loaned it out with the VHS video cassettes of my television show like they were rare, first-edition books from the Smithsonian.

"Have you ever seen Episode 101, 'Flower Power'? Or maybe you'd like to watch 'A Sheila Bridges Holiday?'" she would ask her friends from church.

"I'll need Chris Rock's movie *Good Hair* back, because Mrs. Hall is taking that video out on Friday. You're welcome to borrow another show, but just make sure to bring it back by Sunday the tenth." She had strict rules and a highly organized enumerative classification system of loaning out magazines, books, and videotapes in which I was featured. Suffice it to say, when I first started my business, my Mother was a JV cheerleader sitting on the bench but now she had become the majority shareholder and self-appointed President and CEO of my fan club. I was embarrassed by it all and told her she should stop boasting, but she was insistent, "Too bad." she said. The way she saw it, she had earned her bragging rights fair and square.

Now it was my responsiblity to pack all those shelter magazines, periodicals, and video cassettes into cardboard moving boxes. But what do you do with all the stuff you know in your heart really meant something to your parents as individuals, the things that have nothing to do with their roles as wife or husband and mother or father but speak to the lives they lived before you even entered the picture, interrupting their best-laid plans and unmanifested dreams? The partially planned trip to Tuscany, a play half-written, an oil canvas sketched but not yet painted? One of the biggest stumbling blocks for Sidney and me was the accumulation of awards, plaques, and commendations that adorned the walls of my Father's study. We were both stumped about what to do with them all—the many certificates of appreciation in recognition of his service to his profession; the fancy, framed ones written in Latin, and signed by the governor and the President but also the ones given to him by churches and pastors for his dedication to community service.

As we grow older, I'd like to believe most of us begin to reflect on our lives, on who we are, on what we've contributed to humanity or if we've contributed at all. How will we be remembered? What is our legacy? What do we leave behind for our children, our parents, our friends, our families? I believe it's important to leave something for those you love. It could be a poem, a still-life painting, a black-and-white photograph, a pencil drawing, or a hand-written letter. Even money, I guess, if that's your inclination. Anything that makes your feelings known, if only for a moment. Whatever it is, it should be—*must* be—meaningful to you. And this is the part that needs to be crystal clear to you and you alone—your grasp of its importance, so they might have something of you and your unmistakable spirit when you're gone.

I am 48 years old and have never been married. I don't have children, which means that at the end of the day I don't really have anyone to give anything to in the traditional sense. But then again, there's really never been anything par-ticularly "traditional" about the way I've lived my life up until now. Somehow, though, I'm confident I'll survive and be just fine. Better than fine. And this is mainly because I have always been part of a family. Not just my parents and my brother, Sidney, all three of whom I love beyond expression. But also the family of my own making, which includes my close friends as well as the furry and feathered companions who are also part of my chosen kin. I am at peace with some of the unconventional choices I've made in attempting to live my life as authentically as I can, having chosen a path that I believe has enabled me to be true to myself along the way. No regrets, but many lessons learned. And while my lifestyle may raise a few eyebrows amongst those who relish the status quo and believe we should all walk on primrose paths in similar shoes, I don't really care—and quite frankly never really have. It has always been those very same people who have wanted to jump ahead, making assumptions about me, feeling compelled to do me a favor and tell me about myself without really knowing me. These are the same people who, I can guarantee, will continue to get it wrong. Get *me* wrong.

Life comes full circle, no matter who we are, no matter how hard we try to make time stand still. Funny, isn't it, how time can slip through even the steadiest of hands? Its intended purpose is to ease forward even while we stand fixed. Its stealthy passing eventually changes everything for all of us.

We can feel time pass but we can't see it, regardless of how closely we are reliant upon it—racing against it by checking our wristwatch, BlackBerry, or clock affixed to the wall. We blindly chase after it and think we can cheat it when we are young—our youthful impatience reflected in our rush to grow up. It continues to move forward earnestly while we forget about it, making plans and going about our business of living our busy and oh-so-important lives. When we experience devastating loss and its accompanying sadness, excruciating physical pain, or inconsolable grief, we wish it would hurry up, move faster, get past us. But when we feel creatively inspired, spiritually stirred, or falling deeply in love, we wish we could slow it down, if only for a minute—or even a few seconds—just to elongate our rapture.

Sometimes though, if we stand perfectly still, opening our hearts and minds to the present, instead of worrying about the future or obsessing about the past, it does pause long enough for us to grab hold of it. We might even gently place it in the palm of our hand. But as soon as we grip it—try to wrap our fingers tightly around it—it will fall away. But in that one fleeting moment when we touch it, we create a stunning new memory we can hold onto forever—or for as long as the Universe allows us to dimly remember. Then it is gone. In an instant. Just like us.

EPILOGUE

Some might say writing a memoir is self-indulgent. Arrogant, almost. That the author feels he or she has some essential wisdom to share with the world. Those of you who know me—not my 1,000 closest confidants on Facebook, but those of you who *really* know me—understand this isn't the case. For me, writing down my story has had less to do with wanting to be the center of attention and more with finding the missing pieces of the complicated jigsaw puzzle of my life. This memoir was born out of a desire to better understand who I am and to weave together the colorful patchwork quilt that is my own family. Had I not lost my hair, I don't know if I would ever have embarked on any such journey of introspection and self-discovery.

That one life-altering event forced me to dig deep—to find out what I was really made of. In the process, I let go of everyone else's expectations of who I should be or how I should live my life, which included how I ought to look. In the aftermath of that defining period, I discovered that if I focused on all the positive things I had gained throughout my lifetime rather than on what I had lost, I could find an abundance of light to see my way out of the hole I had fallen into. I made a conscious decision to find joy in life's seasons instead of being jaded by them.

My hair loss created a unique opportunity for me to get to know myself better. It allowed me to get reacquainted with myself, first, and with my new image in the mirror, second. It gave me a chance to redefine beauty on my own terms. For me, beauty became the courage to be myself, to feel comfortable in my own skin, to trust in my own strength.

Many of my perceptions have to do with how I was brought up. Our parents raised my brother and me as black children, rather than as children who happened to be black. They felt this distinction was important. They wanted us to grow up with a clear understanding of the challenges we were likely to face in a world where racism can still be a decisive factor. The way they saw it, it was a matter of self-preservation. For black boys, this meant developing a toughness and heightened self-awareness that could mean the difference between life and death. For black girls, it was about a type of strength and self-esteem that won't quit. While this is not to say I haven't been

---

OVERLEAF I drew my family in Crayola crayons in 1970. I even included Mickey, our Irish Setter.

rattled at times, it ultimately meant I would have fewer doubts about my ability to stand tall in the face of adversity. No matter how difficult those moments have been, there has never been a second in my life when I felt ashamed about who I am or where I come from. I have never wanted to occupy someone else's life, never desired to switch places with another person who seemed to enjoy an easier, tidier existence.

My parents taught us, by example, that ultimately it didn't matter what anyone else thought as long as you stayed true to yourself and took ownership of your beliefs. Say what you mean and mean what you say. They also taught us that when you work hard to pursue your dreams, it makes achieving them so much sweeter. Through their influence, I gained a deep appreciation of the arts, photography, and travel. A love of books and music. The value of close friendship. A capacity for compassion. An overwhelming curiosity about nature. The importance of humility. An understanding that kindness is timeless. Not just to show up, but to be on time.

When I was little, I used to hate that my Mother constantly told me "You are just like your Father" whenever I was quiet, subdued, or inwardly focused. My friends were always afraid of my Father, so I didn't want to be like him. Whenever I was overly talkative my Father would say, "You're acting just like your Mother." Some days I found her chattiness and affection overbearing, so I didn't want to be like her either. *Which is it?* I wondered. I couldn't possibly be both. But recently, with years of perspective, it all started to make sense. Sometimes I am like my Mother, sometimes like my Father. Predisposed by a genetic code, I have inherited some of *both* of their individual quirks and distinctive traits. But, in the end, I found out that what constitutes the majority of my personality is mostly just me being me.

One of the problems I've recently run into, being me, is that I am not interested in communicating or sharing in the ways that most people find preferable nowadays: blogging my opinions, tweeting my whereabouts, posting designs on Tumblr and Pinterest, videos on YouTube, or poking friends on Facebook. I don't want to Skype you. Nor do I want to read a truncated email message from you. What I want is to see you in the flesh and look you in the eyes—maybe have a glass of rosé or a root beer float, and catch up in person. Still, my cell phone is vibrating, land line ringing, emails flooding in, and I admit I sometimes do text while I drive. It's mind boggling, really—this phenomenon called technology. But no matter how much I use it, it still falls short. Our relationship remains adversarial. I suspect it always will.

Forever a tomboy at heart, I am sitting up high in our dogwood tree, in May 1974.

Google me. Most people I meet do. And when you do, many "facts" will appear on your screen—some of them true, some not. You can find out when I was born, and where I grew up. There's even a photo gallery. Let's not forget that. Me with hair, me without. Snippets and quotes about me, misquotes by me, a rapid screen-shot and thumbnail sketch of my life summed up quickly. Yesterday I read on my computer (thanks to Google Alerts) that I was at a fancy fundraising event in Manhattan on Thursday evening, although I was actually in the country, mucking out horse stalls and trying to kill a new bed of poison ivy that seems to have magically blossomed overnight under one of my Norway Spruces.

You can find out my Zodiac sign, whether or not I've been married, had cancer, or ever made a sex tape. You can pose a hundred different questions and your computer will promptly answer back. Unfortunately, you won't ever get to really know me that way.

The internet won't tell you that I've never been kissed under mistletoe. But more important, it won't explain to you that my middle name is Anne, after my grandfather's younger sister, who lived for only one month after she was born. It can't capture or express my feelings or give you a glimpse into my core—or tell you whether or not I feel coquettish, criticized, or cosseted today. It will

The bathroom sink in my Harlem apartment was where I shaved my head for the first time.

also not tell you that the most challenging period of my life so far was the year immediately following the loss of my hair. While that one event was traumatic enough on its own, what really sent me reeling was the fear of tackling all the other emotionally heady events the Universe sent my way to make sure it had my full attention. And just in case losing my hair wasn't enough, the Universe stacked them up in front of me like a big pile of concrete cinder blocks: a nasty break-up, the end of my TV show, my Mother's heart attack, my Father's diagnosis of Alzheimer's, and the death of a close friend from cancer.

I simply didn't know where to begin. So I decided to tackle everything the same way I did when I was in college or design school and felt completely overwhelmed by a huge workload and looming deadlines. One day at a time. One thing at a time. No matter how enormously heavy that mountain of bricks appeared, I figured it would be far less intimidating if I were willing to take the time to dismantle it slowly and carefully—piece by piece, brick by brick. Luckily, I've never been afraid of heavy lifting.

For me, acknowledging then grieving all the losses I had suffered seemed like a good place to start. It didn't help that, in the process of trying to heal, I could not seem to make a move without being accosted by strangers about my bald head. But in the end, this was only a temporary distraction. The choice I made to shave my head was mine and mine alone. I quite simply wanted to stop obsessing over losing my hair and get on with living my life. It was a highly personal decision that I have never regretted, despite the difficulties that continue to be presented for me some days. I feel reassured that I trusted myself enough to make the right decision—for myself.

And while my intention was never to become a poster child for *Alopecia*, nowadays I receive almost as many emails with questions about baldness as I do about decorating. Unfortunately I do not feel nearly as qualified to give advice on hair-loss. It's just not as straightforward as advising you on the optimal height to hang your hand-forged iron chandelier. I wish it were as simple as telling you why you should consider staining your parquet floors walnut instead of cherry. I often wish I were more gifted at saying exactly the right words to magically soothe and heal those women and men who reach out to me, struggling emotionally for themselves or their children. I also wish I could shield them from what I know will ensue. Instead, I do my best to empathize, to validate their feelings, to acknowledge their sense of loss as devastatingly real, to confirm what I learned from experience—that it's no picnic, for sure.

I sometimes try to describe to close friends the anguish and weightiness I felt during the months following my hair loss. It was as if I were forced to wear a heavy, rain-soaked, buttoned-up black wool coat in the middle of August while I trudged back and forth, moving those cinder blocks out of my way, one by one. I cannot begin to explain what a relief it was to finally shed the weight of that wet winter coat and see the sunlight that was blocked by that pile of concrete, obscured only by my own fear.

One of the best rewards of getting older has been attaining greater clarity about all aspects of my life, including the important role I play in my family. Dr. Knapp was right: The more I distanced myself, the closer I could ultimately get when I circled back around. And that the anger I feared had metastasized in my bones would one day disperse and dissipate, only to be replaced by feelings of love and trust that had been buried deep inside.

My brother and I probably have very different recollections of shared events. We grew up in the same household with the same parents, but became very different people. I know how to push his buttons and he knows how to push mine. As adults, we respect one another enough not to "go there" as we did as kids. We are bound by blood but also by what we have in common, including our love of travel, photography, literature, soft pretzels, tennis, cheese-steaks, and sticky buns. We are both creative and equally passionate about our chosen professions.

Like most siblings, we have our moments of discord but I know Sidney's got my back for sure. I hope he knows he can always rely on me to hold it down for him—anytime, anywhere. When I asked him if I could borrow his hair clippers several years ago, there were no questions asked, even though I'm sure he suspected what I planned to do. And while the blades were too dull to shave my head, he still offered to help—without judgment.

My Mother has always been my Mother first. She became my friend second. I may not have been born the prissy little princess she dreamed of having—swaddled in a velveteen dress, white gloves, and black patent-leather shoes—but I grew into a woman she is proud to call her daughter *and* her best friend. My Mother is the only person in my life who calls me on the phone daily and, with remarkable sincerity, asks questions like "What's Molly doing right now?" and "Where's my little Wickham? Did he come home last night?" I've shared so many stories and photos of my favorite hen and my rascal of a cat that my Mom feels nearly as connected to them as I do. She knows Wickham regularly disappears at dusk and reappears at dawn to climb trees like a monkey and play with the oak leaves and acorns littering my gutters.

My Father never seemed to care that, as a child, I was more rough-tough-and-tumble tomboy than girly-girl. He taught me how to throw a football and to properly hold a fishing rod. He let me tag along on all those deep-sea fishing trips with the guys, and never seemed to worry about me climbing all over the boat deck, slippery with fish guts, and sticky from all those cans of spilled Budweiser. My Mother recently found his old tackle box and fishing knife. "You should have these," was all she said as she handed them to me.

I'd be lying if I said I didn't miss the conversations my Father and I used to have about the unique challenges (and rewards) of having your own business; his advice about crabgrass inhibitor or a certain brand of peat moss; whether or not I should hard prune my roses in the early spring or late fall. He may not remember these conversations, but I still do, which is part of why I wanted to write it all down. And truth be told, some days I seriously wonder if I will soon begin to forget things, seemingly out of the blue, as he did. If I spend too much time dwelling on the possibility, though, I start to worry. From time to time, in my mind's eye, I find myself looking over my shoulder just to make sure the coast is clear. I no longer feel chased or intensely dogged by the immense sadness I felt when he was first diagnosed, but I still experience unpredictable moments of melancholy. Time has helped ease that. There are still days when I feel saddened

My Father set a self-timer to take this photograph of the two of us in January
1969, when I was five years old. It is the only portrait I have of just the two of us.

by the loss of his memory, but mostly it's about the loss of his independence,
knowing how much he valued it—and how much I value mine.

Have I mentioned how relieved I am that we resolved many of the issues that
we used to butt heads about when I was young—before he got too sick to
remember that I'm his only daughter? Otherwise I might be left to live out the
rest of my years burdened with the thought that my Father didn't love me, the
weight of which would have been way too much to bear—and which, I trust,
would have been far worse than losing my hair.

On Saturday, December 1, 2012, my Father, Sidney Riddick Bridges, passed away from complications of Alzheimer's. He was 81 years old.

I had already finished writing *The Bald Mermaid*.

Photographer Andrew French took this image of me and Dolby in Manhattan's Central Park.

I never met a vertical stripe I didn't like. These were hand painted by a decorative painter in black, orange, and grey on the walls of my home office.

ACKNOWLEDGMENTS

The first two people I need to acknowledge are Bridget O'Connor and Bridget Casey, the two lovely Irish lasses and fellow writers who convinced me to keep writing because I had a story worth telling. I'd also like to thank the TriBeCa Tribe including Sara Saffian and Wickham Boyle in particular, who introduced me to her erstwhile Puerto Rican, closeted hairdresser–twin brother, my editor David Gibbons. All jokes aside, thank you, Dave, for pushing and prodding with a poised pen to make me go deeper. I also want to thank Janet Hill-Talbert, Faith Childs, Caroline Clarke, Veronica Chambers, and Cherise Davis Fisher for letting me pick their brains as I stumbled to make this project happen; Suzanne Slesin, Frederico Farina, and the folks at Pointed Leaf Press for believing this was more than just a sappy magazine article about hair loss. Thank you for understanding that design is in my DNA and helping to create a beautiful book that reflects it. And while she is not referenced in this memoir, I want to thank my good friend and consigliera Josephine Ciallella for all her support. She is the only person I fully confided in about this memoir while I was writing it. I also want to thank my clients, who kindly granted me permission to reprint photographs of their homes in this book. The stories I've shared in the preceding pages are not necessarily connected to the specific images represented or to the clients themselves. Most of the homes and interiors presented (in addition to the book cover headshot of me) were shot by photographer Dana Meilijson. Thank you, Dana, for your significant contribution to this book. It is both a rarity and a gift to work with someone who is as kind as they are talented. Most important, I owe a special thank you to my Mother for her incomparable strength, spirit, and stellar memory—for helping me fill in the wide gaps, particularly about our family history. Thanks, Mom, for letting me air some dirty family laundry that now, for sure, has been washed Clorox clean.

ABOUT THE AUTHOR

Originally from Philadelphia, Pennsylvania, Sheila Bridges moved to New York in 1986. She holds degrees from Brown University, in Providence, Rhode Island, and the Parsons School of Design, in New York, and studied decorative arts at the Polimoda Institute in Florence, Italy. She lives and works in Harlem, New York, and relaxes at her weekend home in New York's Hudson Valley. *The Bald Mermaid* is her second book.

PHOTOGRAPHY CREDITS

Unless noted below, all photographs are from the personal collection of Sheila Bridges. Every effort has been made to locate copyright holders; any omission will be corrected in future printings.
Reprinted with permission from American Media, Inc.: 58-59
William Boyd: 220
R. Lawrence Bradley: 318, bottom
Sidney E. Bridges: 285
Reprinted with permission from the *Brown Alumni Magazine*: 53
Luis Castaneda Inc./Getty Images: 131
"The Octoroon Girl," painting by Archibald J. Motley, Jr. 1925. Collection of Mara Motley, M.D., and Valerie Gerrard Browne, courtesy of the Chicago History Museum: 35
George Chinsee: 283, 331
Reprinted with permission from Condé Nast: 68
Brian Doben: 127
Cover reprinted with permission from *Elle Decor*: 209
Pieter Estersohn: 68, 70-71, 76
Courtesy of Everett Collection: 36
Andrew French: 343

Garry Gay/Getty Images: 3
Hulton Archive/Getty Images: 170
Pawel Kaminski: 20, 124-125, 178, 188, 228, 286, 298, 309
Michael Lavine: 138, 175, center
Furnishing Forward, Courtesy of Little, Brown and Company: 54
Dana Meilijson: front cover head, endpapers, 5, 73, 77, 78-79, 84, 85, 86, 87, 119, 198, 200-201, 214, 248-249, 250, 251, 252, 253, 254, 255, 256-257, 288, 338
Carl Posey: 175, bottom
Laura Resen: 204, 265, 266, 267, 308
Michelle Rose: front cover and back cover ocean and sky
The Dave Brubeck Quartet, *Time Out* album cover. Courtesy of Sony Music Entertainment: 22
Michael Steinberg: 132
Reprinted with permission by Time Inc.: 114, 115
Luca Travato: 137, 175, top
Marvin Gaye, *What's Going On* album cover. Courtesy of Universal Music Enterprise: 22
William Waldron: 57, 209, 210, 211, 344
Nick Xatzis: 280, 281

The Bald Mermaid is a work of nonfiction. Some names and identifying details have been changed.

PUBLISHER/EDITORIAL DIRECTOR: Suzanne Slesin
CREATIVE DIRECTOR: Frederico Farina

Pointed Leaf Press is pleased to offer special discounts for publications and can provide signed copies upon request. Please contact info@pointedleafpress.com for details, or visit our website www.pointedleafpress.com.

DESIGN BY FREDERICO FARINA

Printed and bound in China.
First edition
ISBN: 978-1-938461-05-7
Library of Congress Control Number: 2012951365